Chips and Change

Chips and Change

How Crisis Reshapes the Semiconductor Industry

Clair Brown and Greg Linden

The MIT Press
Cambridge, Massachusetts
London, England

MIT Press books may be purchased at special quantity discounts fro business or sales promotional use. For information, please email special_sales@mitpress.mit.edu or write to Special Sales Department, The MIT Press, 55 Hayward Street, Cambridge, MA 02142.

This book was set in Sabon on 3B2 by Asco Typesetters, Hong Kong and was printed and bound in the United States of America.

Library of Congress Cataloging-in-Publication Data

Brown, Clair, 1946–
Chips and change : how crisis reshapes the semiconductor industry / Clair Brown and Greg Linden.
 p. cm.
Includes bibliographical references and index.
ISBN 978-0-262-01346-8 (hbk. : alk. paper) 1. Semiconductor industry—Management. 2. Business cycles. I. Linden, Greg, 1959 II. Title.
HD9696.S42B76 2009
338.4′762138152dc22   2009007072

10 9 8 7 6 5 4 3 2 1

Clair dedicates this book to Richard, Daniel, and Jason, with love and appreciation for making coming home from fieldwork a joy.

Greg gratefully dedicates this book to Pam, for her tough love, gentle patience, and wise support.

Contents

Acknowledgments

The authors thank the Alfred P. Sloan Foundation, the Institute for Research on Labor and Employment at UC Berkeley, and the Institute for Technology, Enterprise and Competitiveness (ITEC/COE) at Doshisha University, Japan, for their support during the many years of the research for this book.

This book represents the knowledge gained through the Sloan Competitive Semiconductor Manufacturing Program at UC Berkeley, directed by David Hodges, then Dean of Engineering, and Robert Leachman. Clair Brown joined the project as head of the human resources group in 1991. Along with an extraordinary group of faculty and graduate students, they spent six years together in the field benchmarking and analyzing semiconductor fabrication. The insights and knowledge gained from working with Hodges and Leachman are to be found throughout the book, along with the invaluable contributions from CSM team members over the years, especially Melissa Appleyard, Diane Bailey, Neil Berglund, Michael Borrus, Benjamin Campbell, Robert Cole, Henry Chesbrough, Jumbi Edulbehram, Rosemarie Ham Ziedonis, Nile Hatch, Jeffrey Macher, David Mowery, Yongwook Paik, Yooki Park, Greg Pinsonnault, Daniel Rascher, Michael Reich, David Teece, Jihong Sanderson, Linda Sattler, Amy Shuen, Vince Valvano, and Katalin Voros. We have also benefited enormously over the years from discussions with and feedback from Gail Pesyna, Frank Mayadas, and Ralph Gomory from the Sloan Foundation.

We are also deeply indebted to many engineers and semiconductor experts outside UCB who have shared their time and expertise with us, especially Hisao Baba, Hiroyuki Chuma, Robert Doering, Jean-Philippe

Dauvin, David Ferrell, Michael Flynn, Venugopal Gopinathan, Norikazu Hashimoto, Paul Horn, Toshiaki Masuhara, Elena Obukhova, Makoto Onodera, Toshihiko Osada, William Spencer, Makoto Sumita, Yasuhiro Takada, Andrew Viterbi, and C.-K. Wang. Our research in other countries could not have been accomplished without the expertise, help, and guidance provided by our colleagues Yoshifumi Nakata, Hugh Whittaker, and Eiichi Yamaguchi, along with Philippe Byosiere, Toshiro Kita, James Lincoln, Mon-Han Tsai, Tsuyoshi Tsuru in Japan; Sandra del Boca in Italy; Yea-Huey Su in Taiwan; Ling Huang and Josh Chen in China; and Poornima Shenoy and the India Semiconductor Association in India.

We are also grateful to Gartner, Global Semiconductor Alliance, Ron Hira, G.Dan Hutcheson, iSuppli, Daya Nadamuni, Ed Pausa, Devadas Pillai, SEMI, the Semiconductor Industry Association, Chintay Shih, Gary Smith, Tim Tredwell and anonymous reviewers for their valuable contributions.

Jason Dedrick, Rafiq Dossani, Richard Freeman, Deepak Gupta, Bradford Jensen, Ken Kraemer, Frank Levy, B. Lindsay Lowell, Tom Murtha, Deepak Somaya, Tim Sturgeon, and Michael Teitelbaum, along with participants at the NAE Workshop on the Offshoring of Engineering and the 2005 Brookings Trade Forum on Offshoring of White-Collar Work and participants at seminar presentations at the Berkeley Innovation Seminar, Doshisha ITEC, Japan Electronics and Information Technologies Industry Association (JEITA), Institute for Innovation Research at Hitotsubashi University, and Association of Super-Advanced Electronics Technologies (ASET) provided thoughtful discussions that improved various chapters.

Dozens of industry participants, interviewed under a confidentiality agreement, have patiently provided us with hours of education and insights, without which this book would not be possible, and unfortunately we cannot thank them by name. Special thanks go to the excellent staff of the electronics trade press, whose work is noted throughout the book. Their efforts helped us understand technologies and keep abreast of business developments.

We have been drawn to the study of the semiconductor industry for many years because it is an exciting industry in constant change. Perhaps even more important for engaging us intellectually has been the amazing engineers we met along the way. These engineers are tireless in their dedication to pushing chip technology and applications forward, and their talents, energy, and knowledge have made being out in the field an intellectual and personal treat. We are especially grateful to them, both as researchers and as users of chips.

Clair Brown and Greg Linden
University of California
Berkeley, CA
March 2009

Introduction

The Global Semiconductor Industry

Since the 1960s the semiconductor industry has been a driver of global economic growth and social change. The widespread application of semiconductors has transformed computing, communications, entertainment, and industry. This young and fast-growing industry embraced rapid technological change, and transmitted it to the rest of the economy. Almost all aspects of the economy have been affected by electronic equipment, which derives its capabilities from microchips.

Steady improvements in semiconductor cost and performance have been a major driver in the improvements in US productivity and growth in the postwar period (Jorgenson and Stiroh 2000). Because of the strategic economic importance of the chip industry in supporting innovation and growth across industries, as well as its importance in military equipment and operations, governments worldwide have taken a keen interest in supporting domestic development of the industry and in regulating export of its technology and products.

Eight Crises

The chip industry's remarkable string of technological successes has been accompanied by public drama about the serious problems or challenges facing the industry, and the dire consequences that would occur if the latest crisis were not met. We will show in this book how a chain of technical and managerial crises forced the industry to adapt both incrementally and radically. We use eight crises as the focal points for examining the recent history of the industry from an economic perspective. These

Table I.1
Eight crises in the semiconductor industry

Crisis	Description
Crisis 1	Loss of competitive advantage
Crisis 2	Rising costs of fabrication
Crisis 3	Rising costs of design
Crisis 4	Consumer price squeeze
Crises 5	Limits to Moore's Law
Crisis 6	Finding talent
Crisis 7	Low returns, high risk
Crisis 8	New global competition

eight interlinked crises have had, and continue to have, a major impact on the industry (see table I.1).

By "crisis," we mean a major issue that was viewed as a turning point in the industry because of the potential threat to technological progress or the dominant business model. Although several of these issues are typically commanding the industry's attention at any given time, they are crises in the sense that their resolution is critical to the industry's collective well-being. Our analysis of these crises and how they are met contributes to understanding how global competitive advantage can be won and lost by countries and companies in this swiftly moving and vital industry; provides insight into how consumers and workers benefit from the industry; and gives perspective to leaders in this and other fast-moving industries. Understanding the industry's complexities and dynamics is also vital for policymakers who wish to influence innovation and competitiveness in this and related industries. (Malerba et al. 2008).

Although the "crisis" mentality of the industry is exaggerated, alarmism has helped stir the industry toward solutions that stave off disaster for at least a while longer. The air of crisis is typically created during conferences and in the trade press well before disaster strikes, which helps build awareness and focus attention on developing solutions.

Our study begins in the mid-1980s, when the US industry, which had dominated the global industry with little challenge up to then, was in fear of losing its leadership to Japan (Crisis 1).[1] In the two decades since then, semiconductor industry revenue has grown from less than $20 billion to more than $200 billion, and the global competitive advantage of semiconductor firms and nations have undergone major changes.

The technology for both design and manufacturing has increased greatly in cost and complexity, exerting steadily mounting cost pressure (Crises 2 and 3). At the same time the pool of final users of chip-containing products shifted from big budget corporations to frugal consumers, who pushed prices downward (Crisis 4). The industry attempted to address this cost–price squeeze through a combination of technological fixes that required cooperation, often among competing firms (Crisis 5), and the expansion of the engineering labor pool to include engineers from around the globe (Crisis 6). The measures have been insufficient to improve the industry's relative inability to capture the value it creates (Crisis 7). Despite this, companies in other countries, often with government support, have continued to join the industry, which keeps global competition at a fever pitch (Crisis 8).

Figure I.1 shows how the crises, which span technology, economics, and global competition, are interrelated and became salient at various points in time. The arrows suggest some of the paths by which the crises influence each other, such as "limits to Moore's Law" (Crisis 5) contributes to the rising costs of fabrication (Crisis 2) and of design (Crisis 3).

The location in time in figure I.1 is only approximate and should not be seen as suggesting that crises have tidy beginnings and ends. Progress in advanced lithography adequate to keep up with Moore's Law, for example, has been a major concern of the industry for decades, and our discussion takes up the story in the 1990s as indicated in the figure. In choosing the order for the chapters, we have sought to balance the historical timeline with the need to present various aspects of the industry (e.g., manufacturing, design, and markets) in a logical fashion for our readers.

As the figure suggests, the current decade is a time when the health of the industry seems imperiled by an unusually large number of challenges. This is an accurate impression. During the 1990s the chip industry

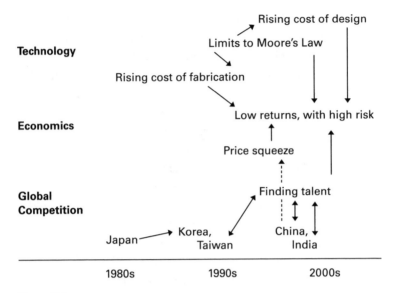

Figure I.1
Timescale and interrelation of the eight crises.

enjoyed a relatively smooth and predictable path of technological and economic progress after the technological and financial ferment of the industry's earlier decades. Since then the industry has increasingly relied on short-term technological and financial fixes, but the deep recession that started in 2008 has brought additional pressures to bear that will likely prove fatal for some chip firms.

None of the crises in this book have yet reached the point of blocking the progress of the industry. However, these forces have caused the industry's structure to change in significant ways that few would have predicted even five years ago, such as the abandonment by Texas Instruments of in-house digital process development, and the private buyout of two chip companies that had started life as the critical chip operations of industry leaders Motorola and Philips. Industry responses typically build on mechanisms that are already in place rather than on radical solutions. This way crises have been defused in less time with less expense than finding a radical solution would have required. In a few cases, such as the emergence of the fabless-foundry model (Crisis 2), the response appears radical in retrospect. And some individual companies embrace radical change as they attempt to find a path through difficult terrain, such as AMD's spin-off of its fabrication operations into a separate company, announced in late 2008.

None of these crises are permanently resolved. The pressure may diminish, but it invariably builds up again, often in a new guise. Thus fear of Japan has re-emerged as fear of China and India. And some problems, like the rising cost of fabrication or the end of Moore's Law, are hardy perennials that resurface every few years. The industry's dynamism drives it again and again into dangerous territory. The financial crisis that has engulfed world markets as we complete this book in November 2008 will aggravate the economic forces in Crises 4 (Price Squeeze) and 7 (Low Returns, High Risk) and reshape the drivers of global competitive advantage.

Whose Perspective?

The primary framework that we use for our analysis is economic: How do costs and market conditions shape a crisis and the industry's response? We invoke technical details only to the extent necessary to understand these economic forces.

The evaluation of a particular crisis and industry response depends on one's perspective. In each crisis we consider the impact at four levels of analysis: the country, the firm, the worker, and the consumer, and here we briefly discuss the context of each of these.

Each country wants to have a large and growing semiconductor industry with profitable firms that provide good jobs to domestic workers. As protectionist barriers became politically less viable, countries resorted to other means to support the industry, including research subsidies, specialized university programs, and outreach to foreign investors, such as through programs to ease costs of land and environmental regulations. Although our focus is primarily US-centric, we also discuss the industry in other countries, particularly in Asia, where much of the industry's activity and growth are taking place.

Firms attempt to maximize revenue by developing technologies and products that are popular across global markets, and to minimize costs, in part through the optimal location of activities globally. Firms face strategy cycles that include a variety of interrelated decisions with different timelines. The consequences of product decisions may become apparent within a year or two, while the development of new underlying technologies, such as a next-generation wireless standard, can take much longer.

Although we will discuss firms in a general way, we will only occasionally discuss specific firms in terms of the strategies they adopted and why they succeeded or not. Our focus at the firm level is on how specific crises are expected to impact the basis of competitive advantage

High-tech workers want to have jobs that continually develop their skills and provide good pay and benefits. As firms focus on career development primarily for key employees, and leave other employees to be in charge of their careers, workers must take advantage of job opportunities across employers. High-tech engineers use labor market mobility to fashion a career path with growing pay and skill development over their forty or more years of work, and these engineers are increasingly part of a global brain circulation.

Consumers, both businesses and individuals, are the big beneficiaries of the continually falling prices and increasing performance of chips. As prices of entry-level phones and computers fall, consumers in developing countries, like China and India, have joined as beneficiaries of the chip revolution that began a half century ago.

A final perspective worth mentioning is that of the world economy as a whole. The spread of the chip industry to new locations has been an important engine of wealth creation in industrializing countries such as Taiwan and South Korea. The global diffusion of activities has also created intense competition that has spurred innovation while keeping prices down. Lower prices spurred downstream innovation and helped spark growth in new geographic and product markets. This global dynamism has helped keep the industry growing and could potentially provide benefits to many more countries, firms, workers, and consumers.

The Semiconductor Industry

For readers who may not be familiar with the semiconductor industry, we offer a short introduction here.

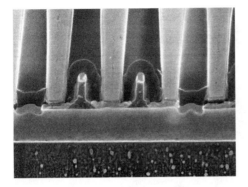

Figure I.2
This cross section of an IBM POWER6 dual-core processor photographed using a scanning electron microscope shows two transistors out of the 790 million on the thumbnail-sized die. Photo courtesy of IBM.

"Semiconductor" is a generic term for any material that conducts electricity imperfectly. Silicon is one such material and the one most widely used by the chip industry. Others, such as gallium arsenide, are used for specialized applications. By introducing various chemicals into a substrate of one of these materials, it is possible to make a transistor that can switch current on or off, which provides the building block for the ones and zeros of computer language (see figure I.2).

The most valuable semiconductors are those that consist of hundreds of millions of transistors constructed on a single slice of silicon. The best-known and most complex of these are microprocessors, such as those made by Intel, which can cost hundreds of dollars. The industry also encompasses a wide array of simpler products such as operational amplifiers, which cost just a few dollars, and single transistors, which cost as little as a few cents (see figure I.4).

Figure I.3 shows the breakdown of the sales of semiconductors by type for 2007, when sales totaled about $250 billion.

The largest category is logic, at 26 percent, which encompasses a variety of digital designs including custom and programmable chips. Close behind, at 23 percent, is memory, including dynamic random access memory (DRAM, the short-term memory of computers) and flash memory (retains its data without power for use in mobile devices). At 22 percent in 2007, the share of microcomponents (including

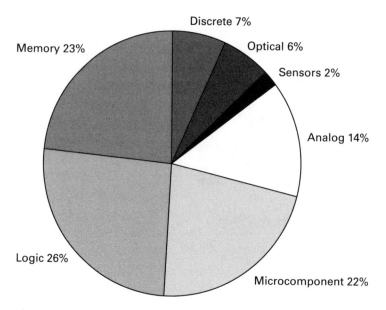

Figure I.3
Semiconductors by type, 2007 (percentage of global sales). Source: WSTS News Release dated November 13, 2007.

Figure I.4
Chips come in many shapes and sizes.
Photo courtesy of Hongjue International Co., Ltd.

microprocessors and digital signal processors) has steadily grown not only with the spread of computers but also with the spread of embedded processing in everything from toasters to cars. Analog chips (14 percent) are designed to process the continuous signals of the real world rather than the binary data of the digital realm; they also convert from one to the other, so almost any machine interface requires some analog circuitry. The smaller categories include discrete semiconductors, such as individual diodes and transistors; optical semiconductors, such as the lasers used to read compact discs; and sensors, such as those used to trigger automobile air bags.

Our primary focus will be on microcomponent, memory, and logic chips, which mainly rely on a fabrication process called CMOS (complementary metal-oxide semiconductor) that became the industry's main manufacturing platform in the 1980s. Other types of semiconductors use specialized processes with different technology trajectories than the one that drives the industry's largest companies.

Moore's Law

The mainstream production of the chip industry has moved for more than thirty years along a steep productivity path known as "Moore's Law," the name given to a projection made by Gordon Moore (Moore 1965) based on early industry trends. A few years later Moore would go on to co-found Intel. Moore forecast that the cost-minimizing number of transistors that could be manufactured on a chip would double every year (later revised to every two years). The industry has maintained this exponential pace ever since, albeit with steadily rising fixed costs (Crisis 2). For the industry Moore's Law became a shared vision, a roadmap that guided investment by firms seeking a leadership position.

Moore's prediction was based on several elements, such as the ability to control manufacturing defects and the ability to manufacture larger chip sizes, but in the decades that followed, the driving technological force has been a steady reduction in the size of transistors. Designer ingenuity about packing more components in less space has also played an important role (Flamm 2004). Over time the number of transistors that leading-edge producers can fabricate in a given area of silicon has doubled roughly every three years, and from 1995 to 2003 the pace accelerated to a doubling every *two* years.[2]

The relentless miniaturization of components is now reaching the molecular level. The smallest "linewidth" (width of feature on the chip surface) shrank from two microns in 1980 to less than a tenth micron (100 nanometers) a quarter-century later. If viewed in cross section, the thickness of horizontal layers of material deposited on the silicon surface is currently about 1.2 nanometers. To give an idea of the scale involved, the width of a human hair is about 100 microns (or 100 millionth parts of a meter), and the width of a molecule is about 1 nanometer (one-thousandth of a micron).

The ability to put more transistors in less space has brought faster processors, higher capacity memory chips, and multifunction chips that improve the cost and portability of electronic end products. The enhanced capabilities of microchips enable new applications, such as cell phones, that raise demand for silicon enough to justify the growing expense of the industry's technological progress.

The Semiconductor Value Chain

Fabrication, the manufacturing process to which Moore's Law applies, is just one step in the semiconductor value chain. Fabrication is preceded by design and followed by chip assembly and test. In this book we are concerned primarily with design and fabrication. Assembly is an important stage of value creation, but a stage that has been less affected by the crises that have roiled the industry since the mid-1980s.

During design, the desired electronic circuits are developed as a series of abstract representations of increasing detail, from a description of the logical operations that the chip will perform to a full mapping of how the circuits are physically laid out. At each stage the design team must verify that the design, which is often made up of various subsystems, does what it is supposed to do. During fabrication, the integrated circuits are built up in successive layers on the surface of a flat, round wafer made of purified silicon (see figure I.5). Next the wafer is cut into *die* (see figure I.6), and a wafer can have thousands of individual die depending

Figure I.5
On this processed wafer each square represents one die for eventual packaging as a chip. Photo courtesy of Infineon Technologies AG.

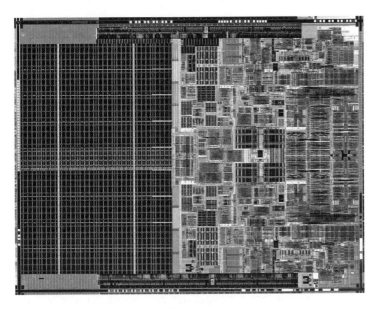

Figure I.6
Intel® Core™2 Duo bare die. This processor has a transistor count of more than 200 million. Photo courtesy of Intel Corp.

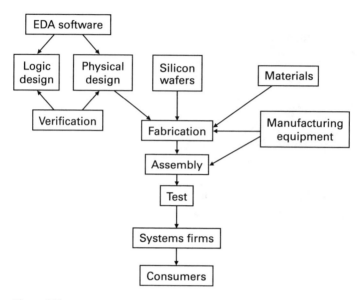

Figure I.7
Semiconductor value chain.

upon their size. Then each delicate die is assembled in a protective package that includes connectors that allow the finished chip to interact with other components. The assembled chips must be tested before they are sent to systems firms such as Dell or Sony for inclusion in electronics products. Figure I.7 provides a graphical representation of a stylized semiconductor value chain.

The economic characteristics of each step of the process differ significantly. Design is skill intensive and requires expensive EDA (electronic design automation) software, which is typically licensed per design engineer. Fabrication of leading-edge logic chips requires a fixed investment of billions of dollars to build a plant (called a *fab*) that holds a wide variety of expensive equipment and that meets requirements for extreme cleanliness. Assembly also requires expensive equipment, but the overall costs of plant and equipment are much lower than for the fab, as are the average skill requirements. Overall, worker skill requirements fall along the value chain (i.e., design is more skill intensive than manufacturing, which is more skill intensive than assembly).

Summary

It is hard to overstate the importance of Moore's Law for the semiconductor industry. The drive to keep the industry on this steep technology trajectory lurks behind each of the eight crises analyzed in this book. Globalization and government intervention add further complexities to the rapid technological change, and the ever-changing industry keeps industry leaders working to maintain their competitive advantage while it provides hope to their rivals that they can move ahead.

We will see in the chapters that follow how the industry has met crises primarily through incremental approaches that maintain as much of the status quo as possible. This is particularly true of engineering challenges, such as the limitations of photolithography (Crisis 5). When business challenges like the industry's price squeeze (Crisis 4) arose, industry managers adopted a variety of strategies including pursuit of new markets, reallocation of assets, and financial restructuring. We will also discuss how we expect these crises to influence the global competitive advantage of firms, and how global competition across nations has been unfolding.

This book is based on our ongoing interview-based research on the globalization of the semiconductor industry. Since the early 1990s, the Berkeley Sloan Semiconductor Program has collected data at semiconductor companies around the world.[3] In the past ten years we have interviewed managers and executives at dozens of semiconductor companies, often with return visits, in the United States, Japan, Taiwan, India, China, and Europe. We also use data from the US Departments of Labor and Commerce, the Semiconductor Industry Association, and the Institute of Electrical and Electronic Engineers (IEEE), as well as other published and proprietary sources, including the trade press, SEC filings, and industry analyst reports.

Our interviews were all conducted under confidentiality agreements, so we generally do not reference our sources. Where possible, we have referenced sources in the online trade press as avenues for further information. Our work is based on knowledge gained from our fieldwork, and we hope that the industry people enjoy the fruits of our many hours of meetings with them.

Crisis 1

Loss of Competitive Advantage

I can only conclude that the common objective of the Japanese government and industry is to dominate the world electronics market. Given the importance of this market to US industry in general and our defense base in particular, we cannot stand by idly.
—Commerce Secretary Malcolm Baldrige
addressing the Senate Finance Committee in March 1987[1]

After its invention in the United States, semiconductor technology steadily spread to other countries during the 1950s and 1960s (Tilton 1971). Western Europe and Japan were the main adopters of the manufacturing and application know-how. In the 1980s, where our analysis of the semiconductor industry begins, strength in process technology determines competitive advantage. In this chapter we discuss how Japanese chip producers raised their share of chip industry revenues above that of US producers by the mid-1980s by improving their manufacturing techniques, which gave rise in the United States to fears of steady US decline. Yet a decade later the United States was again the global leader. We explore the factors behind Japan's rise, the responses of US policy and US corporations, and the circumstances, particularly in Japan, that contributed to a US resurgence.

1.1 Japan's Rise

Japan's rise to prominence in the semiconductor industry was widely chronicled and analyzed in the 1980s. A consensus emerged around a few key factors that we summarize here. Perhaps first among these was government support. In the 1960s, powerful government agencies demanded tough terms, including technology transfers, from foreign companies such as IBM and Texas Instruments that wanted access to the growing Japanese market (Prestowitz 1988). In the 1970s, Japan's government pursued an active policy of subsidizing research and promoting cooperation between its fiercely competitive business groups; this helped them close the technology gap with US firms in chips and related technologies (Fransman 1990). Import protection of the Japanese market and an overvalued dollar were other factors that helped Japanese producers expand their sales to the domestic and US markets and reach economies of scale in production (Flamm 1996).

Japanese firms also benefited from access to capital on more favorable terms than were available to US rivals, which helped them to pursue costly long-term strategies (Borrus 1988; Warshofsky 1989). A major source of this capital advantage was the vertical and horizontal integration of the semiconductor divisions within large electronics firms, which were in turn linked to banks belonging to a common business group (*keiretsu*). A company's internal electronics division could become a source of cross-subsidies when chip sales were down, and a related bank afforded a ready source of patient funds that most stand-alone US chip companies could not match (Okimoto and Nishi 1994).

The main product on which the Japanese firms rose to market dominance was dynamic random-access memory (DRAM), the memory chips used in computer hardware, a technology area where the Japanese government was anxious to establish national autonomy. In the 1970s, IBM's internally produced memory chips were a key source of advantage for its successful System/370 mainframe computer system, with which Japanese companies such as Fujitsu and Hitachi were competing (Fransman 1995).

DRAM was considered strategic because it was process-driven and a perfect vehicle to learn about each new generation of process technology. Every two to three years a process using a finer linewidth would enable companies to fit the most memory cells into the smallest chip size, which minimizes unit production cost. Because of the high investment costs for both process and product development, market leadership in memory chips required high capital expenditures. This could be justified by the large demand for memories, which accounted for 15 to 20 percent of semiconductor revenues during the late 1980s. The long production runs of a single design permitted learning about the process, which raised yield (the percentage of defect-free die on a wafer) and further lowered unit cost. The process and the lessons learned could then be applied to other types of chips, such as microprocessors. Because of the importance of volume production to take advantage of economies of scale, the ability to ramp quickly to high volumes with high yield for the latest-generation memory chip provided competitive advantage through lower costs.

Japanese companies excelled in the process-oriented business of high-volume memory production. In the industry's early years, getting a process to work at minimum acceptable yield was a sufficient foundation for competitive advantage, but as the DRAM market matured, fab efficiency in terms of yield and cycle time became critical (Burgelman 1994). A 1987 report by a US Defense Science Board task force reported that of the twenty-five major semiconductor products and processes considered, Japanese companies were better in twelve and US companies were better in five, with rough parity in five more.[2] By the mid-1980s, the best Japanese producers were achieving yields of 70 to 80 percent, while the best US firms were in the 50 to 60 percent range (Prestowitz 1988). The reliability of Japanese memory chips was also higher (ibid.). US memory producers saw their market share fall from 75 percent in 1980 to just over 25 percent in 1986, while that of Japanese producers rose from 24 to 65 percent during the same period (Borrus 1988, fig. 7.1).

The shift in the memory market was reflected in the industry as a whole. Table 1.1 shows the top ten firms in the overall semiconductor industry for 1980 and 1990, a decade during which industry revenue expanded almost fivefold. The rise of Japanese producers (shaded gray) in the 1980s, mirrored in the relative fall of US producers, can be seen clearly. In 1980, Texas Instruments (TI) was the leader with 14 percent of the market, and the six US companies in the top ten accounted for 43 percent. In 1990, TI's share, despite a doubling of its annual revenue, had fallen to sixth place, and two of the top five chip suppliers (NEC and Toshiba) were Japanese, with the five Japanese companies in the top ten accounting for 31 percent, while the four US companies totaled only 23 percent. This changing of the guard was a great source of

Table 1.1
Change in industry leadership, 1980 to 2000

1980		1990		2000	
Total market $9.4 billion		Total market $44.6 billion		Total market $197.1 billion	
Texas Instruments	14%	NEC (Japan)	8%	Intel	15%
National Semi.	7%	Toshiba (Japan)	7%	Samsung (Korea)	5%
Motorola	7%	Intel	7%	NEC (Japan)	5%
Philips (Europe)	7%	Hitachi (Japan)	7%	Texas Instruments	5%
Intel	6%	Motorola	6%	Toshiba (Japan)	4%
NEC (Japan)	6%	Texas Instruments	6%	STMicro. (Europe)	4%
Fairchild	5%	Fujitsu (Japan)	5%	Motorola	4%
Hitachi (Japan)	4%	Mitsubishi (Japan)	4%	Micron	3%
Toshiba (Japan)	4%	National Semi.	4%	Hyundai (Korea)	3%
Mostek	4%	Philips (Europe)	3%	Hitachi (Japan)	3%

Source: Market research data.
Note: Companies without a geographic designation are US-based companies.

concern in the United States. Some industry observers feared the shift would be permanent: "Japanese producers' dominance of the world chip market threatens to be more or less assured, *even if US producers were to recapture parity in process R&D and manufacturing*" (Borrus 1988, p. 7; italics in original). Government pronouncements, as typified by the Commerce Secretary's quote at the beginning of the chapter, were also grave.

1.2   The US Response

US companies had multiple responses to the challenge from Japan, including improvements in manufacturing quality, politically oriented strategies toward Japan, and strategic shifts in their product mix. The government played an important role with both macroeconomic and industry-level policies.

US firms worked hard to raise the yield of their factories and the quality of their output. One of the best-known examples is Motorola's Six Sigma quality program, which was developed starting in the early 1980s and has since been adopted in a wide range of industries.[3] The "sigma" refers to a statistic that measures the share of output that is acceptable, and "six sigma" corresponds to a defect rate of 3.4 parts per million. The tools involved, such as statistical process control, already existed, but Six Sigma marshaled them in a long-term effort that emphasized employee involvement in preventing, rather than detecting, problems.

US chip firms also overcame their aversion to "not invented here" know-how. Many companies participated in benchmarking efforts such as UC Berkeley's Competitive Semiconductor Manufacturing (CSM) program (http://microlab.berkeley.edu/csm/), which launched a comparative study in 1992 that made detailed analyses of operations at more than 30 fabs worldwide to develop a set of performance-tied best practices based on comparative benchmarks.

Meanwhile the industry pursued political strategies to improve their competitive position vis-à-vis Japan in concert with the US government. In 1977, five leading US chip producers joined together to form the Semiconductor Industry Association, which gave the industry a more unified voice for lobbying the federal government. In 1985, the Semiconductor Industry Association (SIA) filed an unfair trading petition with the US government, claiming that Japan was continuing to protect its market in violation of intergovernment semiconductor agreements that had been reached in 1982 and 1983. This, along with dumping actions on specific types of chips, helped pressure Japan to agree in 1986 to even more drastic measures, although US penetration of the Japan market remained limited (Prestowitz, op. cit.). In 1987, the US imposed penalties of $300 million on Japanese imports to bring further pressure for the enforcement of existing agreements. The Japanese chipmakers found the US pressure very strong, particularly under the first Semiconductor Trade Agreement, which lasted until 1991 (Chuma and Hashimoto 2008).

On the macroeconomic level, US government policy to lower the value of the dollar was also helpful. The 1985 Plaza Accord devalued the dollar relative to the yen, and over the following two years, coordinated central bank action helped lower the exchange value of the dollar against the yen by 51 percent.

On the home front, the US government relaxed the antitrust laws affecting interfirm cooperation and provided half the $200 million annual budget for a research consortium of fourteen US chip companies called SEMATECH, which was formed in 1987 (Ham et al. 1998). The general goal was to pool resources for the improvement of manufacturing technology.

After an uneven start, SEMATECH eventually made strides by getting US semiconductor manufacturers and their specialized equipment suppliers working together on ways to improve US chip manufacturing (Grindley et al. 1994). The model of horizontal and vertical cooperation was based on the earlier successful collaboration that was believed to have contributed to the Japanese success in the chip industry (Fransman 1990). Major government support ended in 1996, and SEMATECH continued forward as a privately funded consortium that has continued to play an important role in equipment innovation and fab productivity.

US firms also responded to the Japanese crisis by adjusting their product mix, most notably by exiting the DRAM market, where the determined investment of the Japanese combined with a dip in demand in 1986 led to a situation of severe overcapacity. As US trade negotiator Clyde Prestowitz put it: "the US semiconductor industry was staring death in the face. It reported losses of nearly $2 billion for 1985 and 1986, while twenty-five thousand people lost their jobs. The Japanese companies lost twice as much money . . . but . . . in a contest of deep pockets theirs were deeper" (1988, p. 55).

Facing red ink and a dismal outlook in memory chips, Intel, which had been one of the first companies to market memory chips, exited in 1986 in order to concentrate on microprocessors, a category it had also pioneered. Around the same time, nine of the eleven US-based producers of high-volume memory chips also exited the memory market (Young 1992). An effort by a group of computer and chip companies to launch a jointly owned memory manufacturer to be called US Memories eventually failed to raise enough funding and was abandoned in 1990. But the firms that remained, such as IBM and Intel, were able to close the technology gap in memory with the Japanese leaders (Iansiti and West 1999).

Intel's microprocessor had been selected for the first IBM PC in 1981. Through a series of strategic moves, including defending its intellectual property and pushing its process technology to the industry forefront, Intel created a competitive wedge between itself and rivals, Intel shored up its position in the microprocessor market during the 1980s by ending its "second-sourcing" agreements with other chip firms, which closed a door to competition. Although Intel's Japanese rivals, such as Fujitsu and NEC, viewed this practice as unfair, they did not push their government to lobby the US government for more competitive practices because the Japanese government was already mired in demands by the US government to open Japanese electronics markets and revalue the yen.[4]

In a series of court cases against one of its licensees, Japan's NEC, Intel established the principal that microcode (the software embedded in a chip's design) is copyrightable, as well as the idea that Intel would vigorously contest challenges to its intellectual property (Afuah 1999). To further separate itself from competitors, Intel sped up its product development cycle and, in 1991, launched an unorthodox branding campaign ("Intel Inside") for its processors.

Intel carved out a quasi-monopoly that grew to account for nearly a fifth of the semiconductor industry's sales at its peak in the late 1990s. In 1999, Intel captured 82 percent of the microprocessor market, even counting non-x86 architecture chips.[5] This is well above the level of market share at which the US Department of Justice considers the industry to be "concentrated."[6]

As US companies were leaving the memory market, dozens of US startups were founded to take advantage of advances in design automation software for designing "application-specific integrated circuits" (ASICs). ASICs, often designed for a particular customer, did not benefit from the cost-reducing volume manufacturing techniques mastered by Japanese firms, but they were able to command a higher profit margin because of their significant advantages, such as reduced unit cost and greater reliability compared with the less-integrated set of chips that would be needed to provide the same functionality.

ASIC entrants from the early 1980s, including LSI Logic and VLSI Technology, generated billions of dollars in revenue and owned their own factories. Beginning in the mid-1980s, a second wave of ASIC start-ups that outsourced production became an important—and US-centric—part of the industry. These "fabless" chip firms will be discussed in the next chapter.

A few US memory producers stayed in the market for most of the 1990s Motorola announced its departure in 1997, and Texas Instruments sold its global DRAM operation to Micron in 1998 in order to concentrate its efforts on building a business in digital signal processors (DSPs), a key component in many of the latest electronics products, from cell phones to anti-lock brakes. IBM, which was a large-scale DRAM producer for its internal needs, announced its exit from DRAM manufacture in 1999 as it ramped up its business in custom logic chips.[7]

The sole US memory survivor, Micron Technology, carved out its niche by using aggressive design methods to trim costs rather than copying the Japanese strategy of relentlessly improving manufacturing technology (Afuah 1999). In addition Micron successfully sued its Japanese rivals in 1985 for violations of US antitrust and antidumping laws. Micron has periodically tried to diversify, first into system-level products like PCs in the 1990s, then into specialized chips like CMOS image sensors for cameras in the 2000s, but memory chips remain its primary line of business.

1.3   The Table Turns

These measures taken by US firms and the government contributed to another dramatic reversal of fortunes, this time with the US industry overtaking its Japanese rivals. Figure 1.1 shows the rise of Japan's global chip market share during the 1980s followed by a steady decline during the 1990s, which caused alarm in Japan.

The increase in the US industry's share largely reflected the growth of one firm—Intel. As shown by the dotted line in figure 1.1, the US share excluding Intel has hovered around 30 percent, only slightly above the Japanese share since 1988.

Table 1.1 shows the top ten firms by revenue in 2000. Intel's share had grown to three times that of the second-ranked firm, Korea's Samsung. Only three Japanese firms were listed, with a combined share of 12 percent. Table 1.2 shows the top ten firms in 2007. Intel occupied the leadership position at 12 percent, but Samsung's share grew to 8 percent.

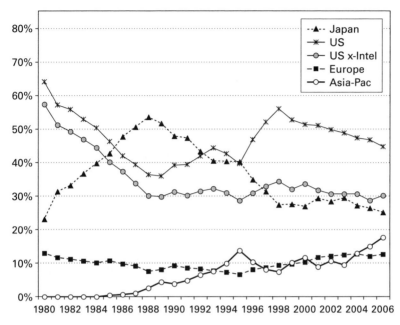

Figure 1.1
Regional shares of semiconductor sales, 1980 to 2006. Source: Authors' calculation using top forty firm data from market research sources. The top forty accounted for 80 to 90 percent of total semiconductor sales during the period.

Samsung Electronics is part of a Korean business group with industrial activities in nontechnology areas such as textiles and sugar. In the 1970s it entered into the semiconductor industry with government inducements in the form of training programs and subsidized credit (Mathews and Cho 2000). Samsung eventually decided to focus on producing DRAM because it's a high volume, standardized product for which the manufacturing skill that it had already developed for complex products such as television tubes was paramount (Hong 1992). Although it initially had to license dated technology from US and Japanese competitors in the early 1980s, it gradually built up its internal technology resources and became the first to demonstrate a working prototype 256-Megabit DRAM in 1994 (Kim 1997). Samsung's leadership of the memory market is also built on a foundation of manufacturing excellence, such as the shortest time required for a wafer to move through the entire fabrication process.[8]

Table 1.2
Top ten semiconductor vendors by revenue, 2007

2007 rank	Company	2007 revenue (US$ millions)	Market share
1	Intel	$33,800	12.3%
2	Samsung (Korea)	$20,464	7.5%
3	Toshiba (Japan)	$11,820	4.3%
4	Texas Instruments	$11,768	4.3%
5	Infineon[a] (Europe)	$10,194	3.7%
6	STMicro. (Europe)	$9,966	3.6%
7	Hynix[b] (Korea)	$9,100	3.3%
8	Renesas (Japan)	$8,001	2.9%
9	AMD	$5,884	2.2%
10	NXP[c] (Europe)	$5,869	2.1%
	Others	$147,045	53.7%
	Total market	$273,911	100.0%

Source: "Worldwide semiconductor revenue increased 4 percent in 2007, according to final results by Gartner," Gartner Press Release, March 31, 2008.
Note: Companies without a geographic designation are US based. If Taiwan foundry TSMC were included, which would be double counting, their $9,828M revenue would put them in seventh place.
a. Infineon's share also reflects sales of its majority-owned memory-chip spin-off Qimonda.
b. Hynix was formerly Hyundai Semiconductor.
c. NXP was formerly Philips' semiconductor division.

In the 2007 top ten, the United States is represented by three firms with a combined share of about 19 percent. Meanwhile Japan's presence among the top ten continued to decline to two companies with 7 percent combined share. The 8th-ranked firm in 2007, Renesas, is a joint venture that took over the logic and flash memory chip divisions of Hitachi and Mitsubishi in 2003.

The reversal of fortunes between the United States and Japan had as much to do with events in Asia as with those in the United States. Even in high-volume memory chips, the top spot was taken from Japanese firms by a Korean producer, Samsung, which followed a relentless investment strategy out of the Japanese playbook in its pursuit of market share. By the mid-1990s, after a decade of effort, it captured the top spot in memory production, which it has held ever since. Another Korean producer, Hyundai Semiconductor (now called Hynix) and, later, Taiwanese producers such as Nanya, Powerchip, and ProMOS grew in importance. The emergence of Korea and Taiwan in the overall industry can be seen in the "Asia–Pacific" line in figure 1.1

Table 1.3 shows the top eight producers of DRAM in 2007. Outside of Taiwan and Korea, the only remaining major DRAM producers are Qimonda in Europe, Micron in the United States, and Elpida in Japan. Qimonda was spun off in 2006 by Infineon, a semiconductor company that was itself spun off from Germany's Siemens in 1999, but is not yet independent as of 2008. Elpida was created in 2000 from the DRAM divisions of Hitachi, NEC, and, later, Mitsubishi. Japan's other leading memory producer, Toshiba, has switched most of its memory efforts to flash chips, which are more expensive but are used in mobile devices because they retain their data even after their power source is switched off.

As mentioned above, DRAM was considered of strategic importance in the 1980s. However, the current domination of the DRAM market by companies based outside the United States, Europe, and Japan is no longer seen as the crisis it would have been twenty years ago. The main reason is that DRAM was knocked off its technology-driver throne by other types of chips that also permit high-volume runs of a single design, with their related learning benefits. In the United States, Intel uses its newest process on its processors, while Texas Instruments uses its

Table 1.3
Worldwide DRAM market shares by revenue, 2007

Rank	Company	Headquarters country	2007 sales ($US millions)	Growth 2006–2007	Market share
1	Samsung	South Korea	$8,699	−11.5%	27.7%
2	Hynix	South Korea	$6,682	18.4%	21.3%
3	Qimonda	Germany	$3,965	−26.2%	12.6%
4	Elpida	Japan	$3,758	7.7%	12.0%
5	Micron	United States	$3,185	−13.8%	10.1%
6	Nanya	Taiwan	$1,479	−29.9%	4.7%
7	Powerchip	Taiwan	$1,229	−16.9%	3.9%
8	ProMOS	Taiwan	$1,071	−26.7%	3.4%
	Others	—	$1,352	12.0%	4.3%
	Total		$31,420	−8.4%	100.0%

Source: Sales, growth, and share data are Gartner estimates reported in Mark LaPedus, "Elpida, Hynix gain in DRAM rankings," *EE Times*, February 4, 2008.

DSP-based cell phone baseband chips as its high-volume learning device. Flash memory, which used to lag by three years, has become the driver at Samsung, the leading DRAM company.[9] Early in the 2000s Samsung foresaw the enormous potential demand for solid-state data storage and began doubling flash density every year, well ahead of the pace predicted by Moore's Law.

DRAM, which has characteristics of a commodity because of the interchangeability of products among vendors, is a particularly cyclical chip market as swings in capacity and demand are often poorly synchronized. During periods of excess capacity, prices fall, sometimes below manufacturing cost for the least efficient producers. The end of 2007 saw the beginning of such a period. The relatively small Taiwanese producers are most at risk because of their reliance on foreign technology partners and a heavy debt burden.[10] The Taiwanese memory firms appear unlikely to emerge in their present form from the deepening recession, with some kind of restructuring expected as part of a new government partnership with Elpida.[11]

1.4   How Japan Stumbled

Beyond steps taken by companies in the United States and the rest of Asia, the relative decline of Japan's chip industry owes a lot to circumstances in Japan.[12] These include a deterioration of the investment climate, an overemphasis on quality, and an overdependence on the domestic market. Another factor, Japan's weak environment for start-up ventures, is addressed in the following section.

One of Japan's biggest impediments to continued market leadership was a decline in investment in new factories brought on by the bursting of Japan's asset bubble in the early 1990s.[13] The end of a real estate bubble led to a credit crunch, and companies found it more expensive and harder to raise funds through issuing bonds or stocks. Already burdened by high debt-to-equity ratios, Japanese firms reduced their capital equipment spending in 1992. Meanwhile Korean firms raised theirs.

Although factors like chip size and cost also influence DRAM market share, steady renewal of leading-edge production capacity is the bare minimum for maintaining or raising market share. The global share of capital expenditures shadows the country shifts in memory leadership (table 1.4). Japan's share of capital expenditures by chip firms rose from 29 percent in 1980 to 50 percent in 1990, and then fell to only 25 percent by 1997. Meanwhile the share of US firms fell from 60 percent in 1980 to 30 percent in 1990, and then recovered only slightly. Meanwhile the "rest of world" category, primarily Korea, starts from zero in 1980, and grows to 33 percent in 1997.

Ironically, the emphasis on quality and reliability that brought Japanese firms to the top of the memory chip industry was part of their undoing, as the primary application markets for memory shifted from mainframes, where long-term reliability was highly valued, to personal computers and consumer products with more limited life spans (Cole and Matsumiya 2007). Japanese DRAM engineers continued to use costly, customized equipment to produce chips that exceeded expectations when

Table 1.4
Capital spending by semiconductor companies, share of world total, selected years

Region	1980	1985	1990	1997
United States	60.4%	35.5%	29.8%	33.0%
Japan	28.9%	46.7%	50.0%	25.0%
Europe	10.7%	8.3%	9.9%	9.0%
Rest of world	0.0%	9.4%	10.3%	33.0%
Total	100.0%	100.0%	100.0%	100.0%

Source: Macher et al. (1999, fig. 4); data supplied by author.
Note: Columns may not total precisely, due to rounding.

most other chip producers were pursuing more standardized solutions (Yunogami 2006).

Japan was also undone by the domestic focus of its chip firms, most of which were part of large conglomerates making a range of electronic and electrical systems. This was a strength when it came to promoting sales opportunities among business group networks, and Japanese companies were able to rely on high prices in Japan to subsidize price-based competition overseas (Prestowitz, op. cit.). But this strength became a major weakness when the Japanese economy, which had roared ahead at more than 3 percent per year in the 1980s, slid into a decade of much slower growth in the 1990s coupled with price deflation.

All the leading Japanese chip producers of the 1990s were vertically integrated with systems divisions. Although Japanese systems companies were strong in mainframe computers, they were less active in personal computers, the major global growth market of the 1990s. The Japanese market was relatively slow to adopt the PC platform, which partly reflected the difficulty of inputting Japanese characters. In 1995 Japan had roughly one-fifth the PCs per capita of the United States.[14] Instead of general-purpose PCs, Japanese business users had favored specialized equipment like dedicated word processors.

The idiosyncrasies of the domestic market had implications for memory chips as well.[15] Although DRAM chips are often referred to as a

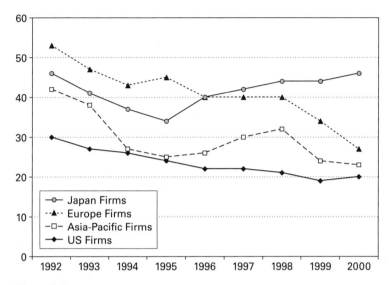

Figure 1.2
Home substitution index for semiconductor sales, 1992 to 2000 (authors' calculation; see appendix for details).

commodity product, there are subtle but important differences of configuration (e.g., number of bits per storage unit, power supply) that would require significant engineering effort to redesign. The DRAM requirements of Japan's consumer electronics makers, which were foremost for their captive chip divisions, were incompatible with those of PC makers in the rest of the world.

Japan has been referred to as a Galapogos market—a market that is vibrant with ideas and original innovation, but this innovation doesn't spread to global markets became Japan is isolated from the rest of the world, which develops in a different way.[16] We think that this describes what has happened in many semiconductors and consumer electronics markets.

To explore Japan chipmakers' dependence on the domestic market and relative isolation from the global market, we constructed a "home substitution index" that shows (figure 1.2) the excess of semiconductor sales to the home market above the home market's share of total global sales (see the chapter appendix for details). For Europe, Asia–Pacific (i.e., Taiwan and Korea) and the United States, the home substitution index ends lower in 2000 than it begins in 1992. In sharp contrast, Japan's reliance on chip sales within Japan starts high and increases during the late 1990s even though Japan's chip consumption declined as a share of the world market, from 32 percent in 1992 to 23 percent in 2000. The global share of Japan's market peaked in 1988 at 40 percent.[17] The US market went from 30.8 percent of world chip consumption to 31.3 percent over the same period.

The dip in Japan's Home Substitution Index (HSI) in the mid-1990s is driven by a boom in the memory market that allowed Japanese chip makers to expand overseas. As Japan's memory market share declined during the later years of the 1990s, Japanese chip makers lost share faster overseas than at home. Japan's HSI for non-memory chips alone was relatively flat, falling slightly from 57 in 1992 to 51 in 2000.

Table 1.5, which shows the regional breakdown of sales by the top ten chip companies in 2005, provides an updated view of Japan's home-market dependence. While most of the non-Japanese companies earn about half of their revenues in "Asia–Pacific" because of the importance of Taiwan and China for electronics manufacturing, the three Japanese firms earned between 57 and 63 percent of their revenues from sales to Japanese customers. Meanwhile the Japan market declined even further in terms of world consumption. By 2005 Japan's market size had fallen to 19 percent (and the United States to 18 percent) as Asia–Pacific (mostly China) grew to 45 percent of the world market.

Japan's largest chip companies have been undertaking organizational restructuring in response to their decline. Hitachi, which was almost out of the top ten by 2000 (table 1.1), divided its chip manufacturing into two joint ventures: a memory venture with NEC called Elpida and a separate venture for logic and flash with Mitsubishi called Renesas, which was the eighth-ranked chip firm in 2007. Among Japan's other major chip producers, Fujitsu put its flash operations into a joint venture called Spansion with US firm AMD, and Sony shifted the manufacturing plants for the processors in its Playstation game consoles into a minority-owned joint venture to be controlled by its development partner, Toshiba. The consolidations and alliances have allowed the newly created firms to achieve greater focus and better scale economies.

Table 1.5
Top ten chip companies' sales by region, 2005 (percentage of global semiconductor revenue)

2005 rank	Company	Americas	Europe–Middle East	Japan	Asia–Pacific
1	Intel	19.6%	21.0%	9.5%	49.9%
2	Samsung (Korea)	28.7%	19.9%	16.4%	35.0%
3	Texas Instruments	14.2%	19.6%	15.3%	50.9%
4	Toshiba (Japan)	6.2%	4.3%	62.7%	26.8%
5	STMicro. (Europe)	16.5%	33.5%	3.4%	46.6%
6	Infineon (Europe)	24.6%	37.7%	4.8%	32.9%
7	Renesas (Japan)	6.2%	9.3%	58.9%	25.6%
8	NEC (Japan)	12.3%	12.2%	56.5%	19.1%
9	Philips (Europe)	9.5%	25.2%	4.3%	61.1%
10	Freescale	26.6%	20.4%	5.1%	48.0%
	Top ten companies	18.0%	20.5%	19.9%	41.6%
	Others	17.5%	12.0%	23.3%	47.2%
	All companies	17.7%	16.1%	21.6%	44.5%

Source: iSuppli, as reported in "iSuppli: Asia Pacific shaped fortunes of key chip suppliers in 2005," *DigiTimes.com*, May 11, 2006.
Note: Companies without a geographic designation are US-based.

Beyond memory, Japanese chip makers clung to broad portfolios of chips while producers elsewhere were pursuing specialization, as exemplified by the processor-centric strategies of Intel and Texas Instruments. Medium-size US chip companies account for about half the firms in the global top fifty. A great many of the US firms are relatively young, having been founded since 1980, and specialize in specific types of analog or digital-logic chips. One area where the United States has achieved global competitive advantage has been with fabless companies, where Japan continues to lag.

1.5   United States and Japan: Start-ups a Defining Difference[18]

Based on the US experience, start-ups are an important way for an economy to exploit new opportunities, but Japan's economy is relatively inhospitable to high-tech start-up ventures. In the fiscal year ending March 2004, Japan had well over fifty companies with electronics revenues of more than US$1 billion, but none of them were established more recently than 1968.[19] The most recently established semiconductor firm among them was Rohm (1958). By contrast, the United States is home to many electronics companies that are much younger and have grown to considerable size, such as Dell (1984), Cisco Systems (1984), and Solectron (1977). Among the top twenty US semiconductor companies in 2004, all with revenue greater than US$1 billion, three were founded in the 1960s (including Intel), six in the 1980s, and two (Nvidia and Broadcom) in the 1990s.

The importance of smaller companies in the innovation process in the United States is highlighted by the fact that National Science Foundation data show companies with less than 250 employees account for 9 percent of manufacturing R&D spending, and have an R&D-to-sales ratio of 7.5 percent.[20] Small and medium enterprises play a more limited role in manufacturing and R&D in Japan, where firms with up to 300 employees account for only 4 percent of manufacturing R&D spending and have an R&D-to-sales ratio of 2.2 percent.[21]

In both the United States and Japan, major semiconductor and electronics producers undertake a great deal of R&D, but less than half of the ideas generated internally are developed further.[22] Start-ups can be an important vehicle for exploiting ideas that industry leaders do not pursue. With low overhead and rapid decision making, start-ups can develop new technology and products faster and cheaper than large companies can.

The primary business model for semiconductor start-ups is the fabless model, in which the company designs and markets its own chips but outsources the manufacturing to another company, most frequently a "foundry" that specializes in manufacturing chips for others (Crisis 2). According to the Fabless Semiconductor Association's report on publicly traded fabless companies in 2005, 84 US companies accounted for 64 percent of global fabless revenues.[23] The second-highest concentration of fabless companies was in Taiwan, with 62 companies and 17 percent of revenues. Fabless companies were scarce in Japan, with three listed companies (MegaChips, RealVision, and THine Electronics) accounting for just over 1 percent of global fabless revenues.

Whittaker's study of Japanese entrepreneurs describes them as "life-work entrepreneurs" whose companies are typically oriented toward the domestic economy, focused on developing technology, and limited in finding first customers or selling business assets (Whittaker 2009). He sees Japanese entrepreneurship as both shaped by and limited by the nature of markets as well as social and cultural factors.

A high-level and comprehensive national report[24] on the state of start-ups reflects Japan's concerns that the country is losing out, especially to the United States, on developing innovation in high-tech industries because of lack of a supportive environment for start-ups, especially in relations with large Japanese enterprises and in operating in domestic labor and financial markets. Our 2004 to 2006 fieldwork at start-ups in Tokyo, Yokohama, Kyushu, and Osaka was consistent with this report. We found that Japanese start-ups face four major difficulties:

1. Acquiring management and marketing skills, since there are a limited number of executives with start-up experience.

2. Finding customers, since large Japanese companies prefer established suppliers.

3. Recruiting engineers, who don't want to lose the status and security provided by a large company.

4. Securing venture capital financing, because the total amount of Japanese venture capital investment was about 3.6 percent of the US amount in 2006.[25]

Japanese start-ups take several forms, and they can be characterized by their independence from, or their ties to, large companies.

The self-funded *independent start-up* model is used by many young Japanese companies in the electronics industry. Initial funding is provided by the founders, who sell services to generate cash flow while a new product is being developed. For example, start-up semiconductor firms in Japan often sell chip design services while developing their own chip. This was the model followed by MegaChips, a fabless semiconductor company founded in 1990 and listed on the Tokyo Stock Exchange in 2000.

Although this model can succeed, it is a slow path to innovation. Independent start-ups suffer from inadequate initial funding and from lack of access to large Japanese companies as customers. The services business, which has limited growth potential, requires as much as 80 percent of the managers' and engineers' time, which slows down the development of an innovative product.

An important but rare variant is the *Silicon Valley model* where the start-up adopts a high-risk, high-return strategy of commercializing innovative technology with funding from venture capitalists instead of using the cash flow from services. This model, pursued by visionary firms like Internet companies Rakuten and Google, is slowly becoming more common in Japan. However, most venture-funded start-ups in Japan are less ambitious than those in the United States. Companies like Sony and Matsushita operate corporate venture capital subsidiaries, but so far most of their investments are outside Japan. Silicon Valley's venture capital model, which targets opportunities for high, rapid growth with a low success rate, is not congruent with Japanese economic institutions and culture where failure carries a heavy penalty, such as the inability to obtain bank financing for a new venture for ten years after a business failure.

A common method of creating new companies in Japan is for a large company to assign a developed technology to a wholly owned *corporate division or subsidiary* that remains under corporate control. We consider these divisions or wholly owned spin-offs to be paths to commercialization rather than innovation because they typically involve a late stage of product development, and employees are still under the large company's umbrella and protected from failure. The employees are also prevented from sharing in high returns from the innovation in the event of a success. An example of this type of company is Hitachi's Mu Solutions, which was set up as an in-house (*shanai*) venture company (i.e., fully owned but with separate management team) to commercialize wireless data tags. After Mu Solutions became a supplier to a large company, Hitachi returned the venture back to Hitachi to facilitate total systems integration.[26]

The *independent spin-out* model, which represents a more autono-mous type of corporate spin-out, is rare in Japan. When a parent com-pany has a technology that it chooses not to develop, the engineers who worked on the technology leave to start a new company that receives an exclusive technology license and only partial funding from the parent company. An example is Fab Solutions, which markets an advanced sys-tem for process control in semiconductor manufacturing. Four engineers from NEC were allowed to take the business private in 2002. They ob-tained two rounds of venture funding and were included in a 2004 list of "Top Emerging Start-ups"[27] but appear to have gone out of business.

The *cooperative venture* involves an independent start-up that enters a strategic alliance with a larger company that provides up-front resources in return for a share of the licensing fees or a share of output. The large company will usually be part of the venture company's supply chain (e.g., an equipment supplier or potential customer). This relationship overcomes some of the problems facing venture companies in Japan. This model has the advantage of providing better resources and, in the case of downstream cooperation, better access to customers. In the com-ponents sector, THine Electronics was founded in 1991 as a joint ven-ture with its customer Samsung Electronics, and the founders were able to buy out Samsung's share in 1997. A younger semiconductor start-up, IPFlex, received a minority investment in 2003 from Fujitsu, which pro-vides fabrication services and development assistance.

The Japanese government has already taken important steps to remove regulatory constraints facing start-ups, such as the liberalization of stock options and abolition of minimum capital requirements. Starting a new company in Japan has become easier and less expensive in recent years according to a World Bank ranking.[28] For example, the administrative steps required for registering a new firm fell from eleven in the 2004 re-port to eight in 2008, but that is still higher than the average of six for the OECD, a group of middle- and high-income countries. The cost of a start-up expressed as a percentage of gross national income per capita has fallen from 10.5 to 7.5 percent, also above the OECD average of 5.1 percent.

The lifetime employment offered to regular employees of large compa-nies coupled with limited participation in the global brain circulation that links the United States and the rest of Asia restrains Japan's labor market mobility. Yet the proportion of the workforce who have lifetime employment in major companies has fallen (Nakata and Miyazaki 2007), and younger Japanese who entered the labor market to diminished opportunities during Japan's long recession are more mobile and more global in their outlook. We expect that the hold of lifetime employment will continue to weaken and mobility will increase over time, which may prove to be an important step in building a foundation for start-ups in Japan.

1.6   Lessons and Conclusions

Shifting global competitive advantage in the 1980s and 1990s created an atmosphere of crisis in the United States in the 1980s and then in Japan in the 1990s, and drove changes in both countries. The key response in the United States was the major change in product mix from memory toward processors and custom logic. This radical repositioning was led by Intel's microprocessor powerhouse, and was supported by a wide range of companies exploiting new technological opportunities. Japan's response in the 1990s was constrained by her weak domestic economy, and her semiconductor industry underinvested in capacity.

One of the primary lessons of the global leadership crisis is that in a rapidly evolving industry like semiconductors, national competitive advantage is often fleeting. Japan's global competitive advantage evaporated with strategic responses by rivals and Japan's own response to a weak domestic economy. This echoed the way that Japan's initial rise highlighted the weaknesses of the US market leaders. American chip companies are again riding high, but as we will see in the rest of this book, any of a number of ongoing crises could unseat them as recent entrants in Asia compete for market share and global competitive advantage.

The struggle for global advantage during the 1980s and 1990s brought considerable benefits to the world's consumers, particularly businesses, in the form of computer platforms with steadily improving performance at steady prices. Of course workers' fortunes reflect the fortunes of their employers and industry, and semiconductor workers suffered from the swings in employment and profits. In Crisis 6 we describe how the weakened market position of US firms resulted in an erosion of employment security and firm-based retraining and an increase of labor mobility.

For governments, the years of US–Japan rivalry established the reduced scope for government intervention in an established industry. In the 1970s a range of policy tools such as tariffs and subsidies were available to the Japanese government in its effort to overtake US chip firms, and international trade agreements forced these to be dropped once Japan's industry was established. The direct policy tools of the past have been sidelined by various agreements under the World Trade Organization (WTO), although developing countries like China are still able to provide subsidies to push their infant industry along.

Nevertheless, governments still have important roles to play in managing their exchange rates, financial markets, and domestic economies, all of which can have a major impact on the semiconductor industry. Governments also fund WTO-compliant precompetitive joint research programs in Europe, Japan, and the United States.

Government can also play a more direct role. The Franco–Italian joint venture STMicroelectronics, which has been a top ten chip firm since the mid-1990s, was majority-owned by French and Italian government entities until 1999 and has benefited from regular participation in EU programs for microelectronics research, so it would be an exaggeration to say it was fully exposed to the free market. Direct intervention still takes place to varying degrees. As the global economic recession spread in 2008, the Taiwan government proposed loan relief for its memory chip firms, and a Chinese government-connected telecommunications firm, Datang, made a major investment in China's leading, but loss-making, chip manufacturer, SMIC.[29] We expect to see more government intervention to help faltering firms worldwide, as companies shift their strategies toward survival rather than global competitive advantage, to which we return in Crisis 7.

The industry has always faced large business cycle swings. However, the challenges of these large demand swings have become more severe because of the rapidly rising fixed costs for manufacturing and design, to which we turn in the next two chapters.

Appendix

The Home Substitution Index (HSI) in figure 1.2 is a statistic that allows us to see whether firms from a chip-producing region realize a greater share of revenue in their "home" (own region) market than we would expect given the size of that market. The measure is standardized for the size of the home market so that the results are comparable across regions.

The HSI is calculated using the following formula:

$$HSI = \frac{[(\% \text{ of Sales in "Home" Region}) - ("Home" \text{ Market as } \% \text{ of World Market})]}{\text{Foreign Markets as } \% \text{ of World Market}} \times 100.$$

The HSI shows to what extent the "excess" sales to the home market (i.e., sales above home's market size) "replace" sales to foreign markets. Given that the share of "home" sales by chip firms in each region was larger than that regional market's share of world sales, the relevant range of the index is from 0 to 100. The lower is the HSI, the more global are the sales distribution of home-based firms. At zero, the share of sales to the home market matches the market's relative size. If true for all regions, this would represent a state of perfect, frictionless globalization. At 100, sales to the home market replace 100 percent of the sales to foreign markets. If true for all regions, the world is broken into isolated regional blocs.

In 1992 the HSI shows that US companies replaced 30 percent of the foreign sales that would have been predicted if the industry were perfectly globalized with sales in the Americas. In other words, in 1992 US companies' sales to foreign markets were 70 percent of what would be expected based on the relative size of the four regional markets.

Companies in all regions except Japan reduced their reliance on home market sales during the 1990s. European, Korean, and Taiwanese firms rapidly became more global in sales as their HSI converged toward the US low value of 20 in 2000.

Crisis 2
Rising Cost of Fabrication

The cost of semiconductor manufacturing is rising at such a tremendous rate that the big challenge will lie not in the ability to make better chips, but in having enough money to do so.
—Robert Doering, senior fellow in Silicon Technology Development, Texas Instruments, December 1996[1]

One of the fundamental economic forces in the semiconductor industry, the rising cost of fabrication, reflects new process technology that allows more complex chips to be designed at lower cost per transistor. However the fabs in which this occurs now carry price tags that few chip firms can afford.

Crisis 2, rising fabrication cost, is related to Crisis 5, which concerns a critical manufacturing step called photolithography. Crisis 2 also plays a role in shifting national advantage as countries willing to directly or indirectly subsidize the cost of new fabs, such as Japan in the 1980s (Crisis 1) and China in the 2000s (Crisis 8), have been able to grab market share.

One possible response to this crisis is consolidation, which allows companies to become large enough to justify investing in new fabs. While some restructuring occurred in the 2000s (see Crisis 7), industry-wide consolidation was largely forestalled by a radical business model innovation that began in the late 1980s with the creation of independent contract manufacturers (foundries) for microchips. This unforeseen response allowed design-only start-ups to flourish, and it also heralded a more rapid shift of fabrication to Asia with Taiwan home to the top two foundries (TSMC and UMC), which together accounted for almost half the global foundry revenue in 2007 (table 2.4).

This chapter begins with a brief discussion of the technical factors contributing to the rising cost of fabrication. The next section discusses changes in the technology of chip design that permitted design-only firms to contract out their fabrication to manufacturing-only foundries, which has profoundly altered the industry's structure. This "solution" has led to new concerns about the shift of manufacturing to Asia.

2.1   Chip Fabrication: the Price Tag Explodes

Semiconductor fabrication creates electronic circuitry on a silicon wafer by transferring patterns from a set of reusable templates called masks onto the wafer surface. Light is passed through a mask to the treated wafer surface in a process step called lithography, and then the wafer is processed by other tools to create one layer of the chip. The fabrication of an integrated circuit requires hundreds of different steps using dozens of different types of equipment (commonly called "tools"). Complex chips can require as many as 30 mask layers and take weeks to process from start to finish. All processes take place in a carefully controlled "clean room" that's classified by standards such as one dust particle per cubic foot of air (class one).

One of the central drivers of fab cost is lithography equipment, which typically accounts for 20 percent of the fixed cost of an advanced fabrication facility.[2] As we will discuss further in Crisis 5, advances in lithography technology are central to the industry's ability to follow Moore's Law, with a new process generation (smaller feature size) introduced every two to three years. While some generations require only new materials, others require new, more complex lithography machines that now cost millions of dollars each.

Another important factor in semiconductor economics is wafer size. The silicon wafers on which the integrated circuits are fabricated are round, and one wafer can hold anywhere from dozens to thousands of raw chips (known as "die"), depending on the die size. After fabrication, the die on a wafer are separated and, in most cases, packaged in a protective shell that includes wires for connecting to other components.

Larger wafers permit more chips to be manufactured for a given wafer throughput and die size, and this reduces the cost per chip. For example, the move from 4-inch to 6-inch wafers (a 1.5× increase in wafer diameter) more than doubled (2.25×) the wafer area. The costly move that began in 2000 from 8-inch (200-mm) to 12-inch (300-mm) wafers (again, a 1.5× increase in wafer diameter) provided a 2.5× increase in wafer size. A further move to 18-inch (450-mm) wafers, which would again impose enormous development costs on industry leaders and equipment makers, entered an early stage of evaluation in 2008 and would provide a similar increase.[3]

As discussed in Crisis 1, semiconductor fabrication is characterized by economies of scale and learning through experience, which favors large-scale facilities that produce products using the most advanced process technology, especially in the case of high-volume digital chips like DRAM (dynamic random-access memory).

The rising cost of lithography and other manufacturing equipment has resulted in the push to expand output in order to capture economies of scale. The typical scale for an 8-inch fab in the 1990s was 20,000 to 30,000 wafers per month. A newer crop of *megafabs*, such as an Intel "flash memory" fab in Albuquerque and a Hynix DRAM fab in Korea have a capacity of 50,000 wafers per month. In 2005 the Taiwanese foundry TSMC announced its intention to build, in stages, a *gigafab* that would eventually process 100,000 wafers per month at an eventual investment cost of $10 billion. One market researcher estimated that this would result in a 10 percent unit cost savings over megafabs because fixed costs, such as software for monitoring and automation, can be spread out over the larger output and because production bottlenecks from equipment failure are less likely to arise as a result of the increased redundancy of each type of equipment.[4] However, even as the unit costs go down, the fixed costs of building fabs have skyrocketed and resulted in fabs that must operate constantly at extremely high volumes to be profitable.

As shown in table 2.1, the cost to build a leading-edge fab in 1983 was about $200 million, but by 2007 the price tag for an advanced fab of minimum efficient scale had climbed to as much as $5 billion. A flash memory fab built in Japan by Toshiba and its joint-venture partner SanDisk reached a scale of more than 100,000 300-mm wafers per month at an estimated capital cost of $7 billion.[5]

Table 2.1
Rising cost of building a leading-edge fab, 1983 to 2003

Year	1983	1990	1997	2001	2007
Wafer (inches in diameter)	4	6	8	12	12
Linewidth (microns)	1.200	0.800	0.250	0.130	0.065
Cost (US$ millions)	$200	$400	$1,250	$3,000	$5,000

Source: Adapted from Hurtarte et al. (2007, fig. 1.14).

The economics and appropriate timeline of developing 450-mm wafer fabs is being debated, even as industry leaders Intel, Samsung, and TSMC have pledged to go forward with development of pilot lines by 2012.[6] Equipment makers are especially concerned about the development costs for equipment to handle the large, delicate wafers, and how much they would be expected to contribute.[7] Cost simulations indicate that wafer demand and volumes will eventually provide competitive advantage to those companies who have 450-mm fabs.[8] This elite club may well be limited to Intel, TSMC, and Samsung, plus a handful of joint-venture fabs.

To the rising cost of infrastructure must be added the rising cost of developing each process generation, which is also increasing at a formidable pace. Development of a basic process flow for a 300-mm wafer fab at the 0.065-micron generation reportedly ran about $1.5 billion per firm, while the comparable expenses for the follow-on 0.045-micron generation jumped to $2.4 billion.[9] This is in sharp contrast to an estimated $10 billion total spent by the *entire worldwide industry* of chip makers and their equipment suppliers to develop the 1-micron process generation in the late 1980s.[10] While some of this increase has been offset by the formation of various R&D consortia, the industry's R&D to sales ratio has been rising since the mid-1990s (Crisis 7).

Not all integrated (fab-owning) chip firms run leading-edge megafabs. Companies with specialized products or processes, such as analog chip firms, are able to remain viable at a smaller scale by using trailing-edge processes and smaller wafers. These companies have older fabs and equipment that are no longer burdened by the heavy depreciation charges that weigh on the industry leaders, and they avoid the painful R&D expenses of leading-edge process development.

Table 2.2
Wafer starts by process generation, fourth quarter 2007

Process generation	Year introduced	Percentage of wafer starts
>0.500 micron		6.5%
0.500 micron	1992	8.0%
0.350 micron	1995	6.7%
0.250 micron	1997	4.5%
0.180 micron	1999	6.9%
0.130 micron	2002	14.1%
0.090 micron	2004	20.7%
0.065 micron	2006	32.6%

Source: calculated from Semiconductor Industry Association SICAS data (http://www.sia-online.org/pre_statistics.cfm). "Year introduced" is based on multiple sources, including *National Technology Roadmap for Semiconductors*, various years, and Intel's *Microprocessor Quick Reference Guide* (http://www.intel.com/pressroom/kits/quickreffam.htm).
Note: "Process generation" is the approximate value of the smallest feature on a wafer; individual companies may use processes whose smallest feature differs from the generation name.

Table 2.2 shows the share of each process generation in the industry's output in terms of wafer area for the fourth quarter of 2007. Roughly one-third of wafers are at the leading edge, 0.065 micron, and another third are at the previous two generations (0.090 and 0.130 micron). These recent-generation chips would account for an even greater share of revenue because their performance and size advantages command a high price. The other one-third of wafers are used for chips in which size or speed are less important than low cost, which is the case for many consumer products such as DVD players or microwave ovens.

Similarly the larger 12-inch (or 300-mm) wafers have not totally displaced smaller wafers. Only about a third of wafers run in 2007 were 12-inch, although their share would be larger if calculated in terms of silicon surface area.[11]

During the 1980s it was still possible for a start-up to enter the industry as an integrated producer because sufficient capital was available for promising projects targeting high-volume markets. In view of the relentless rise in fab cost, the mid-1990s saw what may well have been the last entries by integrated producers, a batch of Taiwanese memory producers including Powerchip Semiconductor and Nanya Technology that are now among the top DRAM suppliers (Crisis 1). But even then, when financial and technical entry barriers were lower than they are today, those entrants were backed by established Taiwanese electronics producers that wanted to expand into semiconductors, not by venture capital. The high cost and relatively unattractive risk-return trade-offs (Crisis 7) make it improbable that any new venture-backed chip firms will include a high-volume fab in their business plan.

2.2 Going To Pieces: The Fabless-Foundry Model

One possibility for industry evolution in the face of the rising cost of fixed investment would have been consolidation to a smaller number of very large integrated manufacturers. Some consolidation and restructuring of the industry has occurred in the 2000s, as discussed in Crisis 7, but much more might have been necessary if not for an organizational innovation that permitted new chip firms to compete without making a massive investment in a fab.

The key development was that chip fabrication and assembly became available as outsourced services. Many of these outsourced service providers are located in Asia, which provides a way for firms based in high-cost countries to tap into Asia's pools of relatively low-cost skilled labor, as we discuss in Crisis 8.

This de-integration of the chip industry has a long history that began with assembly, the postfabrication stage of production when the bare chips are packaged for use in an electronic system. In the 1960s US chip companies started moving assembly, a very labor-intensive process at the time, to low-wage locations in Asia to meet the low-cost competition from Japan, and most large chip makers eventually followed suit (Brown and Linden 2006). Before long, local Asian producers emerged to offer assembly services. In 2006, 43.5 percent of all chip assembly and test

Table 2.3
Independent assembly and test providers, 2007

2006 rank	Company	HQ location	2006 revenue (US$ millions)	Market share
1	ASE Group	Taiwan	$3,080	15.0%
2	Amkor	United States	$2,739	13.3%
3	SPIL	Taiwan	$1,967	9.5%
4	STATS ChipPAC	Singapore	$1,631	7.9%
5	UTAC	Singapore	$756	3.7%
	Others		$10,427	50.6%
	Total market		$20,600	100.0%

Source: "Gartner says worldwide semiconductor assembly and test services revenue increased 7.4 percent in 2007," Gartner Press Release, March 12, 2008.
Note: Data are preliminary as of their reporting date.

was outsourced, and the figure has been growing rapidly in recent years as the complexity and diversity of packages has increased.[12] The top five assembly contractors (table 2.3), with nearly half the total contracting revenue in 2007, are Asia-based, except Amkor, which shifted its headquarters from South Korea to Arizona in 1999.[13]

Fabrication and design remained firmly integrated within companies during the 1970s. Most chips at that time were for general-purpose use, and competitive advantage lay primarily in process knowledge, so splitting off design as a separate function would have made little sense. But the importance of design as a differentiator for chips and for the systems that use them has grown as continued miniaturization permitted the placement of ever more dense and complex functions on a single chip.

New technologies permitted the emergence in the mid-1980s of design-only (*fabless*) chip companies that outsourced the manufacturing of their chips to an integrated chip company with spare capacity. Developments that spurred the rise of fabless companies include the automation of chip design with EDA software and technologies that provide an interface between semiconductor design and manufacturing, which we now describe in more detail.

Chip design, which was initially done entirely by hand, has steadily become more automated, and electronic design automation (EDA) software has grown into a $5 billion industry.[14] Designs were digitized in the 1970s, and new design methods such as "standard cell" design, which employs reusable blocks of design data, were developed (Hilbert 1991). True automation began in the 1980s with automated mapping of transistors across the area of a chip, followed later by logic synthesis, which converts a higher level abstraction of a chip's functionality into the circuits (MacMillen et al. 2000).

Over the same period the interface between chip designers and fabrication plants became more standardized. In the early 1970s, researchers at UC Berkeley developed a circuit simulation system called SPICE (Simulation Program with Integrated Circuit Emphasis) that continues to be useful for allowing fabs to communicate fab-specific circuit characteristics to designers. In the late 1970s, the industry adopted the GDSII (Graphic Data System II) data format as a de facto standard for conveying a design to the fab, and this format is still in use in 2009.

Meanwhile, changes on the manufacturing side also supported the separation of design. During the 1980s, the metal-oxide–semiconductor (MOS) process gradually became the mainstream semiconductor fabrication technology. Unlike the power-hungry bipolar process that dominated through the 1970s, MOS offered the long-term advantage that the performance of its microcomponents improved uniformly as their physical dimensions shrunk (Bassett 2002, p. 44). MOS therefore provided a predictable technology trajectory for designers to target. Around the same time the Berkeley transistor simulation model (BSIM) appeared and was formally adopted in 1994 over competing models as an industry standard for conveying manufacturing information from the factory to design automation software.

Because of the idiosyncrasies of semiconductor manufacturing, chip designers need to know technical details about the process technology in each fab where their chip will be manufactured. This information is conveyed in two primary ways. First, *technical models* like BSIM detail the precise characteristics of each type of microcomponent, such as a transistor, that the manufacturer offers; subtle variations can occur even in different factories of a single company. Second, *design rules* specify the technical boundaries for physically arranging these devices in a chip layout; designs must follow the rules to be manufacturable.

These developments allowed the separation of semiconductor design and manufacturing even as manufacturing became more technically complex (Crisis 5). In other words, firms could potentially sell chips of their own design without the expense of building a fab.

"Fabless" chip firms began to appear in the mid-1980s, including Xilinx and Chips and Technologies. Of 124 semiconductor start-ups in the United States from 1978 to 1987, nearly two-thirds (79) did not own a fab (Angel 1990). In the fabless-foundry business model, the fabless firms are able to compete with other chip firms by creating designs based on their own intellectual property, such as an algorithm for compressing video, without having to master the complex process technology or bear the heavy investment of chip manufacturing. This division of labor proved very successful, and the fabless sector has grown much faster than the chip industry as a whole.

US venture capitalists were initially skeptical of the fabless business model, and early fabless start-ups turned to Japan, where companies were interested in opportunities to learn from Silicon Valley innovators, for financing and spare manufacturing capacity.[15] However, relying on vertically integrated firms for fabrication raised intellectual property issues because of the information revealed when the design was passed to the fab, and the possibility that the fab owner might decide to enter the fabless company's market. There were also issues of capacity availability since the fab owner might place a higher priority on its internal capacity needs during a market upturn, just when the fabless company also wanted to raise output.

In response to the opportunity presented by fabless firms, new manufacturing-only (*foundry*) firms that sold no products of their own were established. The term "silicon foundry" was coined in the 1970s by Gordon Moore of Moore's Law renown and popularized in the industry by Carver Mead, one of the pioneers of design automation.[16] Use of a foundry solves the intellectual property and capacity commitment issues that arose when fabless companies used potential competitors for their manufacturing.

Table 2.4
Top ten foundries, 2007

Company (location)	Business model	Revenue 2007 (US$ millions)	Growth (%) 2006– 2007	Share of foundry sales (%)
TSMC (Taiwan)	Pure-play	$9,828	1.2%	44.3%
UMC (Taiwan)	Pure-play	$3,263	2.3%	14.7%
SMIC (China)	Pure-play	$1,550	5.8%	7.0%
Chartered (Singapore)	Pure-play	$1,445	−5.4%	6.5%
IBM (US)	Hybrid	$605	−12.1%	2.7%
Vanguard (Taiwan)	Pure-play	$488	22.6%	2.2%
X-Fab (Germany)	Pure-play	$411	40.3%	1.9%
Dongbu (Korea)	Pure-play	$405	−12.4%	1.8%
MagnaChip (Korea)	Hybrid	$370	−8.4%	1.7%
HuaHong NEC (China)	Hybrid	$321	7.0%	1.4%
Others		$3,506	9.5%	15.8%
Total		$22,192		100.0%

Source: Revenue, growth and share data are from Gartner as reported in Mark LaPedus, "Big changes seen in foundry rankings," *EE Times*, April 28, 2008.

The dedicated, or *pure-play*, foundry model was first implemented in Taiwan in 1987, when the government brought together investors, licensed mature production technology from the United States, and attracted Taiwanese engineers and managers with experience from the US chip industry. That first foundry, Taiwan Semiconductor Manufacturing Corporation (TSMC), remains the largest by a considerable margin, as shown in table 2.4. TSMC was founded by Morris Chang, a Chinese-born, MIT-educated executive with twenty-five years' experience at Texas Instruments who moved to Taiwan in 1985.

TSMC started life with older generation processes that the Taiwanese could license and transfer relatively easily. Once established, TSMC gradually developed process capability that was comparable to that of the leading integrated chip companies by the late 1990s. Fabless firms today have little incentive to invest in their own fab that would cost billions of dollars and incur losses if capacity is underutilized. Some integrated chip firms, including IBM, Samsung, and Fujitsu, operate a hybrid model in which they also offer foundry services to help keep their fab capacity utilized, but they generally don't provide the same level of customer support as pure-play foundries. The revenue share of these hybrid foundries fell steadily from 27 percent in 1999 to 15 percent in 2004.[17]

TSMC's revenue of $9.8 billion in 2007 was large enough to have made the chip industry's top ten list at number seven, but it is usually excluded from such lists since the chips it sells are resold by other companies under their own brands. To include the foundries with their integrated and fabless customers would constitute double counting.

Looked at another way, the foundry price is about one-third of the final chip value, so TSMC manufactured over $29 billion worth of chips, which would have placed it number two behind Intel. By the same one-third estimation, the foundry sector as a whole can be seen to have produced 24 percent of the world's chip output, whose final market value was $274 billion in 2007.

Among the top five foundries in table 2.4, the fastest growing is Semiconductor Manufacturing International Corporation (SMIC) of mainland China. SMIC was founded in 2000 by Richard Chang, a Taiwanese expatriate with experience in Taiwan's foundry business following a US graduate education and twenty years' experience at Texas Instruments. SMIC, whose initial funders included Motorola and the Shanghai municipal government, attracted a range of technology partners and customers, hired hundreds of Taiwanese engineers with foundry experience,[18] and listed its shares on the New York Stock Exchange in 2004. The company's fortunes turned after that, however, with annual net losses from 2005 through 2008.

Foundries are critical for fabless companies, but they also permit fab-owning firms to hedge the enormous risk of building new factories by using the foundries for buffer capacity in response to upward demand swings, for fabricating chips that have a short product life or uncertain volume, and for benchmarking their in-house manufacturing operation.

In 2007 Texas Instruments, the world's third-largest chip firm, surprised the industry by announcing that it would cease internal digital process development after the 0.045-micron generation and rely on TSMC and UMC for process development, beginning with the 0.032-micron process that had just started the development cycle.[19] Earlier, medium-size integrated producers, such as LSI Logic, went completely fabless because of the attractive economics of the business model. Fab owners began shifting business to foundries in the mid-1990s and by the mid-2000s accounted for approximately 45 percent of foundry revenue.[20]

Foundries have been expanding the range of services they provide, such as offering design cores (see Crisis 3) tailored to their in-house processes and collaborating with customers on the complex task of designing for leading-edge processes (see Crisis 5), as well as building extensive libraries of simple design elements to aid their customers in chip design.

The availability of buffer capacity in Asia has allowed chip producers to build less fabrication capacity, which reduces the risk of facing unutilized capacity with a large fixed depreciation expense. In the early stage of this *fab-lite* strategy, the fab-owning companies tried to keep their own fabs fully booked and shifted excess demand to the foundries as needed. However, fab-lite is evolving to mean that companies end their own development of leading-edge capability and shift leading-edge manufacturing to manufacturing partners while they continue to run their older fabs.

We do not expect the entire semiconductor industry to go "fabless." For example, Intel will continue internal fabrication of its PC microprocessors because leading-edge process technology is part of the company's competitive advantage. Samsung, the leading memory maker, will continue internal fabrication of its memory chips because DRAM designers must work closely with process development engineers to push the technical parameters of the fabrication process (Monteverde 1995). Intel and Samsung alone account for over one-fifth of semiconductor industry sales. Other companies like TI and Micron benefit from running nonstandard processes for part of their output. The major category of chips that are manufactured by foundries are logic and mixed-signal chips, which primarily use standard processes. All told, outsourced manufacturing will probably never exceed 50 percent of the semiconductor industry because older or specialized processes are still appropriate for a range of semiconductor products from discrete transistors to sophisticated sensors that are made by small, specialized integrated producers.[21]

Fabless start-ups have been the main beneficiaries of the foundry phenomenon. Initially the fabless business model was expected by some to be short-lived (Angel 1990), and the prevailing view in the industry was that "real men have fabs."[22]

Far from being a fad, however, fabless companies have become an integral part of the chip industry and one of the forces underlying the US resurgence in global market share seen in Crisis 1. From 1987 to 2007 fabless revenue (compound annual growth rate, CAGR, of 26 percent) grew much faster than the semiconductor industry as a whole (CAGR of 10 percent) to become more than one-fifth the chip industry total.[23] This record of growth with a near-total reliance on contract fabrication is a powerful indicator of the strength of the foundries' value proposition.

Today, with the cost of a leading-edge fab at least $3 billion, not even the largest fabless firms (table 2.5) have sufficient revenue to contemplate making such an investment on their own, since the industry norm is that capital expense should be less than a third of revenue.[24] The last fabless company to build its own fab was Silicon Integrated Systems (SiS), a Taiwanese designer of logic chip sets for computers and other systems. SiS built an 8-inch wafer fab in 1999 but sold it off to a foundry, UMC, five years later after running into financial difficulties.[25]

In the 1990s, rather than build modest-sized fabs of their own, a few fabless firms invested in joint-venture fabs with a manufacturing partner. For example, several US-based fabless companies co-invested in fabs with Taiwan's UMC to guarantee access to capacity. UMC bought out all these alliances after a few years to improve its ability to manage its resources.[26] The Singapore foundry, Chartered, had joint ventures with vertically integrated companies Hewlett-Packard and Lucent that continued with their otherwise fabless chip spin-offs Avago and Agere, respectively. The other co-investor among the leading fabless firms is SanDisk, which since 2000 has invested in several advanced Japanese fabs with its manufacturing partner Toshiba.

Table 2.5
Top ten fabless companies, 2007

Company	Semiconductor revenue (US$ millions)	Remarks
Qualcomm	$5,619	Excludes revenue from technology licensing
NVIDIA	$4,098	
SanDisk	$3,896	Excludes revenue from sale of consumer products (music players, etc.); Co-invests in fabs with Toshiba
Broadcom	$3,776	
Marvell	$2,895	
LSI Logic[a]	$2,604	Sold last in-house fab in April 2006
MediaTek	$2,473	
Xilinx	$1,809	
Avago[a]	$1,554	Owns a fab jointly with Chartered (Singapore)
Altera	$1,264	

Source: Global Semiconductor Alliance.
a. Former integrated manufacturer.

To date, successful fabless companies are a mainly US phenomenon. Of the top ten fabless companies in 2007 (table 2.5), only one, Taiwan's MediaTek, was based outside North America.

Competitive advantage can potentially be easily won and lost, however, because the barriers to entry in the fabless sector are relatively low (at least compared with fabrication). There are now hundreds of fabless start-ups in countries with a good supply of engineers and a supportive entrepreneurial infrastructure, including China, Israel, South Korea, Taiwan, and the United Kingdom. In 2007, according to the Global Semiconductor Alliance (GSA) database of publicly listed fabless companies, US-based fabless companies accounted for 74 percent of the $40 billion of fabless chip sales, followed by Taiwanese (19 percent), European (4

Table 2.6
Fabless revenue of publicly listed firms by region, 2007

Location	2007 revenue (US$ millions)	Share of total	Total number of firms	Firms with revenue >$100,000
United States	$37,826	73.90%	84	47
Taiwan	$9,752	19.05%	56	21
Europe	$1,842	3.60%	13	4
Japan	$612	1.20%	3	2
China	$584	1.14%	6	3
Korea	$374	0.73%	13	2
Canada	$189	0.37%	2	1
India	$6	0.01%	1	0
Total	$51,185		178	80

Source: Authors' calculations from Global Semiconductor Alliance data.
Note: The only privately owned fabless firm with significant revenue in 2007 was Avago, with estimated 2007 sales of $1.5 billion; it was taken private in 2005.

percent), and Japan and China at 1 percent each (table 2.6). The Japan share is noticeably low given the depth of semiconductor skills there, but Japanese start-ups face a range of difficulties, as we discussed in Crisis 1.

Fabless start-ups, in addition to their potential to grow to importance in their own right, can be an important source of technology for established firms. In 2007 the Global Semiconductor Alliance recorded 71 mergers or acquisitions of fabless start-ups. Although the deal value of many private acquisitions is undisclosed, the reported values totaled $6.2 billion.[27] An example of a typical acquisition is that of TransChip, an Israeli CMOS image sensor developer, by Samsung Electronics in October 2007. The acquired company became Samsung Semiconductor Israel R&D Center, which is typical of the way a start-up can bring an infusion of technology and talent to the acquiring firm.[28]

There is some concern in the industry that start-ups will become scarcer as venture capitalists balk at the growing cost of R&D even for design-only firms (Crisis 3). Annual investment in fabless start-ups was relatively stable from 2002 to 2007 and averaged $1.8 billion.[29] The severe financial crisis that began in 2008 is likely to herald a period of reduced venture investment; however we expect this to be a temporary decline.

2.3   Global Shift of Manufacturing

The increasing importance of a fabless sector dependent on Asian manufacturing gave rise to concerns about a loss of chip fabrication in the United States. A 2005 report by an advisory panel to the US Department of Defense looked at the rising use of Asian foundries to produce advanced chips and recommended "a broad national effort to offset foreign polices designed to encourage movement of leading edge semiconductor manufacturing facilities to offshore locations" (Defense Science Board 2005, p. 6).

Data confirm a striking shift of fab investment away from the United States and Japan to the rest of Asia, primarily South Korea and Taiwan (table 2.7).[30] Japan and the United States accounted for a combined total of 80 percent of linewidth-adjusted fab capacity in 1980, but only 49 percent of capacity in 2001.

However, from the same data in terms of region of ownership (shown in parenthesis), the decline of capacity owned by US and Japanese companies can be seen to be less severe than the fall in capacity located in the two countries. Although only 29 percent of linewidth-adjusted fab capacity in 2001 was in the United States, US companies had ownership stakes in almost 40 percent of global capacity. Japan's fall to 20 percent of capacity was less offset, with only an additional 4 percent of offshore investments.

Meanwhile about 22 percent of the fab capacity located in North America in 2001 was owned by companies based in other regions.[31] Foreign companies still find the United States an attractive place to invest, as evidenced by Samsung's 2006 commitment to a new, multibillion-dollar fab in Austin.[32]

Table 2.7
Regional location and ownership of worldwide fabrication capacity

Year	Asia ex-Japan	Europe	Japan	United States
1980	4% (3%)	16% (15%)	38% (37%)	42% (44%)
1990	12% (12%)	13% (9%)	45% (45%)	30% (36%)
2001	38% (39%)	13% (8%)	20% (24%)	29% (38%)

Source: Leachman and Leachman (2004, tabs. 8.2, 8.4); the data were normalized by the theoretical number of manufacturable functions to adjust for the different linewidth capabilities of each fab.
Note: For each year, capacity location is shown on top and capacity ownership is shown beneath it in parentheses. The ownership row total for 2001 adds to more than 100 because jointly owned capacity was credited in full to all owners.

Table 2.8
Distribution of North American-owned fab capacity, 2001

North America	65.4%
Europe/Middle East	18.6%
Japan	13.0%
Asia ex-Japan	3.0%

Source: Calculations courtesy of Rob Leachman.

The US capacity ownership data reflect decisions by US companies to build fabs offshore.[33] In 2001 the offshore share of US-owned fabs was approximately one-third, primarily in Japan and Europe, as shown in table 2.8. This preference for locating manufacturing capacity in other developed countries reflects the historical presence of tariffs and other trade barriers, and the more recent availability of subsidies and skilled labor.

An update of the regional location of capacity, table 2.9, comes from a different data source based on silicon surface area instead of the linewidth-adjusted values in table 2.7. The shift to Asia continued

Table 2.9
Fab capacity by region, 2000 to 2008

Country	2000	2008
Japan	34%	25%
United States	22%	16%
Europe	15%	11%
South Korea	11%	18%
Taiwan	13%	16%
Southeast Asia	3%	6%
China	2%	8%

Source: SEMI, World Fab Watch Reports and World Fab Forecast Reports, October 2008.

through 2008, with South Korea and mainland China gaining the most in capacity share (7 and 6 percent of world capacity, respectively).

A look at where the newest fabs are located reinforces this picture. The largest, most advanced, and potentially most cost-efficient fabs today utilize 300-mm (12-inch) diameter wafers. Many of the 300-mm generation of fabs have not been expanded to efficient scale, because of lack of demand to run at higher volume. When new fabs are not running at full volume, losses mount quickly because of rapid equipment depreciation. Projected cost savings of about 30 percent per chip are expected from these fabs when they are equipped to efficient scale and running at full capacity.[34]

Table 2.10 shows the geographical distribution of installed 300-mm capacity as of late 2008. South Korea and Taiwan have the largest concentrations of these megafactories, which are needed by the foundries and memory chip producers to keep their unit costs low, even though their risk of excess capacity increases as a result. The major Japanese companies have also made a significant commitment to 300-mm fabs. Leading US firms, such as Texas Instruments, were early adopters of the 300-mm technology but have slowed their investments in new fabs, in

Table 2.10
Installed 300-mm fabs capacity by region, October 2008

Country	Share of worldwide 300-mm capacity
South Korea	27%
Taiwan	24%
Japan	19%
United States	15%
Europe	6%
China	6%
Singapore	3%

Source: SEMI World Fab Forecast, October 2008, based on theoretical full capacity and on fab location (not ownership).

part because of their use of foundries for leading-edge manufacturing as well as buffer capacity.

Although the shift to Asia is well underway, we expect some fabs to continue to be built in "expensive" locations such as the United States and Japan. Fabrication is capital intensive, so the advantages of investing in countries with lower cost labor are relatively small. Labor typically accounts for 16 percent of costs (including depreciation) in US fabs producing 200-mm wafers, and less than 10 percent in the newer 300-mm fabs.[35]

A survey of industry executives found that the top five reasons, rated very close in importance, for fab site selection were tax advantages, supply of engineering and technical talent, quality of water supply and reliability of utilities, proximity to existing company facilities, and environmental permitting process and/or other regulations (Leachman and Leachman 2004, p. 226). Empirical research on fab investment data shows that host country political institutions, the presence of other fabs, and a firm's prior investment experience also affect the location of fab investments (Henisz and Macher 2004). This multiplicity of concerns surrounding such a major investment accounts for the relatively few cases of US-owned fabs in low-cost locations, even with the rich subsidies that have been offered by countries like Singapore.

2.4   Lessons and Conclusions

The supply economics of the semiconductor industry have been evolving inexorably to favor enormous factories requiring huge investments. The industry responded with an organizational innovation, the fabless-foundry model, in which companies specialized in either design or manufacturing.

The soaring cost of fabs favored countries where governments and investors were willing to shoulder the burden, which led to expansion of the industry in Taiwan, Singapore, Malaysia, and, eventually, China. As the fabless-foundry model thrived, the growth of foundry capacity occurred almost exclusively in Asia.

While Asian foundries have probably contributed to a long-run reduction in chip manufacturing in the developed countries, the net loss of engineering jobs has been offset to some extent by the increase in design jobs at fabless companies that were made possible by the foundry capacity. As a back of the envelope calculation, we estimate that if all foundry production had been based in the United States instead of Asia in 2005, it might have added 11,000 jobs, of which some 2,600 would be highly paid engineers.[36] As a point of comparison, the Fabless Semiconductor Association (now the Global Semiconductor Alliance) reported that publicly traded fabless companies in North America as of December 2005 employed over 50,000 workers,[37] more than half of whom would have been software or hardware engineers. The number of these engineers located offshore is not known, although the proportion was about one-third for the US industry as a whole (see Crisis 4, figure 4.4), which would leave about 16,000 US fabless engineers, or six times the number of jobs possibly "lost" to Asian foundries. The trade-off is probably negative for Europe, with relatively few fabless firms but whose integrated firms use foundries, while Japan has made little use of either foundries or the fabless model.

Nevertheless, the shift of so much manufacturing capacity to Asia has raised US concerns. One is the possible loss of competitiveness if design follows manufacturing, which we discuss in Crisis 8. Another is the risk associated with the concentration of so much foundry capacity in Taiwan, which is prone to earthquakes and in an ongoing cold conflict with the mainland.

The unforeseen development of semiconductor foundries greatly relieved the pressure on the industry from the rising costs of building fabs. However, as with other crises, this one was only postponed, and the current price tag for leading-edge fabs has spurred some integrated firms to go fab-lite or even fabless (see Crisis 7).

The economics of chip making have continued to work in the consumer's favor. Despite the sizable fixed cost of building a fab, the unit costs of the chips that are manufactured are lower. The lower costs help keep demand growing, which permits firms to achieve economies of scale. Consumers continue to benefit from increased performance and lower prices even as companies face escalating and risky capital investments (Crisis 7). Meanwhile the cost of designing the complex chips made possible by advances in fabrication has also skyrocketed, and this has created a parallel design cost crisis to which we turn in the next chapter.

Crisis 3
Rising Cost of Design

As the capability to build 10 million to 20 million-gate ASICs has arrived, designs of great functional complexity are now possible. So complex in fact that designers would be very hard-pressed to complete these designs in a reasonable amount of time—if at all.

—Rich Wawrzyniak, Semico Research, January 2000[1]

Parallel to the rising cost of fabrication (Crisis 2), the chip industry experienced an increase in the cost of design as the complexity of design skyrocketed. While developments in technology rapidly expanded the ability to fabricate circuits, the ability to design chips that took advantage of the large number of circuits available did not keep pace. So there is an urgency to improve design productivity in order to fully use the advances in fabrication and create chips that are being called on to perform an increasing number of functions with improved power usage and networking capability. In this chapter we first discuss the design challenges facing the industry, and then we look at two incremental industry responses: design reuse and system-level design. In both cases attempts to achieve a collective response have been slow and have achieved only partial success.

3.1 The Chip Becomes the System

The Moore's Law trajectory has produced a doubling of transistor density every two to three years. The increased number of transistors that can be fabricated on a chip at smaller linewidths permits designs to encompass greater complexity than ever before even as their size decreases. Over several technology generations, it also means that functions previously implemented as separate components, often by different companies, can be integrated within a single chip design. The increase in functional integration has reached a point where a single chip often integrates most of the individual components that populated the circuit board of earlier systems, giving rise to the name "system on a chip" (SOC).

System-level integration in semiconductors has a long history, although the systems themselves have become more complex. As far back as 1969, for example, a company called Mostek produced the first single-chip calculator, which integrated basic functions like addition, subtraction, multiplication, and division (Borrus 1988, p. 77). The current SOC movement reflects a qualitatively different level of integration that places highly complex, multifunction electronic circuits on a single chip. Today's system-on-a-chip incorporates at least one processor, memory, and any number of other functions such as protocol converters, signal processors, and input and output controllers.

System-level integration on a single chip has several advantages over the use of an equivalent set of simpler, separate chips on a conventional printed circuit board (PCB). First, it enables faster operating speeds, since data flows over microscopic, rather than visible, distances. A related advantage is lower power consumption, since lower voltages are required for each bit of data. A third major advantage of SOCs is a reduction in the size of end-use products resulting from fewer chips and minimal off-chip circuitry. Fourth, the consolidation of functions on a single chip leads to lower costs relative to the use of separate chips. Fifth, the replacement of PCB interconnects with pathways on a single chip improves system reliability.

SOC is often uneconomical for the *entire* system, and certain specialty functions that are best executed in non-CMOS manufacturing technologies will be implemented on separate ICs. In cases where integration is desirable but the process technologies appropriate for different functions are incompatible, companies can choose a system in package (SIP), an option that lies between SOC integration and separately packaged components on a circuit board. An SIP, sometimes also called a multichip module, consists of a single package that contains the bare die of different types of chips, for example, a processor combined with logic and memory die plus non-chip components. SIP brings some of the cost, performance, and size advantages of SOC with reduced complexity and lower development costs.

SOC has steadily expanded its share of the semiconductor market. SOC revenue in 1997 was $7.6 billion (Linden and Somaya 2003), and it grew faster than the industry as a whole through 2005 to reach $46 billion, roughly 20 percent of total chip revenues.[2]

The growth of SOC is being driven, in part, by a shift in the electronics market from performance-oriented, computer-centric devices to other applications that include low-end computers, networked and wireless consumer products, and mobile devices. During the 1990s with corporate PC sales the primary driver of the chip business, semiconductor firms competed aggressively to be the first to market with cutting-edge "performance components" that were able to earn a premium over current technology. As will be discussed in Crisis 4, the increasingly important consumer markets demanded the low-cost and portability made possible by SOC integration.

3.2 The Design Productivity Challenge

The advantages of SOC come with a cost. Although the unit manufacturing cost of an SOC is smaller than the combined cost of the separate components it replaces, the fixed costs of a complex design can be significantly higher. For that reason SOCs only make sense for high-volume markets where the fixed cost can be spread over many units. The development cost of an SOC for manufacturing at a 0.130-micron linewidth was reportedly $2 to $5 million in 2004.[3] By late 2007, when the first 0.045-micron chips came into production, the cost of a leading-edge design had ballooned to the $20 to $50 million range.[4] According to an industry analyst, a $20 million design would need $400 million in sales to produce a normal level of profitability for a chip company. As discussed in Crisis 4, the shift from corporate to consumer users fragmented markets so that opportunities for products with this volume are more and more rare.[5]

The factors driving the rise in the cost of design are less obvious than those driving the rising cost of manufacturing. To better understand these forces, we must step back and unpack the craft of digital chip design.

With considerable simplification, the process of chip design can be split into four sequential stages: specification, logic design, physical design, and validation, also known as verification. Specification is the highest level design stage, which determines how the chip as a whole should behave within the system of which it's a part. This is a high value-added function that applies the company's market knowledge and intellectual property in deciding what feature set and performance level will be most profitable. The next stage, logic design, uses symbolic abstractions to describe how signals will be processed within the chip, first at the register level, then at the gate level. The final stage, physical design, involves the translation of the abstract version into a map of actual wires and devices interconnecting across multiple layers on the silicon surface. The design must be verified at each stage, then, once a prototype chip has been produced, it must be validated in a mock-up of the final system-level product to make sure it performs as expected before the design can be released for volume production.

Parallel with this process is the generation of the basic software code that will run on the chip to allow it to respond to higher level applications. Such firmware may be embedded on the chip or in a separate read-only or reprogrammable memory chip. The chip company might also create programming interfaces that customers use when they write applications for the system of which the chip is a part.

Table 3.1 shows the change in the effort required at each stage of design over succeeding generations of process technology, from 0.350-micron linewidths, first introduced in the mid-1990s, to 0.130 micron, which entered volume production in 2003. The underlying project is assumed to be a digital logic design, the industry's typical product. Other types of design, such as analog or memory chips, require different engineering inputs. The overall chip is assumed to be more complex at each linewidth as miniaturization allows more functions to be packed onto a chip. It is the complexity that raises the design cost of successive generations of chips. In raw terms (transistors per engineer per year), design engineer productivity improved by a factor of more than 20 during the 1990s (SIA 2003).

Table 3.1
Engineer hours to design one million logic transistors

	0.35 micron	0.25 micron	0.18 micron	0.13 micron	Change from 0.35 to 0.13 micron
Specification	23.0	29.8	91.4	271.6	1,081%
Logic design	714.2	738.4	756.4	837.7	17%
Physical design	311.0	357.2	391.7	473.5	52%
Validation	103.7	127.6	164.5	197.4	90%
Software	378.4	672.4	985.7	1798.3	375%
Totals	1,530.3	1,925.4	2,389.7	3,578.5	134%

Source: *International Business Strategies* (2002), used with permission.
Note: The average number of transistors in a typical logic design increases by a factor of about two with each reduction in linewidth. The table normalizes the hours required for 1 million transistors at each generation based on the assumption that the underlying project is increasingly complex: 2 million transistors at 0.35 micron, 5 million at 0.25, 20 million at 0.18 micron, and 40 million at 0.13 micron.

As the table makes clear, the biggest increase in engineering hours (and hence development cost) is from software, which now accounts for about half of the total engineer hours. The system-level integration of an SOC has shifted much of the burden of software programming from the customer, such as system firms making portable music players or cell phones, to the chip maker. Software expertise is increasingly important for the competitive advantage of semiconductor firms, who may hire as many software engineers as electrical engineers (Linden et al. 2004).

This has happened in part because chip companies try to differentiate their offerings by providing a complete package of hardware and software that will help the customer get its final product to market more quickly. Many chip buyers, who in the past would have developed their own system and software around simple components, have come to expect a "reference design" as part of their SOC purchase. A "reference design" is a generic blueprint for a specific kind of product such as a portable digital music player. The design encompasses a recommended circuit and set of components, and typically includes a menu of possible features and functions enabled by the SOC that the buyer can choose whether or not to implement in the final product. The reference package typically also includes some basic software applications and tools that customers can use for developing their own programs.

To some extent, the shift of software engineering to the chip companies is also occurring for technical reasons. A system and its software are more likely to fit together seamlessly when they emerge from a unified project team. The need for hardware-software co-design has caused the specification portion of chip designs, which includes the partition of functions between hardware and software, to explode by 1081 percent over the last four technology generations.

The software effort alone increased by 375 percent. This growth is driven in part by companies choosing to implement more algorithms in software rather than hardware to deal with shorter product lives, since hardware solutions typically take more time to develop and involve a higher fixed cost for R&D. According to one software executive, a typical chip in 1995 went into a stand-alone product and required 100,000 lines of code. In 2002 a typical chip for a networked programmable product required a million lines of code.[6] The effort needed to write software grows exponentially, and one expert estimates that a million lines of code require about 223 person-years to write and test.[7] In the 0.090-micron process generation, which is the one following those shown in table 3.1, the software for representative chips accounted for about 45 percent of the total design investment.[8]

The expanding numbers of lines of code, plus the greater hardware complexity of system-level chips, caused the hours needed for design validation to grow by 90 percent for each million transistors.

By comparison, the growth levels for the actual design engineering jobs of logic and physical design for each million transistors were a relatively modest 17 and 52 percent respectively. This is largely because, as chips have gotten more complex, the process of chip design has become more automated (Hemani 2004). Still, physical design at the "deep submicron" feature sizes that the industry has reached involves dealing with complex phenomena, and the engineers with the requisite training and experience are highly prized.

Design automation has reduced the need for more engineers than would have otherwise been required by the increase in chip complexity and continued expansion of the industry to new applications. In the early years of the industry, designs were hand-drawn and hand-transferred to a template that was used to manufacture the circuit. In the 1970s, the later stages of the process were computerized using computer-aided design (CAD) tools, and in the 1980s, they were automated, giving rise to the electronic design automation (EDA) industry in which the three leading firms since the mid-1990s have been Cadence Design Systems, Synopsys, and Mentor Graphics, who had a combined market share of 80 percent in 2007.[9] In the 1990s, the combination of computerization and high-bandwidth telecommunications gave chip companies the ability to divide the design process across multiple locations, which enabled the offshoring to lower cost locations discussed in Crisis 4.

These advances in design automation pertain primarily to digital designs, namely those that work on binary streams of data. Designs that utilize all, or mostly, analog circuits, which process continuous signals such as sound waves, are also developed with EDA tools but are less automated and require more experienced designers with specific training.

According to the Semiconductor Industry Association's International Technology Roadmap for Semiconductors, the rate of EDA-based productivity improvement for digital design was about 39 percent a year during the 1990s (SIA 2003). However, the increase of manufacturing capability under Moore's Law translates to 58 percent a year. In other words, the ability of factories to place transistors on silicon is theoretically outstripping the ability of the existing pool of engineers to design them, a phenomenon sometimes called the "design productivity gap" (ibid.). Fortunately, this gap is not as serious in practice since a relatively small percentage of designs are done at the leading edge in any one year.[10] Nevertheless, there is an acknowledged need for more design engineers as the number of potential applications for chips continues to expand alongside the increase in design complexity.

The productivity gap may actually be widening because power usage, an aspect of design that engineers were able to manage with relative ease in the past, has added another dimension of complexity as linewidths have shrunk even smaller than those shown in table 3.1. One power-related issue is leakage. CMOS transistors leak power in their inactive state, but designers were able to ignore the leakage in most instances. However, as more transistors are placed on a chip, the power consumption of the chip increases nonlinearly. This could be addressed by designing transistors that work at a lower voltage, but then the leakage accounts for an ever-increasing share of the chip's power consumption. At 0.090 nm, the linewidth introduced by major producers in 2004, leakage accounted for as much as half of a chip's power consumption.[11]

Fab owners have been able to produce transistors with less power leakage by introducing exotic techniques such as "strained silicon," in which the wafer substrate includes a layer of silicon where the silicon atoms are literally stretched by attraction to different atoms in an underlayer; "silicon on insulator," another layered wafer technique; and "high-k dielectric gates," in which thicker materials with more attractive electrical characteristics are used for building some of the structures of a chip. Some or all of these techniques have been introduced by leading chip makers including Intel and TSMC since the 0.090-micron generation, but they add design complexity (and higher fabrication costs).

In addition to the leakage problem, the Internet era of battery-powered mobile products and power-hungry data warehouses demands minimal power consumption, even as rising processing speeds drive up heat dissipation. In response, a variety of low-power design techniques are becoming common, including the subdivision of chips into sections that run on different voltages or that can be turned off when not needed. Such adjustments, however, impact all aspects of the design from architecture to physical layout. According to a design officer at NXP (formerly Philips Semiconductor), the use of low-power design methods led to as much as a 50 percent reduction in design productivity.[12]

3.3 An Industry Response: Reusable Design Cores

The industry is pursuing several approaches to design complexity, including avoidance, brute force, design reuse, and new design methods, such as the system-level approach. In this section we focus on design reuse and then turn to system-level design in the next section.

Avoiding the complexity of leading-edge chip design is an increasingly attractive option. In the past, companies would routinely design for the latest process available because of the attendant advantages in terms of size and speed. In recent process generations (0.180 to 0.090 micron) a smaller share of designs use each new process as more designers stay at the trailing edge, which offers satisfactory results for many applications.[13] For companies competing on processing speed or die size, however, avoidance is not an option.

The brute force approach—using more engineers—primarily takes the form of hiring lower cost engineers abroad. This will be discussed in the context of cost reduction as part of Crisis 4, the consumerization of the industry. We note here that the hiring of overseas design engineers is also a response to the design productivity challenge: companies tap into new pools of engineers abroad to supply the growing number of engineering hours required for the design of complex, large-scale chips.

The response that concerns us in the rest of this section is design reuse, in which functional subunits of a chip design can be integrated, ideally with little or no modification, in subsequent designs. Design reuse is practiced extensively within chip firms that require teams to document design elements sufficiently so that they can be reused in future designs. According to an estimate from Semico Research, the value of this internal design reuse is greater than 25 percent of design costs, or about five times that of the merchant market, to which we now turn.[14]

There is a growing market for interfirm trade in reusable design elements known in the industry as "cores" or "IP blocks" (Linden and Somaya 2003). When properly handled by vendor and customer, the use of design cores will speed time to market, reduce project cost, and improve performance with best-in-class capability.

A typical example of a design core is a USB interface, a standard feature in many computer peripherals and an increasing number of consumer products. Acquiring a predesigned version from an outside source allows a company's engineers to focus on higher value portions of a system-level chip.

At the other extreme, designing a high-value microprocessor core is so complicated and time-consuming that to do so for each chip where one is needed would delay most SOC projects unacceptably. Microprocessors

Table 3.2
Top ten semiconductor design core vendors by total revenue, 2007

Rank	Company	Revenue (US$ millions)	Growth 2006–2007	2007 share
1	ARM	$458.9	7%	33%
2	MIPS Technologies	$120.3	55%	9%
3	Synopsys	$99.7	8%	7%
4	Imagination Technologies	$50.2	29%	4%
5	Virage Logic	$49.1	−14%	4%
6	Rambus	$47.0	22%	3%
7	Silicon Image	$45.9	40%	3%
8	Faraday Technology	$37.4	12%	3%
9	Ceva	$33.2	2%	2%
10	ARC International	$28.9	17%	2%
	Other design cores	$407.7	0%	30%
	Total	$1,378.3	9%	100%

Source: Ganesh Ramamoorthy and Christian Heidarson, "Market share: Semiconductor intellectual property, worldwide, 2007," *Gartner*, May 2008.

also benefit from network effects because of the need for writers of software applications to learn a processor-specific command set. Many SOCs use one of a small group of processor cores, particularly those made by ARM and MIPS, which represent the high end of the design core market.

Design core revenue in 1998 was around $140 million according to one estimate.[15] By 2007, the amount had grown to nearly $1.4 billion (table 3.2), growing at roughly twice the rate of the chip industry as a whole.

To put this in perspective, design costs are typically about 10 percent of chip value, which would place design costs for the industry as a whole in 2007 around $27 billion. The $1.4 billion market for design cores is thus around 5 percent of the industry's total design cost.

The market for design cores is relatively concentrated, with the top ten firms accounting for 70 percent of design core revenue in 2007 (table 3.2), but there are dozens of smaller vendors worldwide.[16] The model has been particularly attractive in Europe, where venture capital is less readily available to early-stage start-ups than in the United States, because of the lower initial cost of selling design cores relative to launching a fabless company. Japan has no significant design core vendors.

The leading core vendor is the British firm ARM Ltd. which sells a microprocessor core widely used in chips for cell phones and other portable devices. Other top ten firms specializing in some type of processor are MIPS, Imagination, and ARC. Rambus and Virage specialize in memory-related technologies. Others, including EDA software vendors Synopsys and Mentor and Taiwanese design services vendor Faraday, offer a range of less-specialized standards-based cores that save customers the need to redesign everything from the ground up. The foundries also provide some basic, process-specific design cores for their customers.

Most of the core vendors, including ARM, are "chipless" firms, which sell no physical semiconductor product of their own and rely entirely on one-time license fees and/or ongoing royalty revenue from chips sold using their design cores. A few, like Silicon Image, a specialist in display interfaces and storage systems, sell chips of their own design as well as license design cores.

Despite the steady growth of the market for design cores, a number of obstacles have prevented them from becoming the panacea for the industry's design productivity problem that some had hoped.

To use design cores in their chip designs, engineers face difficulty in evaluating competing cores, a time-consuming licensing process, and problems with integrating the core that may require a great deal of vendor support. This last factor has in fact blurred the line between IP cores and design services, with most companies that license IP cores also offering various levels of design support.

Integration of design cores in a design project can be difficult. We heard reports of projects that have been derailed by design cores that were not suitable or were otherwise difficult to integrate because they were inadequately supported. Design cores are especially helpful to customers when they have been "tuned" to a particular foundry process, since cores can also be sold as more abstract descriptions still in need of physical layout for a specific fab. For this reason foundries often subsidize the validation, and increasingly also the design, of a wide range of design cores for use in their own fabs as an enhanced service to their potential customers.

Design cores have not provided the easy path to entry by start-ups that was once foreseen. Start-ups find it hard to provide the required levels of customer support; most start-ups can ill afford to spare their high-skilled engineers from R&D activities. Customers are reluctant to start working with a small vendor's core that they would need for several product generations in case the start-up goes out of business and deprives the customer of technical support and upgrades. Small companies may also be unable to indemnify customers from potential patent infringement involving their design core. For all these reasons the design core business model favors larger companies offering either a few complex, high-value cores, like ARM, or a wide range of cores over which they can spread their costs, like the EDA companies.

A lack of technical standards remains a barrier to both the use and marketing of design cores. Industry groups including the Virtual Socket Interface Alliance (VSIA), the Open Core Protocol International Partnership, and SPIRIT[17] have worked to develop standards to facilitate use of design cores by moving the technology closer to the "plug-and-play" ideal. But many initiatives that initially seemed promising, such as the now-defunct Virtual Component Exchange, a state-subsidized design core trading infrastructure that was created in Scotland in 1998, have failed or remained small. And the VSIA, perhaps the highest profile group working to establish design core standards, voted to disband in 2007, suggesting that some of the barriers to "plug-and-play" design cores may prove intractable.[18]

3.4   An Emerging Response: System-Level Design Approaches

A different and still-developing response to the design productivity challenge is to add a higher layer of abstraction to the design hierarchy that describes a system's behavior, guides the implementation of the later stages of design, and assists in the simultaneous validation of the software and hardware implementations. Design automation programs that have these capabilities are called Electronic System-Level (ESL) tools. Some form of ESL has been in development since the 1990s, but it was only in 1999 that 45 companies from all parts of the global electronics industry came together to create a nonprofit organization called the Open SystemC Initiative (OSCI). SystemC was initially promoted primarily by Synopsys, one of the largest design automation suppliers, but the creation of an open standards organization eased competitive fears, and Synopsys' two main rivals, Mentor and Cadence, are also members of OSCI.

Another ESL language, known as SystemVerilog, has also been developed and has broad use. Whereas SystemC emerged from the C++ language widely used to write chip software, SystemVerilog is related to the Verilog language used to design chip hardware. SystemVerilog's origins lie with a British start-up (later acquired by Synopsys) that offered to contribute the language to Accellera, a design automation industry standards body, which chose the language over competing options in 2002. Accellera also counts Synopsys, Mentor, and Cadence among its members.

Both SystemC and SystemVerilog were approved as IEEE standards in 2005. Although one ESL language could in theory eclipse the other, in practice, they have proved to be complementary because of their respective hardware and software origins. A 2007 survey indicates, however, that neither one has been widely adopted for design implementation, although they are being adopted for high-level modeling and for simultaneous hardware–software validation.[19]

Observers have suggested that one reason for the slow uptake of ESL design methods is the nature of engineering jobs, which are often too pressured by the next deadline to allow engineers time to learn new techniques.[20] As the support for these standards by software companies expands and more engineers are trained in the new methods, ESL tools may eventually bring the long-expected and much-needed productivity boost.

Low-power design, one of the drags on productivity discussed above, is also the focus of competing standards efforts. Industry participants agreed on the need for a common system to specify power aspects of the design across stages of the design process and across tools from different design software vendors. Cadence developed the Common Power Format (CPF) and provided it in 2007 to an industry group called the Silicon Integration Initiative (Si2) for development as an industry standard. Meanwhile Cadence's rivals had worked together through Accellera to develop a similar standard called the Unified Power Format (UPF). Despite attempts to combine the efforts and a strong preference on the part of customers for a single standard, CPF and UPF have remained separate because of concerns about ownership and control. In May 2007 the IEEE approved UPF as a formal standard for chip design, but what actually gets implemented by EDA firms and adopted by design engineers will be determined by the market, where both already have committed users.

3.5   Lessons and Conclusions

The rising cost of design reflects the growing complexity of low-power, system-level chips, which continue to pose a challenge that firms have been meeting in ad hoc ways while the industry tries to move cooperatively toward comprehensive responses. Among firms, complexity can provide competitive advantage to incumbents, who creatively use their design infrastructure and experience to manage the complexity effectively. For developing countries and for start-ups, the complexities add costs that limit entry opportunities into the chip business.

Two prospective approaches to mitigating design complexity, tradable design cores and standards for system-level design, have proved harder than anticipated to develop and implement.

Despite initial enthusiasm about trade in reusable design cores, this incremental restructuring of the chip industry has run into a host of problems that have overwhelmed most of the organizations attempting to create the necessary market infrastructure. Most firms that hoped to specialize in design cores have found it too hard to build a unique advantage, and growth in the market has been dominated by a few standout specialists like ARM.

Efforts at cooperation, like the open standards committees created to support design core reuse and system-level design, can be cumbersome and tangled in the differing agendas of participating companies. Moreover standards, once adopted by the industry, may be implemented slowly (if at all) by engineering teams. Engineers who master the skills used to design complex chips, such as those for system-level design or for deep submicron physical design, find themselves in high demand.

For consumers, higher levels of on-chip integration bring smaller portable gadgets and more reliable systems. As the key customer base for electronics goods shifted from performance-minded businesses to price-sensitive consumers, the cost pressures on chip companies, already coping with both rising design and fabrication costs, became even more constraining, as we discuss in Crisis 4.

Crisis 4

Consumer Price Squeeze

Under the old [business] model, increasing design and process costs simply required higher volume markets to reach profitability. For 25 years expanding markets were there. . . . But today the emphasis is on finer and finer segmentation, and consumer tastes are more fickle and value oriented. . . . The old financial plan that fab costs will be amortized over a large volume market is gone.
—Charles DiLisio, President, D-Side Advisors, March 2003[1]

As the technology complexity for both manufacturing and design boosted the cost side of semiconductors (Crises 2 and 3), the economic challenge facing chip firms was compounded by pressure on the demand side as price-sensitive consumers were becoming more important relative to performance-minded corporate purchasers. This consumerization of demand led to a profit squeeze as chip producers could not easily pass along higher costs in consumer markets. Producers had to search for ways to lower costs in order to attractively price new consumer products and keep consumer markets growing.

This chapter provides an overview of the evolution of semiconductor markets from corporate purchases of computers to consumer purchases of PCs, cell phones, game consoles, and mobile devices, fueled by the widespread use of the Internet beginning in the mid-1990s. We then analyze the industry response of seeking lower costs by locating selected operations offshore and using lower prices to expand consumer markets, especially in rapidly-growing less-developed economies.

4.1 From Corporations to Consumers

Although semiconductors have long found a home in high-volume consumer markets, beginning with the transistor radio, corporate computing

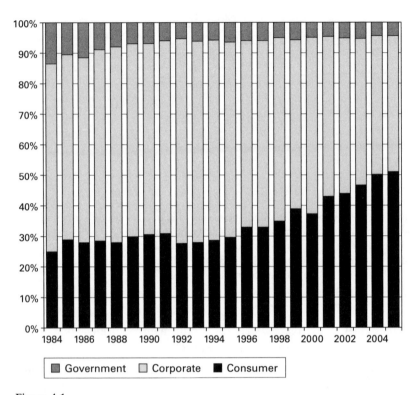

Figure 4.1
Semiconductor consumption by end use, 1984 to 2005 (as percentage of total global revenue). Source: Courtesy of Doug Andrey, SIA.

—from mainframes to PCs and servers—drove the industry forward technologically by paying for rapid performance improvements. Since the 1990s a decisive shift toward consumer markets has taken place (see figure 4.1). In 1995, consumers accounted for 30 percent of semiconductor consumption, and corporations accounted for over 60 percent (with government accounting for less than 10 percent). By 2005, consumers accounted for 50 percent of the semiconductor market, and corporations for 45 percent.

This evolution is harder to detect in the traditional market segments. Figure 4.2 shows the application markets for semiconductors since the mid-1980s. The share of the computer market dominates, although it is eroded somewhat by the growth of communications, including network-

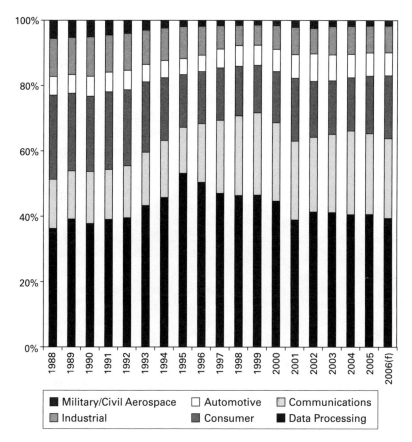

Figure 4.2
Semiconductor application markets, 1988 to 2006 (percentage). Source: Market research data and authors' calculations.

ing equipment and cell phones. The narrowly defined "consumer" market, which consists mostly of audiovisual products, accounted for less than 20 percent of semiconductor sales in 2005. But sales to consumers (as opposed to sales of consumer electronics) are embedded in the other application markets. Most cell phones, to take a key example, are sold to consumers.

The personal computer (PC) market, which alone accounts for more than a quarter of semiconductor sales, provides a clear example of the consumerization of the data processing sector. The explosive growth of

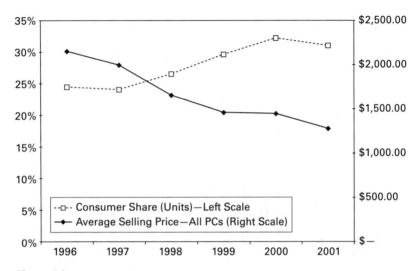

Figure 4.3
Evolution of PC market, 1996 to 2001. Source: Market research data; 2001 was estimated as of July 2001.

the PC market in the 1980s was driven by corporate purchasers, who placed a high value on functions like word processing and spreadsheets. Although some consumers, such as those playing video games, were willing to buy high-powered computers at a high price, a "value" segment of the market was waiting to be served that opened up opportunities for competitors. As technological advances kept chip capabilities on the Moore's Law trajectory, PCs were able to support richer graphical user interfaces. By late 1996 personal computers selling for less than $1,000 —a previously unbreakable barrier—had come to market (Curry and Kenney 1999). Figure 4.3 recaps this evolution with two intersecting lines spanning the period 1996 to 2001. The downward-sloping line is the average selling price of all PCs, which fell from about $2,150 to $1,460, a drop of more than 30 percent. The upward-sloping line shows that the steady price reductions expanded the market in part by attracting relatively more consumers, whose share of total unit purchases grew from 24 to 32 percent.

The Internet was a driving force behind the shift of sales to consumers. The Internet also sparked a convergence of once-separate markets, so that the computing, communications, and consumer electronics sectors increasingly overlapped. Multimedia PCs, cell phones that can download songs and play broadcast television, and videogame consoles that can engage in multiplayer games across the Internet are all part of this market convergence.

Even Intel, which rode the long wave of PC growth to chip industry dominance, has sought growth opportunities beyond the PC market. Intel moved into communications and consumer markets through a series of more than 30 communications-related acquisitions for more than $10 billion between 1997 and 2002.[2] Intel's efforts during this period included the development of portable devices such as an Internet music player, around a non–Intel processor architecture;[3] an aggressive entry in the small but lucrative market for chips in communications infrastructure;[4] and the pursuit of a proprietary digital signal processor in partnership with Analog Devices for use in Internet-capable cell phones.[5] Yet, in a clear indication of the difficulty of serving converged markets, Intel eventually unwound its positions in some of these application areas.[6]

Consumers are now effectively driving the chip industry in high-performance computing as well as in sales. For example, the 8-core "Cell" chip at the heart of Sony's PlayStation 3 game console was a "bleeding-edge" design delivering computing power well beyond that of a PC and manufactured using the latest manufacturing process at the time (0.065 micron). The same is true for memory chips such as the "flash" chips that store songs in an iPod Nano and are designed and manufactured with advanced process technology before other types of chips.[7]

4.2   The Challenges of Consumer Markets

Consumer markets pose three major challenges to chip producers—consumers are more price conscious than corporate buyers, they're more prone to follow trends that appear and vanish with equal rapidity, and consumer product markets are more fragmented than corporate markets. For semiconductor companies the increasing reliance on consumer markets translates into more price-sensitive demand for their products with even shorter product cycles (i.e., the time before a new model is introduced). In addition fragmented consumer markets increase the risk that a product will not sell in sufficient volume to cover its fixed development costs.

The shortening of product cycles and market windows (the time before the price begins dropping) has been a trend over a long period. In the personal computer market, for example, the average product life cycle dropped from about five years in the very early years of the industry to less than two years in 1989 (Wesson 1994). By 1997 the length of time a new model commanded the highest price before being superseded by a better model had fallen to three months (Curry and Kenney 1999).

These forces were heightened by increased global competition, as trade negotiations reduced tariffs. Chip tariffs were eliminated between the United States and Japan in the mid-1980s and by most major trading countries, including the European Union, under the World Trade Organization's Information Technology Agreement in 1997. China became a signatory to the ITA in 2003, solidifying the liberalization of a chip market that has become the world's largest.[8] Multilateral liberalization meant that companies could no longer depend on a competitive advantage in their home markets.

Even as the global opportunities became potentially larger, more firms were vying for the same prize. Recent entrants, primarily from Asia, rapidly produced low-cost versions of successful chips (see Crisis 8). This further ratcheted down the width of market windows. Although there are still some areas of the industry, particularly in standards-based sectors such as communications infrastructure, where the same chip can be sold for years, most high-volume applications have seen a decrease in product life and a corresponding rise in time-to-market pressure on design teams.

Market fragmentation increased the risks of developing new products and expanding to new markets. Whereas the computing market offered huge scale that allowed chipmakers, such as Intel, to field a narrow range of general-purpose chips, consumer electronics and communications require much more specialized chips because of the constant efforts of competing systems firms to create a competitive advantage by offering a different feature set from their rivals. While some of this variation is addressed by software, much of it is hardware-based. Digital TVs, for example, use a variety of display technologies, such as liquid crystal displays, plasma displays, digital light processors, and cathode ray tubes, each of which requires different supporting chips.

Fragmentation is also caused by competing standards, which are particularly pervasive in the important, but unsettled, wireless networking market. WiMax, UltraWideBand, 3G, 802.11n, Zigbee, and Bluetooth are examples of standards that permit wireless transmission of data over various distances using incompatible technologies, and wireless chip companies must choose to support some subset of these in an attempt to create a de facto standard.

Even DRAM chips, one of the most commoditized semiconductor devices of the PC era, have been fragmented by multiple standards such as Rambus' Double-Data Rate. Application-specific memory variants have also appeared, for example, in fast networking infrastructure equipment. Memory chips in mobile consumer products have still another set of technology requirements, such as low power consumption, which further fragments the memory category.

Market fragmentation opens opportunities for start-ups, unburdened by the high fixed costs of large incumbent firms. Small companies are often able to develop projects that have been rejected by large companies, even though they have commercial potential. We learned in our interviews in Japan and the United States that about 70 percent of the ideas will never be developed because:

• the company lacks the resources to pursue all the available ideas;

• some ideas are not related to the company's core capabilities;

• some ideas compete with the company's existing products; or

• the potential market appears too small, and so the company's high overhead costs make the project unprofitable.

Large companies may find that even their most attractive prospective markets are smaller than required by the higher fixed costs of chip manufacturing (Crises 2) and design (Crises 3) that they must cover.[9] Chip companies have dealt with this in part by developing application-specific "platforms" with circuitry dedicated to a general class of products (e.g., multimedia) that can be rapidly customized and mass produced for a number of related products (e.g., DVD recorder and digital TV). They have also reduced costs by shifting certain activities to lower cost areas.

We discussed the shift of fabrication to Asian foundries in response to Crisis 2. In the following section we discuss the shift of design to lower cost areas, especially India, in response to consumerization.

4.3   An Industry Response: Designing in Low-Cost Locations

One of the chip industry's responses to the price-sensitivity and fragmentation of consumer markets is to open design centers in locations with a supply of lower cost engineers. There are other factors driving the expansion of offshore design, such as the cost pressures of increased design complexity, discussed in Crisis 3. Firms also claim that offshore investments are necessitated by an engineer shortage at home (Lewin and Peeters 2006), a claim we evaluate for the United States in Crisis 6.

All parts of chip design and development, from specification to finished chips, can be done by different teams, either in-house or out-sourced, and either locally or offshore. Locational decisions for chip design are based on three primary factors related to competitive advantage: closer contact with customers, access to specialized skilled labor, and cost reduction. Here we focus on cost reduction, although the other two factors play a role that may or may not overlap with lower costs for a specific design project (Brown and Linden 2005).

The easiest part of chip design to offshore or outsource is physical design because it is a relatively standardized task. It is also the least sensitive part of design in terms of revealing the customer's intellectual property. However, for designs requiring leading-edge process technology, layout has become much less straightforward because of the sensitivity of the atomic-scale wiring. In such a case the physical design is likely to be outsourced only by small and medium companies that lack the resources to develop the necessary expertise in-house.

Another design function that is frequently offshored or outsourced is logic verification, the resource-intensive task of making sure that first stages of the physical implementation are a correct translation of the abstract logic. At the other extreme, architectural design, or the design of key functional blocks containing proprietary algorithms, is the least likely to be outsourced because of the risk of exposing valuable intellectual property.[10]

For firms in the high-cost Silicon Valley, which is home to companies accounting for roughly a quarter of US chip industry revenue with Intel accounting for nearly half of these revenues in 2007,[11] cost reduction is available by opening satellite design centers elsewhere in the United States, where some locations have average engineering salaries as much as 20 percent lower. But these salaries are still much higher than salaries in India and elsewhere (Crisis 8, table 8.2).[12]

Reducing cost by going offshore has become much more feasible with the availability of the global high-bandwidth network infrastructure and the economic liberalization of large parts of Eastern Europe and Asia (Ernst 2004). Moreover the chip industry has extensive experience with offshore activities in the fabrication and assembly parts of the value chain. Offshore operations will be discussed further in Crisis 8, but here we look at the location of design centers.

Dividing chip design projects across locations presents a number of managerial challenges. The sacrifice of face-to-face interaction between different parts of the design team can adversely affect productivity, and distance makes it harder to evaluate and reward individual contributions to team performance. Task assignments must be more carefully codified for offshore teams than for locally based engineers to compensate for the lack of personal communication, and managers will need to travel periodically between locations. When the separation is across borders, there are also cultural differences that can make communication less effective. A high-level manager at the Bangalore, India, design center of a US multinational told us about communication problems between teams in India and the United States, especially when projects were in early development. A major cultural difference was the Indian engineers' reluctance to disagree with their superiors or to speak up with suggestions for improvements, since this might appear to be critical of others. Indian engineers would agree to proposed timelines even when they were unrealistic, since saying that the time was too short indicated the engineers were not up to the task.[13]

Cost-driven offshoring incurs other costs that partially offset the difference in salaries, especially during the early stages of establishing an offshore design center. One cost that was often mentioned during our fieldwork is the lower quality and productivity of inexperienced engineers, which can harm productivity. In one instance we studied, a chip design project took twice as long to complete as planned.[14] Weaknesses, often unanticipated, in foreign engineering teams raise monitoring costs, as compared with domestic design teams, and offshore engineers may also require a longer training period than a US team would need. Additional controls may also need to be implemented to protect key intellectual property. According to a venture capitalist, the actual savings from going offshore is more likely to be 25 to 50 percent rather than the 80 to 90 percent suggested by a simple salary comparison.[15]

Design offshoring can run up against national security barriers. For example, the US government has placed limits on the export of advanced encryption technology. Communications chips that employ such technology are difficult to design offshore. Either the chip design must be compartmentalized, with the encryption block designed only in the United States, or government approval, subject to possible delays, must be obtained in advance.[16]

Yet despite these pitfalls the amount of offshore design in industrializing economies has noticeably expanded in recent years, especially in India (Bangalore in particular). Among the top twenty US semiconductor companies in 2005, only two had *not* established a design center in India (see table 4.1). Nine of these companies opened their Indian operations since 2004, and so their operations are in an early stage. The company with the most mature Indian design operations is Texas Instruments (TI), which in 1985 became the first chip company to establish engineering operations in India, in this case the programming of design automation software. In the mid- to late-1990s, six US companies, including Intel, Motorola (now Freescale), and Broadcom, also set up Indian design centers. The size of the operations varies widely, from Intel employing 2,700 engineers (as of 2006) to Maxim hiring 25 engineers (in 2002). The range of activities is quite broad, and can be limited to simple parts of the design flow of a mature technology or can encompass the entire design flow.

The experience of TI India shows the potential for offshore chip design centers that begin with a limited range of activities to develop over time. TI India started out in 1985 writing software for internal use, and added its first chip design activity in 1988.[17] In 1998 TI India announced that it had taken a digital signal processor core all the way from specification to working silicon over the preceding two years.[18] The subsidiary has gone on to create award-winning chip designs, earn hundreds of US patents, and become integral to TI to the point of dealing directly with customers, which is so far rare among offshore design centers.

In a marked difference with India, few major chip companies have opened design centers in China. Concerns over intellectual property protection appear to pose a greater barrier to foreign design activity there than in India.[19] Table 4.2 shows that only a handful of US companies had opened chip design centers (vs. embedded software or application engineering centers) in China as of 2005. Motorola, which had made a large commitment to China by opening a fab there, which it has since sold, has several design centers with different specialties. Only four other US companies in the global top fifty chip firms have set up design centers in China.

Table 4.2 also shows design centers opened in China by Japanese and European chip companies. In India, of the Japanese only Sanyo had opened a design center, while several others have hired Indian outsourcing companies to run dedicated design centers for them.[20] Japanese firms have shown a relatively greater readiness to open China design centers, perhaps because of geographical and linguistic proximity. The three major European chip producers have chip design centers in China; two, STMicroelectronics and NXP, also have large Indian design centers.

Some chip companies with foreign design subsidiaries value the opportunity to design on a 24-hour cycle because of the enormous pressure to reach the market ahead of, or no later than, competitors. One established US chip company adopted a rolling cycle between design centers in the United States, Europe, and India.[21] More common is the bi-national arrangement used by a Silicon Valley start-up that had all of its design beyond the initial specification done by a China subsidiary established within months of the company's founding. Ten executives in the head office had to train the mostly inexperienced staff in Beijing, which was about 30 strong.[22] The Silicon Valley staff would review Beijing's work from the previous day, then spend up to three hours on the phone (starting around 5 pm California time) providing feedback and reviewing

Table 4.1
India design centers of the twenty largest US chip companies

2005 Rank by global sales	Company	City (year began)	Employees (given date)	Remarks
1	Intel	Bangalore (1999)	2,700 (5/06)	
3	TI	Bangalore (1985)	1,100 (8/04)	Pioneering investment in India by a US chip company
12	Freescale	Delhi area (1998)	780 (7/06)	
14	Micron	No investment		
16	AMD	Bangalore (2004)	200 (2008)	
17	IBM	Bangalore (2003)	100 (2003-f)	IBM employs 53,000 in India as of December 2007, making it the largest foreign employer
18	Qualcomm	Bangalore (2004)	150 (9/04)	Acquired a local company
23	Broadcom	Bangalore (1999)	150 (10/05)	Acquired local design team and expanded
24	Analog Devices	Bangalore (1995)	100 (3/04)	Also acquired a Hyderabad design team in 2001
25	Nvidia	Bangalore (2005)	80 (2005-f)	Acquired a Pune software team in 2006
26	SanDisk	Bangalore (2005)	60 (2/06)	
27	National	Bangalore (1995)	25 (1/99)	

30	Avago (Agilent)	Delhi area (2004)	50 (2004-f)	
31	ATI	Hyderabad (2005)	100 (2005-f)	Acquired local design team
34	Atmel	No investment		
35	Maxim	Bangalore (2002)	25 (2002-f)	
36	Agere	Bangalore (1998)	250 (2/05)	
37	Xilinx	Hyderabad (2006)	75 (10/06)	Acquired design center that had been operated for 3 years by a local company
38	Marvell	Bangalore (2005)	75 (12/05)	Design team acquired from a smaller US company
43	LSI Logic	Bangalore (2004), Pune (2006)		Customer support center, including design services

Sources: Sales rank: IC insights; design center information: press reports confirmed in some cases by local interviews.

Notes: "-f" in the "employees" column indicates a forecast rather than an actual headcount; "employees" includes both software and hardware engineers, but none of the centers listed are software only.

Table 4.2
China design centers of leading US and Japanese companies, 2005

2005 rank by global sales	Parent company (name when started)	City (year established)
United States		
12	Freescale (Motorola)	Hong Kong (1988)
12	Freescale (Motorola)	Suzhou (1999)
12	Freescale (Motorola)	Tianjin (2002)
12	Freescale	Shanghai (2005)
23	Broadcom	Shanghai (pre-2004)
24	Analog Devices	Beijing (2000)
36	Agere	Shanghai (2001)
43	LSI Logic	Beijing (1998)
Japan		
4	Toshiba	Shanghai (1994)
7	Renesas (Hitachi)	Suzhou (1995)
7	Renesas (Mitsubishi)	Beijing (1995)
13	NEC	Beijing (1998)
13	NEC	Shanghai (2000)
19	Fujitsu	Shanghai (2003)
33	Sanyo	Shenzhen (2002)
European Union		
5	STMicroelectronics	Shenzhen (1994)
11	Philips (now NXP)	Shanghai (2000)
8	Infineon	Xi'an (2004)

Source: Sales rank: IC insights; design center information: press reports confirmed in some cases by local interviews.

assignments for that day in Beijing. In a single-location firm this work-feedback cycle would take two days instead of one.

Venture capitalists have reportedly begun to require start-ups to include some offshoring in their business plans in order to better leverage their resources. A typical comment is, "We don't fund chip designs that don't outsource to India. If you rely on Indian contractors for the things they do well, you can get a chip out for under $10 million. If you don't, you can't, and you won't be competitive. It's that simple."[23] Portal-Player, the company behind the key multimedia chip in Apple's original iPod, was a high-profile example of a start-up that included an Indian software and chip design subsidiary as part of its operation from the outset.[24] However the position of most chip suppliers is seldom secure. PortalPlayer lost the Apple business after several generations of iPod, and was purchased by Nvidia in 2006.

Low-cost design engineering resources can also be tapped through international outsourcing, although most design outsourcing by US companies takes place domestically. Many interviewees reported that they outsource physical design to small local companies on an as-needed basis. The leading suppliers of design services worldwide are the leading design automation software vendors, Cadence Design Systems, Synopsys, and Mentor Graphics. Their annual services revenue is about $300 million out of a total outsourced design market estimated at $2.5 billion.[25] As this suggests, the remaining market is highly fragmented.

The availability of outsourcing (foreign or domestic) is particularly important for small companies and start-ups because of the relatively large fixed cost of EDA tools, which are typically licensed per engineer. One consultant estimated that the minimum annual design software expense for a small company in 2002 was $10 million (International Business Strategies 2002). For the industry as a whole, EDA expense runs close to 1 percent of revenue. The $10 million start-up amount suggests then that a company earning less than $1 billion in revenue would be at a competitive disadvantage by trying to do its designs in-house. In 2007, only the ten largest fabless companies passed the billion-dollar threshold. By one estimate, outsourcing a design, even within the United States, would save a small start-up designing fewer than five chips a year up to two-thirds the cost of doing the work in-house.[26]

Another type of customer for outsourced design services is the systems company, such as Apple Computer or Cisco. Although these companies often design chips in-house either to protect intellectual property or to reduce the cost of custom chips, they may turn to outside (and possibly offshore) service providers for part of the design process.

4.4   The Location of Engineering Jobs at US Companies

The growing importance of China and India as providers of various activities in the supply chain, especially manufacturing in China and design in India, and as the fastest expanding markets for cell phones and computers, will lead to crises covered later, such as Crisis 6 (the state of the US engineering labor market) and Crisis 8 (renewed concern over loss of leadership). Here we examine data on the extent to which US chip companies have expanded engineering jobs abroad over the past decade.

Data based on annual workforce surveys by the US-based Semiconductor Industry Association (SIA) show that the estimated total engineering workforce at US chip companies increased from under 60,000 in 1997 to over twice that number, 136,905, in 2007. Over the same period the share of engineers located in the United States among these companies fell dramatically from 87 to 57 percent (figure 4.4, right scale). The number of engineers located offshore (left scale) rose steadily even during periods when US employment declined, as in 2003.

This trend was apparent from our field research at offshore design centers. A wave of investment in offshore design took place at the height of the dot-com bubble, and during the subsequent downturn chip companies cut more staff at home than abroad. As the recovery required expansion of design operations, chip companies expanded design operations abroad faster than at home.[27] We do not know if the relative shift in the geographic distribution of employment will occur again during the next recovery period.

Decision making and advanced tasks are not evenly distributed across locations. For the time being, patentable R&D remains centered in chip companies' home regions (Macher et al. 2007) even as the work is relocating globally.

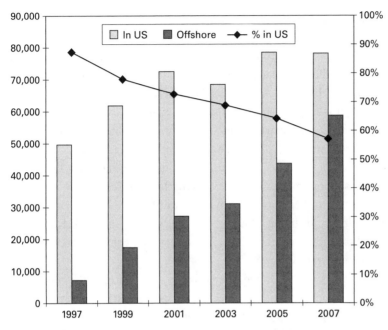

Figure 4.4
Semiconductor engineers at US companies, by location, 1997 to 2007. Source: SIA survey results, various years; values may not be comparable from one year to the next due to changes in sample group and estimation technique.

Perhaps unsurprisingly, industry participants are split on the significance of offshoring for the US job market. A 2004 survey of more than 1,453 chip and board design engineers and managers by *EE Times* shows that about half saw foreign outsourcing as leading to a reduction in headcount.[28] Qualitative opinions in the survey were also divided, with optimists noting that reduced costs made for a stronger company and a more secure job, while the pessimists bemoaned downward pressure on wages and employment plus a possible loss of intellectual property and, in the long run, industry leadership.

4.5 Lessons and Conclusions

The consumerization of chip markets, such as PCs and cell phones, has added downward price pressure to the upward cost pressures discussed in previous chapters (Crises 2 and 3). The industry has responded with incremental adjustments to operations. In particular, adding design operations in low-cost locations helped the industry to keep its costs (and prices) within the range needed to keep consumer product markets growing. An added bonus was that design centers in India and China gave firms a foothold in two large, fast-growing markets.

Because firms headquartered in any country are able to pursue a similar locational strategy, the long-term competitive advantage from investing offshore is limited. Nevertheless, offshore design has become a means for staying in the race for consumer markets, especially in emerging economies, rather than for moving out in front.

For China and India, this foreign investment in local R&D has increased the inflow of technology. We discuss the rise of local chip firms in both countries in Crisis 8.

For engineers in the United States, Japan, and Europe, the offshoring of design has meant that they find themselves, at least indirectly, in competition with young engineers overseas. For many engineers, it also meant working at odd hours in order to collaborate across time zones and traveling more internationally for face-to-face meetings.

Consumers experienced this industry crisis in a decidedly more positive way. As chip firms learned how to develop low-cost products, consumers were flooded with affordable devices of steadily improving performance. In advanced countries, digital music players, car navigation systems, and smartphones are just some of the newer products that have found widespread adoption. In developing economies, consumers of limited means are also experiencing benefits from low-cost, specially engineered products like the rugged "One Laptop Per Child" notebook designed to operate in isolated rural areas.[29] Competition in the extremely low-cost market continues to expand the potential for computing and online access.

We have so far considered strategic and market factors that put cost and price pressure on the industry. In the next chapter (Crisis 5) we explore how the industry is responding to some of the technological challenges that it faces.

Crisis 5

Limits to Moore's Law

If we don't find [new lithography] solutions, Moore's Law breaks down.
—G. Dan Hutcheson, VLSI Research Inc., March 2007[1]

Moore's Law, which provides the economic basis for the industry's dominant business model, is approaching certain physical limits. Although industry leaders have so far stayed on the technology path defined by Moore's Law, they face growing challenges, such as the power leakage discussed in Crisis 3, that are forcing companies to search for innovative solutions to ensure that continued miniaturization of circuits results in significant performance improvement.

In our discussion of the rising cost of fabrication (Crisis 2), we touched on photolithography, the central process for achieving Moore's Law miniaturization of circuits. Here we take a closer look at chip lithography, which is facing one of its most challenging transitions yet.

For most of the 1990s lithography progressed along a relatively predictable path, with steady benefits to chip density and performance. As chip design nears an atomic scale, the ability to extend the existing lithography technology is being questioned, and each new process generation forces chip design to become more responsive to the physics of fabrication, adding a set of design complications beyond those discussed in Crisis 3.

These developments have been particularly hard on the fabless-foundry model (Crisis 2), which is based on the technical separation of design and manufacturing. As that separation becomes counter-productive for leading-edge design, some observers have suggested that integrated companies would gain a competitive advantage over fabless rivals because integrated companies have natural communication between design and manufacturing. However, as we discuss below, the foundries worked with their EDA partners and customers to deepen their collaboration and keep the fabless-foundry model viable.

In this chapter we begin with a brief overview of lithography and its evolution. Next we describe the industry's efforts to take lithography beyond its current "optical" infrastructure. The remainder of the chapter explores the challenge posed to the fabless-foundry model by the repercussions of continued lithographic technical progress and the industry's incremental responses.

5.1   Photolithography

Photolithography involves the transfer of the chip design from a set of reusable templates (a "mask set") onto the wafer surface, which has been treated with a light-sensitive chemical called photoresist. For each layer of chip circuitry, light is passed through one mask from the set, then through a reduction lens (typically 4× reduction or greater) to the treated wafer surface. Next the exposed resist is removed, allowing the underlying areas of the wafer to be processed by other tools to create one layer of the chip. A complex chip will go through this process dozens of times over a period of weeks to build up the interconnected circuit layers.

A set of lithographic equipment typically accounts for 20 percent of the multibillion dollar fixed cost of an advanced fabrication facility (Crisis 2).[2] Because lithography tools are the most expensive machines in the fab, the rest of the fab is planned around them, so they are directly responsible for the rising cost of fabs. It is important to bear in mind that despite these rising fixed costs, the cost per transistor has continued to fall throughout the industry's history.

The lithography market has had a tortuous competitive history. In 1980 most lithography suppliers were US-based, selling tools capable of 2.0-micron linewidths. A quarter-century later, tools capable of creating linewidths of less than a tenth micron (100 nanometers) are being manufactured only by Japanese and European companies.[3]

The last US producer of leading-edge lithography tools was Silicon Valley Group (SVG), which was acquired by Dutch company ASM Lithography (ASML) in 2001, after careful vetting by the US government. The deal was approved after ASML agreed to divest SVG's advanced optics lab that did some defense-related work. The SVG acquisition put ASML ahead of its Japanese lithography rivals Canon and Nikon. In 2006 ASML earned 61 percent of the lithography industry's $6.7 billion in revenue.[4]

5.1.1 The Evolution of Optical Lithography

The photolithography methods employed by the industry over the past four decades are known collectively as "optical lithography," since light passes through a lens to the wafer. For many years experts have predicted that optical lithography would run into physical limits that would necessitate the development of an alternative method to continue moving along the Moore's Law path. However, continued advances in light sources, lenses, and wafer processing have kept the basic architecture of optical lithography in use despite serious, long-running research efforts on alternative technologies.

Engineers, including Gordon Moore of Moore's Law fame, have periodically declared that photolithography would cease to work "within ten years" because of the physical limitations of the process, but this terminal point has proved to be a moving target.[5] Around 1980, the expectation was that Moore's Law would cease to operate at about 0.8-micron linewidths. By the mid-1980s, when 1.0-micron lines were in volume production, the predicted end shifted to 0.5 micron, but this also proved wrong as engineers in industry and academia worked together to extend the capabilities of the existing tools.

To accomplish this feat, the pace of change in optical lithography technology has accelerated. For more than twenty years, lithography tools primarily used a 0.436-micron light beam (which lies in the blue range of the color spectrum). By the early 1990s, blue-light tools were being used to produce circuit lines as narrow as 0.6 micron.

The next generation of tools, which used wavelengths of 0.365 micron (ultraviolet), was brought to market in the mid-1980s and was supplanted by the next wavelength (0.248-micron "deep ultraviolet") starting only ten years later. Thanks to developments in lenses and mask technologies, the 0.365-micron machines were eventually used for feature sizes down to 0.350 micron—the beginning of "subwavelength" lithography.

Subwavelength lithography is analogous to painting a one-inch line with a two-inch paintbrush, and a number of technological innovations were needed to make it possible. These advances primarily involved mask enhancements known as "optical proximity correction" (OPC) and "phase shifting," which correct for the limitations of lithographic systems to create sharp-edged shapes of microscopic dimensions in the horizontal and vertical sense respectively. Both methods distort the image on the mask so that it no longer looks exactly like the desired circuit layout, yet—because of the physics of light and the manufacturing process—it produces a better result than would a one-to-one mask image. The mask adjustments add cost, complexity, and delay to design projects but are preferable to a failed prototype chip, which would require either a new mask or changes to the design, both of which are expensive and time-consuming.

When a new generation of lithography tools using a 0.193-micron wavelength was brought to market in 1999, it was used immediately for subwavelength manufacturing at 0.130-micron linewidths. This meant that the 0.248-micron wavelength stayed at the leading edge for barely five years.

By 2006, when 0.065-micron chips came into production, mask adjustments moved beyond OPC and phase shifting to incorporate data about characteristics of the photoresist and the lithography tool. These techniques, all part of "computational lithography," require tremendous computing resources involving banks of processors working in parallel. The computational requirements of the mask optimization for a microprocessor in 2006 were pegged at ten "CPU-years"; in other words the calculations would require a single processor to work constantly for a decade, whereas the actual process occurs within a matter of weeks.[6]

The advent of 0.032-micron (32-nanometer) designs with the existing 0.193-micron wavelength lithography infrastructure further raises the computational requirements with a technique called double-patterning, which involves twice as many exposures per layer of the chip.[7] While lithography and mask breakthroughs have kept the chip industry on the steep path of Moore's Law, the progress has come with a high price tag beyond even the hundreds of millions of dollars spent on R&D. A single lithography tool in a 1983 fab cost about $400,000.[8] Tools using a 0.193-micron light source came on the market for more than $10 million each—and about twenty of them are needed in a fab of efficient scale.[9]

5.1.2 The Hunt for Postoptical Solutions

While these advances in the incumbent optical systems have continued steadily, leading firms have pursued a variety of "just in case" technologies for use when optical lithography ceases to be viable. Research into alternatives to optical lithography started before 1970 (Henderson 1995). One such alternative was a system that draws patterns directly on the wafer using an electron beam, which has seen limited use for small-batch production of very advanced chips. Another alternative proposed the use of X rays with a full-size mask and no reducing lens. IBM is rumored to have poured as much as $1 billion into X-ray lithography, with the US government having added hundreds of millions more. According to a 1984 forecast, these technologies were supposed to see use in volume production by 1987, but their day has still not come.[10]

More recently Intel and other companies have spent hundreds of millions of dollars on an alternative technology called "extreme ultraviolet" (EUV) lithography (Linden et al. 2000).[11] EUV is a type of radiation whose wavelength is approximately 0.013 micron. Since no lens can transmit such waves, they are reflected off a series of mirrors, one of which contains a 4× mask. Each aspherical mirror must be precisely shaped and coated with dozens of superfine alternating layers of molybdenum and silicon. Since all the elements of the technology—wave source, mirrors, and layered masks—are new, the development process has been lengthy.

EUV technology was originally developed within the Department of Energy's labs as a possible element of a 1980s missile defense system but was also recognized for its potential in the semiconductor industry. Government labs entered a series of cooperative research agreements with semiconductor industry firms during the early 1990s, and when Congress wanted to cut funding, one of the partners, Intel, offered to pay for continued development using assets at three national labs (Livermore, Sandia, and Berkeley). In 1997 Intel was also able to attract support from AMD and Motorola for a three-year, $250-million project. The goal, a proof-of-concept machine, was achieved roughly on time in 2001, and a parallel Japanese effort yielded a similar result soon after.[12] Production-worthy versions are under development by independent lithography companies. But obstacles remain, and even Intel is hedging its bets by focusing on another optical extension for production of 0.022-micron linewidths, which is expected to begin around 2011— long past the initially projected 2005 introduction of EUV machines.[13]

As these examples suggest, the industry is making large bets on lithography alternatives. A host of exotic lithography technologies, with names like "nano-imprint" and "electron beam direct-write," are under development and evaluation at considerable cost and risk for the companies involved.

To mitigate the technological uncertainty, industry representatives have gathered regularly since the late 1980s to share technology projections and to drive toward a consensus over which options seemed most worth pursuing.[14] This "roadmap" process, which has been formalized and updated periodically since 1992, began as a US-only effort, but the preparatory meetings were expanded to include foreign participants in 1998, when the "National Technology Roadmap" officially became "International."[15]

However even a roadmap based on global consensus can scarcely keep up with the evolution of lithography technology. Technologies come and go, such as an optical extension based on 0.157-micron wavelengths, which appeared on the roadmap from 1998 to 2004. Or they see their insertion date delayed repeatedly, like the EUV system, which was originally listed for possible adoption at the 0.130-micron node in the mid-1990s.

Other technologies spring up and are adopted comparatively soon after the roadmap takes official notice of them. An extension of optical lithography known as "immersion," which places fluid between the lens and the wafer, didn't appear on the roadmap until 2003, but production versions of immersion tools were shipped to chip makers beginning in 2006.[16]

As one executive put it in 2006: "Realistically, in this industry when you try to look out beyond three to five years, the probability of you being right is almost zero."[17] Most in the industry expect Moore's Law to continue for at least another decade, although the fabrication methods will resemble current photolithography less and less.

5.2   The Impact of Lithography on Design

The advent of subwavelength lithography through the use of mask-based techniques such as phase-shifting, discussed above, created a new problem for chip designers. In the past the designers specifying a physical layout for a chip could be relatively confident that the structures they specified would emerge from the fab much as they expected because the design data were used directly in the manufacture of a photomask set.

For chips at 0.130-micron and smaller linewidths that require phase-shifting and optical proximity correction, the design database is reprocessed by software that purposely distorts the image used for the photomask in a way that nevertheless creates a result closer to the designer's intent on the wafer surface than would an exact mask image. In addition to adding weeks to the design process, this intermediate step could erode some of the desirable performance characteristics of the chip while expending effort on possibly irrelevant details of the chip, such as dummy metal fill used to even out density of the interconnect layers, that don't need to be reproduced precisely on the wafer. In the worst cases it leads to functional failures of the design. According to one industry participant, "starting at 180 nm [0.180 micron] and now to 65 nm [0.065 micron], we're getting more failures due to lithography problems and yield indications and a lack of good expectations of how those OPC structures we apply to the patterns are actually printing."[18]

5.3   An Industry Response: Design for Manufacturing

In response to these problems that manufacturing creates for designers, companies have been blurring the lines between design and manufacturing. Fabless firms, who face the possibility that integrated producers have gained an advantage from the natural integration of their design teams and in-house fabs, have paid special attention to the issue, in concert with the foundries that manufacture their chips.

The potentially costly disconnect between the designer and the fabrication process around lithography problems was the first major issue in a growing wave of concern over "design for manufacturing" (DFM). As the industry's leading-edge designers continued to 0.090 micron and below, similar issues became too important to ignore. As one industry analyst put it: "At 65 nm [0.065 micron], the wall between design and manufacturing comes down."[19]

In the past, problems around a design that did not mesh well with some aspect of a process could often be fixed in a fab. In the subwavelength era these issues became too serious and too common. If the issues weren't addressed before the design went to the fab, a costly redesign cycle and new photomask set would be required.

One such issue is the instability of new processes. As time-to-market demands have increased (Crisis 4) and development of each new process requires more time, it has become harder for leading-edge designers, who are trying to complete the design at the same time the process will go into volume production, to get stable process characterizations to guide their designs. There is a risk that if the designers adjust the design to accommodate a feature of the process that the fab engineers later change, then some features on the chip may not be fabricated as planned (Sawicki 2004).

Another major concern is process variability, which has gone from being a secondary cause of low fab yield to a major cause (Berglund 2003). According to one expert, some elements on a chip are so thin that a change of one atom can cause a 25 percent difference in various aspects of performance.[20]

Rather than a comprehensive solution, the industry has adopted a variety of approaches to mitigate the problem. One of the most basic approaches was the adoption of restrictive design rules that accommodate known process variability issues in order to avoid "worst-case" outcomes. Engineers like to design chips in a way that exploits the full capability of a process in at least some dimensions, but as process performance became less predictable, the simplest solution was to narrow the expected performance window. This approach was adopted by Intel, among others.[21] However, as smaller linewidths increase the sensitivity of chips to process variation, restrictive design rules could lead to the perverse outcome of worse performance than in a trailing-edge process with less-restrictive rules. This was reportedly an issue in the transition between the 0.090- and 0.065-micron processes.[22] An increasing number of designers are in fact deciding they don't need, or don't want to learn how to use, the latest process, which is a major break with the industry's history.[23]

Another approach is tighter integration of design with process characteristics. Some EDA software has become lithography-aware, allowing lithography-related issues to be handled during the design process rather than after its conclusion. Another way is to build process information into the standard cell library, which involves simpler design elements than the design cores discussed in Crisis 3. While this has worked for designs using mature technology, it is of no use for the leading-edge chip designs, which cannot wait for the process to be frozen in its final form and encoded in a cell library.

A variant is an architectural approach. Since process variability leads to differences in circuit timing between chips, it has been proposed to design chip with built-in controllers that respond to the full range of variability.[24] Or, alternatively, adding buffers could help regulate inter-chip variability in terms of power leakage or temperature.[25]

One of the most promising approaches is statistical design, which utilizes data on the observed distribution of process parameters and optimizes designs within them. This results in designs that take greater advantage of the potential performance of the process than was possible under restrictive design rules because it is not defined by worst-case limitations. However, statistical analysis requires considerably more computing resources, which significantly raises the fixed cost of a design. IBM has adopted a hybrid model that combines restrictive design rules and statistical analysis.[26]

Another difficulty with implementing a statistical approach is the need to get process data from the fab. While this is not a concern in integrated chip firms, it was a barrier in the fabless-foundry model because foundries consider the performance data for their process to be highly sensitive. Foundries eventually began to offer data on yield and other variables to their largest customers and to the major EDA companies.[27] By 2007 foundry data were increasingly available for 0.065-micron (65-nm) processes, but the EDA tools weren't yet available to incorporate it.[28]

5.4   Virtual Re-aggregation of the Foundry-Fabless Model

Some observers have suggested that the growing interaction of process and design- would favor integrated firms, who both design and manufacture their own chips.[29] These companies face fewer barriers to the exchange of sensitive information between the fab and the design team.

In actuality the fabless-foundry model, with a fair amount of added cross-skilling, appears to be quite robust. As mentioned in Crisis 2, some integrated firms have even become fabless.

Changes at the largest fabless company, Qualcomm, show how the chip industry is being re-integrated in terms of knowledge flows rather than through integration within a single company. As one industry participant put it: "[Design for manufacturing] is a contact sport. You've got to be communicating closely, effectively and systematically."[30]

Since 2004, Qualcomm has developed a skills base related to manufacturing, including expertise in materials, packaging, and equipment, so that it can work with its foundry partners on process development and negotiate over design rules.[31] Qualcomm worked with TSMC and an IBM-led foundry consortium known as the Common Platform Alliance for more than a year prior to the introduction of 0.065-micron manufacturing. The advance collaboration will last even longer for 0.045 micron, which entered production in 2008. The close collaboration has permitted Qualcomm to narrow its technology gap with the integrated firms, particularly its chief rival Texas Instruments, from a year or more at the 0.090-micron generation to about 6 months at 0.065 micron.[32]

On the foundry side, TSMC has become steadily more involved with design. Although most of its customers rely on their own design teams or those at service providers allied with TSMC, the foundry has found it increasingly necessary to develop in-house expertise in order to help its customers create manufacturable designs and, not incidentally, fill TSMC's fabs.[33] TSMC's internal design division has developed standard cell libraries and functional design cores for new processes, much as an integrated or advanced fabless chip company would do, to help its customers complete their designs successfully and in less time, at lower cost.[34]

These are just some examples of the way the fabless-foundry model has risen to the challenge of the subwavelength lithography era with incremental changes. The model matured during a decade of relatively straightforward technical progress that made it easy to separate design and manufacturing. Although the way forward has become much more difficult, the economics of the chip industry—especially the multibillion-dollar cost of fabs—continue to favor the foundry model for products that can be manufactured in a mainstream digital process.

5.5   Lessons and Conclusions

The semiconductor industry thrives on its ability to push its technology along the trajectory of Moore's Law, although the physical challenges have grown. In this chapter we have focused on the mounting crisis in photolithography, a key to continued improvement. First, the familiar optical lithography technology is reaching the end of its usefulness following a series of increasingly exotic extensions such as immersion lithography. Second, the industry's very success at continuing along Moore's Law has brought designers up against undesirable physical effects of the incredibly small circuitry.

The industry's responses have so far been incremental. The extension of optical lithography is a classic example of engineers preferring the known (optical infrastructure) to the unknown (untried postoptical alternatives). A postoptical solution, such as EUV, may bring about a radical break with the past. To get there, the industry is moving cooperatively within the industry roadmap framework. In this instance cooperation is imperative because of the considerable development costs involved. The success of these efforts would maintain the technology trajectory predicted by Moore's Law that continues to offer consumers quality improvements at declining prices.

The design-for-manufacturing challenge has been met by an incremental blurring of the separation between leading-edge fabless companies and their foundries that relies on a small but highly skilled set of engineers who can bridge the gap between the two spheres. All parts of the industry, including foundries, EDA, fabless and fabbed chip companies, are moving toward a transparent solution in which EDA tools that receive manufacturing data from an in-house fab or foundry can ensure that designs are compatible with the idiosyncrasies of a leading-edge process.

As discussed in Crisis 3, cooperative efforts such as roadmapping and transparent design for manufacturing are subject to strategic moves by participants that can undermine collective progress. There is no guarantee that a postoptical lithography solution will appear on schedule, or that the intellectual property concerns of foundries will be addressed to allow them to share data from their leading-edge processes with a wide range of customers. These efforts are all expensive, and are occurring in the context of the industry's rising R&D-to-sales ratio and generally low return on investment (Crisis 7) amid a severe economic downturn. If the industry falls off the Moore's Law curve, it may well be because of the failure of cooperation rather than the limits of physics.

Crisis 6

Finding Talent

The fast-paced evolution and continued growth of the semiconductor industry in the US demands a pipeline of talented and highly-trained workers. What's flowing through that pipeline is becoming increasingly insufficient.
—Kevin Lyman, Sr VP, Human Resources, AMD, December 2006.[1]

In the long run, the nation as a whole will suffer from the lack of new talent that could have been discovered and nurtured in affordable, accessible, high-quality public schools, colleges, and universities.
—*Rising above the Gathering Storm: Energizing and Employing America for a Brighter Economic Future*, National Academy of Sciences Report, 2007[2]

In this chapter we switch to a close-up on the United States and ask if the US chip industry is facing a talent crisis. High-tech companies have been issuing the "crisis warning" about engineering shortages for at least the past two decades. The warnings from AMD and the National Academies quoted above are only two in a long line issued by companies and government-sponsored panels.

We saw in Crisis 4 that the price squeeze that led the US industry to globalize its supply chain also led to the fear that engineers in high-cost locations would lose jobs to lower cost foreign engineers. Moreover the deep recession that began in 2008 brought a string of layoff announcements from chip companies around the world, including Intel, Texas Instruments, IBM, Elpida, Renesas, STMicroelectronics, AMD, National Semiconductor, and a host of smaller companies. The US layoffs further raised anxiety over the future of chip jobs in the United States.

The pre-downturn worries seem inconsistent. How can the US fear of loss of engineering jobs if it is experiencing a shortage of engineers? Experts cannot agree if the United States is educating or granting visas to too few or too many engineers and scientists.[3] This is partly because economists find it hard to believe a shortage exists in a labor market when real earnings are *not rising* across the board, as we will see describes the situation in the high-tech engineering labor market. The debate also reflects the difference in opinion of engineers and their employers on the proper government policies to regulate immigration and fund higher education of engineers and scientists.

Economists have generally believed that any imbalance in the engineering labor market is short lived while the market equilibrates through changes in earnings and in the supply of newly educated engineers— earnings increase (or decrease) and result in an increase (or decrease) in supply of engineers and decrease (or increase) in demand. Eventually the supply of engineers should satisfy the demand, although the transition requires time to train new engineers or to retire or relocate experienced engineers.

At the heart of the public debate is the fact that engineers and their employers represent the two sides of the marketplace: employers want low-cost hard-working engineers with state-of-the-art knowledge, and engineers want well-paid challenging jobs that provide continual skill and career development. Employers prefer a surplus of engineers in their hiring queue in order to find new hires with exactly the right state-of-the-art skills and without competition from other employers that drives up earnings. Engineers prefer a shortage of engineers, so employers are willing to (re)train their current workforce in the required skills, or the engineers have challenging job options with other employers, which tends to drive up earnings.

The US government plays a powerful role in the US engineering labor market and can speed up or slow down the transition towards equilibrium. Here we focus on the impact on the supply of US engineers through visa regulations, which determine the number of foreign engineers and foreign students coming into the United States. These policies can quickly increase or decrease the supply of engineers and directly affect the bargaining power of engineers and their employers. No wonder the two sides present very different arguments to the federal government about how many foreign engineers should be allowed to study and work in the United States.

Our own interviews with semiconductor executives since the early 1990s indicate that companies continually worry about a "future shortage" even as they report being able to recruit excellent engineers. Companies also have increasing educational requirements, and most want to hire only MS (or PhD) engineers for design and product or process development. Their worries about hiring talented engineers seem to reflect their fears that competition will push salaries up for those with graduate training, and of course the companies would prefer that the graduate premium stay low.

In order to evaluate the crisis warnings issued about inadequate high-tech talent in the United States, we look in detail at the labor market for semiconductor engineers—the earnings and employment opportunities over the past five years, the career paths engineers face as they age, and the returns to investing in advanced degrees. Then we look at the influence of graduate education and H-1B visa policies on the demand and supply for semiconductor engineers. We close by discussing lessons from the global brain circulation.

6.1 The US Labor Market for Engineers

In a highly cyclical industry like semiconductors, we often have a hard time disentangling the cyclical fluctuations from the long-run trends. Just since 2000, the US semiconductor industry has experienced ups and downs in demand—a severe recession in 2001, a recovery that stalled in 2004, a large decline in US venture funding for start-ups that began to pick up in 2006, and another severe recession and fall in venture funding in 2008. Meanwhile federal policies affected the foreigners who wanted to join the US high-tech economy with an increase and then decrease in the number of H-1B visas, and a drop and then recovery in foreign student applications to US graduate engineering schools since 9/11. Meanwhile US firms were busy opening design centers offshore, especially in India. The long-run impact on US engineering jobs from this confluence of forces and the engineers' responses cannot be predicted and disentangled, and this caveat should be borne in mind in any analysis of the labor market for semiconductor engineers.

Because of the complexity of the situation, we look at multiple data sources with different strengths and weaknesses, to see how US semiconductor engineers are faring. First we use occupational employment statistics (OES) data from firms to look at how employment and earnings of various types of engineers have changed during 2000 to 2005, and how engineers have fared compared to other professionals.[4] Then we use American Community Survey (ACS) data from households to see how engineers with different levels of education and at various stages of their careers were doing in 2005. We then use a longitudinal employer-household dynamics (LEHD) data set that links employees and firms to look in some detail at career paths of semiconductor workers, as they piece together the jobs offered by firms over the 1992 through 2001 period.[5] Together these data sets provide us with a rich and complex view of the high-tech engineering labor market.

6.1.1   Employment and Earnings

Nationally in 2005, 2.4 million engineers averaged yearly earnings of $63,920 (see table 6.1). Another 2.9 million engineers had jobs in computer occupations with average yearly earnings of $67,100.

The semiconductor industry[6] employed 450,000 US workers in 2005, with 27 percent in engineering and computer occupations (or 17 percent if lower level subcategories such as technicians and computer support are excluded). These two occupation groups do not include managers, who are 8.2 percent of employment.

A significant percentage of engineers work in the semiconductor industry, especially in the most relevant subcategories—12 percent of electronics engineers, 7.3 percent of electrical engineers, 18 percent of computer hardware engineers, 5.8 percent of industrial engineers, and 2 percent of computer software (applications and systems) engineers. Together these six occupations account for 85 percent of engineering jobs in the semiconductor industry.[7]

Although national employment in engineering occupations, which includes a category called "technicians" for workers with less than a BS degree, fell 7.5 percent from 2000 to 2005, engineering jobs in the semiconductor industry fell a surprising 28 percent.[8] However, when we look at the major categories for semiconductor engineers, we see that jobs increased for electrical engineers (6 percent), electronic engineers (11 percent), and computer hardware engineers (141 percent), while jobs for industrial engineers fell 12 percent, which is the only specialty where job growth for semiconductor engineers was lower than for comparable engineers nationally.

Software engineers have become increasingly important in the semiconductor industry (Crisis 3), and semiconductor software jobs grew 6 percent between 2000 and 2005, while national software employment stagnated. However, the growth was in software applications jobs, which grew 40 percent, while software systems jobs fell 14 percent.

Of course, the years between 2000 and 2005 exhibit variations in employment rather than a smooth increase. For example, applications software engineers experienced strong employment growth in 2003 followed by a dip in employment in 2004, and electrical and electronics engineers experienced a dip in employment in 2003 followed by very strong employment growth in 2004. Nationally the unemployment rate for electrical and electronics engineers attracted attention as it reached 6.2 percent in 2003, converging for the first time in thirty years with the general unemployment rate, and then falling back in 2004 to a more typical rate of 2.2 percent.[9]

Engineers in the semiconductor industry typically command a higher salary than their counterparts in other industries. Semiconductor engineers received average annual earnings that were anywhere from 3 percent higher for electronic engineers (EEs) to 9 percent higher for computer software application engineers compared to engineers nationally. The premium paid to semiconductor engineers is much higher if we make the more appropriate comparison to comparable engineers in all other industries (excluding semiconductors). For example, the 12 percent of EEs who work in the semiconductor industry average about 23 percent higher earnings compared to EEs working in all other industries (OES data, not shown). These comparisons are crude since they are not adjusted for experience and education.

The main six semiconductor engineering specialties all experienced real earnings growth. Real (inflation-corrected) growth ranged from 1.6 percent for industrial engineers to 12 percent for computer hardware engineers.

Table 6.1
Engineer employment and earnings, 2000 and 2005

	2000		2005		Change in employment	Change in earnings
	Employment	Average annual earnings	Employment	Average annual earnings		
Engineering occupations (total)	2,575,620	$61,312	2,382,480	$63,920	−7.50%	4.25%
Engineers in SC	132,150	$59,089	95,520	$68,720	−27.72%	16.30%
Electrical engineers (total)	162,400	$75,217	144,920	$76,060	−10.76%	1.12%
Electrical engineers in SC	10,050	$78,891	10,620	$82,400	5.67%	4.45%
Electronic engineers (total)	123,690	$75,409	130,050	$79,990	5.14%	6.07%
Electronic engineers in SC	14,170	$74,173	15,700	$82,430	10.80%	11.13%
Aerospace engineers (total)	71,550	$78,301	81,100	$85,450	13.35%	9.13%
Chemical engineers (total)	31,530	$76,169	27,550	$79,230	−12.62%	4.02%
Civil engineers (total)	207,080	$66,211	229,700	$69,480	10.92%	4.94%
Computer hardware engineers (total)	63,680	$79,504	78,580	$87,170	23.40%	9.64%
Hardware engineers in SC	5,990	$80,275	14,440	$89,870	141.07%	11.95%

Industrial engineers (total)	171,810	$67,935	191,640	$68,500	11.54%	0.83%
Industrial engineers in SC	12,580	$73,062	11,030	$74,250	-12.32%	1.63%
Mechanical engineers (total)	207,300	$69,024	220,750	$70,000	6.49%	1.41%
Computer occupations (total)	2,932,810	$65,837	2,952,740	$67,100	0.68%	1.92%
Computer occupations in SC	27,080	$75,602	28,770	$77,800	6.24%	2.91%
Computer programmers (total)	530,730	$69,149	389,090	$67,400	-26.69%	-2.53%
Programmers in SC	3,310	$74,627	1,900	$74,370	-42.60%	-0.34%
Software engineers, applications (total)	374,640	$79,730	455,980	$79,540	21.71%	-0.24%
Software engineers (applications) in SC	5,890	$82,430	8,250	$86,860	40.07%	5.37%
Computer software engineers, systems (total)	264,610	$80,400	320,720	$84,310	21.20%	4.86%
Software engineers (systems) in SC	8,280	$86,944	7,090	$90,820	-14.37%	4.46%

Note: SC = semiconductors at the lowest level of aggregation available from BLS: SIC 367 in 2000 and NAICS 3344 in 2005. Earnings are in constant 2005 dollars (adjusted by CPI-U).

These data indicate that the labor market for semiconductor engineers appears to be relatively strong in the five years since the dot.com bust in 2000 because nationally for all occupations, earnings mostly stagnated during the economic recovery with income gains going disproportionately to those at the very top. Semiconductor engineers have also experienced better job and earnings growth than engineers in the same specialty in other industries. Although earnings growth was relatively high only for computer hardware engineers and electronic engineers in the semiconductor industry, all six specialties of semiconductor engineers had high 2005 average annual earnings, which ranged from $74,250 for industrial engineers to $90,820 for software systems engineers.

Overall, the data indicate that the labor market for high-tech engineers does not seem to be out of balance in either supply or demand. High-tech engineers appear able to move among various industries as demand shifts, and overall wages appear stable. However, these average data do not tell the full story, since we don't know how engineers are doing over

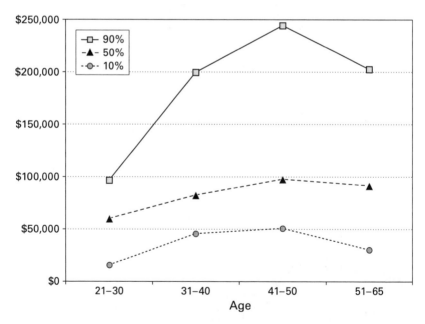

Figure 6.1
2005 age-earning profile, BS holders. Source: Authors' calculations from 2005 ACS data.

their careers as they age, or how engineers at the top and bottom of the
salary distribution are faring.

6.1.2   Age-Earnings Profiles by Education[10]

American Community Survey (ACS) data allow us to compare earnings
of engineers with different levels of education and at various stages of
their careers.[11] A rough snapshot of how semiconductor engineers are
doing as they age and their returns to experience is provided by looking
at the earnings of engineers of various age groups in a given year. We use
2005 ACS data to look at earnings of engineers ages 21 to 65 years (a
proxy for experience) in the semiconductor industry by education (BS,
MS/PhD).[12] The 2005 age-earnings profiles of semiconductor engineers
with BS degree (figure 6.1) and MS/PhD degrees (figure 6.2) show how
engineers at the high (90th percentile), median, and low (10th percentile)
points of the salary distribution fare as they age. These results are
also shown in table 6.2.[13] Of course, we do not know if the returns to

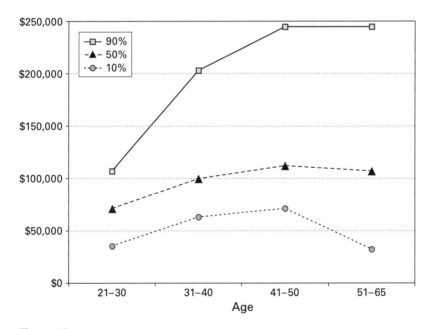

Figure 6.2
2005 age-earnings profile, MS and PhD holders. Source: Authors' calculations
from 2005 ACS data.

Table 6.2
Age-earnings profile, 2005

		Age ranges			
		21–30	31–40	41–50	51–65
Less than Bachelor's degree	10%	11,358	37,691	38,710	35,144
	50%	32,597	61,120	63,667	63,157
	90%	62,648	91,680	99,830	96,773
	90/10 ratio	5.52	2.43	2.58	2.75
	Mean	35,256	61,261	71,027	63,968
Bachelor's degree	10%	15,687	45,840	50,933	30,560
	50%	60,102	82,512	97,792	91,680
	90%	96,773	199,659	244,480	202,715
	90/10 ratio	2.74	3.26	3.44	3.17
	Mean	58,522	95,093	121,700	101,024
Master's or PhD degree	10%	35,653	63,157	71,307	32,394
	50%	71,307	99,830	112,054	106,960
	90%	106,960	202,715	244,480	244,480
	90/10 ratio	3.00	3.21	3.43	7.55
	Mean	72,791	111,742	137,356	118,549

Note: Repetition of earnings in some cells, especially for the 90 percent group, appears to reflect the data collection, which is done by asking employers to give earnings in specific ranges.

Table 6.3
Proportion working less than full year (48 weeks), 2005

	Age ranges			
	21–30	31–40	41–50	51–65
Bachelor's degree	20.3%	9.3%	6.6%	17.4%
Master's or PhD degree	17.7%	9.3%	6.0%	17.5%

Note: Value in each cell is the proportion of that age group with the indicated degree who were employed less than 48 weeks in the indicated year.

experience indicated by the 2005 data are the actual returns experienced by the cohorts of engineers over time.

All engineers—at the top, middle, and bottom of the salary distribution in both education groups—show earnings that increase with experience (age) through prime ages (21 to 50 years). Then older workers (51 to 65 years) experienced labor market problems as earnings declined (see figures 6.1 and 6.2). Only engineers with advanced degrees at the top of the salary distribution did not experience a decline in earnings after age 50.

At least part of the decline in earnings for older engineers can be explained by looking at weeks worked (table 6.3). Workers over age 50 are much more likely than workers in their 30s and 40s to work less than a full year (defined conservatively here as less than 48 weeks of paid work). One in six engineers aged 51 to 65 years reported being paid for less than a full year of work in 2005, when the labor market was relatively strong. During the 2002 downturn more than one in four older engineers had less than a full year of paid work (Brown and Linden 2005). Feedback from our interviews with engineers and stories from the public press indicate that the reduced hours are mostly involuntary.

The inequality in earnings increases with age (see 90/10 ratio and graphs) with one exception—the earnings inequality is lower for engineers over 50 compared to those in their 40s with a bachelor's degree, as both earners at the top and bottom of the distribution experience lower earnings. In contrast, the earnings inequality for engineers over 50 with graduate degrees jumps up. Typically the growing inequality is thought to reflect faster growing pay for the higher performers, and pay for the top earners would be expected to increase as some engineers become managers. However, we see that pay at the top flattens out with age and pay at the bottom end suffers a sharp drop for these engineers with graduate degrees. The increase in inequality between prime-aged and older engineers reflects holding on at the top and losing ground at the bottom, rather than the top performers doing even better. These profiles indicate that many engineers with college and advanced degrees are facing declining and inadequate job opportunities after age 50.

6.1.3   Returns to Education

Although we expect earnings to increase with education, figures 6.1 and 6.2 show fairly similar earnings for semiconductor engineers with college degrees and advanced degrees. What is the return to an advanced degree?

In 2005 the graduate degree premium for the typical engineer in the early stage of a career (median earnings at age 31 to 40) was 21 percent, but the premium fell to only 15 percent for engineers over 40 (calculated from table 6.2). Using the national earnings figures as a guide, we made a rough estimate of the earnings and earnings growth of a semiconductor engineer with a BS degree and one with a PhD up to age 40. We assumed the BS earns $50,000 in the first job (age 21) and earns $90,000 at age 40; the MS/PhD takes three years to complete graduate training and earns $70,000 in the first job (age 24) and earns $105,000 at age 40. If earnings grow at a constant annual rate, the BS engineer's earnings are growing at 3.3 percent annually, and the MS/PhD engineer's earnings are growing at 2.75 percent annually.[14] At age 40, the MS/PhD is earning 17 percent (or $15,500) more than the BS engineer, but career earnings are $51,000 *lower*, since the graduate training involved giving up pay for three years.[15]

The negative graduate degree premium indicates that no financial incentives exist for domestic engineers to pursue graduate degrees. However, the graduate degree premium for students born abroad in a developing country is high, since entrance into a graduate program in the United States allows them access to much higher paying jobs in the United States upon graduation. If they go to work with a BS in their home countries, their pay is a fraction of the US pay, as we saw in India, although the Indian salary may rise very quickly for several years.[16] By coming to the United States for graduate training, they dramatically improve their job opportunities, both in the United States and abroad, so their graduate degree premium is extremely high. For foreign engineers, obtaining a graduate degree at a US university provides a high-income career relative to what they could earn at home with a domestic BS degree.

For domestic US students, the return to a BS degree provides financial incentives to finish college, with the college graduate experiencing median earnings that are 35 to 84 percent higher than the earnings of engineers (usually technicians) who finished high school but not college in 2005. The typical engineer with a BS degree experienced steady earnings improvements with age until reaching the 50s. In contrast, the typical engineer who did not finish college experienced a jump in earnings between the 20s and 30s, and then median earnings flattened out after age 30.

6.1.4 Career Paths for Semiconductor Professionals

Let's look briefly at the actual career paths of prime-aged (aged 35 to 54) high-education (college degree and graduate degrees) male semiconductor workers to see if they are consistent with our results based on comparing engineers of different ages.[17] Here workers cannot be broken out by occupation, so they include engineers as well as managers and others. We describe the career paths for these workers by how many jobs they have—one, two, or three jobs over the decade 1992 to 2001.[18]

Semiconductor workers exhibit two distinct types of career paths— loyalists and job changers (see table 6.4). Workers who have landed a good semiconductor job (high initial earnings and good earnings growth) become loyalists, namely they do not change jobs over the decade. Loyalists have career paths that are considerably better than the career paths of job changers, who have inferior jobs and change jobs, either voluntary or involuntary (we don't know which), to land a better job. These job changers have relatively low initial earnings in a job outside the semiconductor industry, and then experience substantial earnings growth (usually 20 to 30 percent for younger and 10 to 20 percent for older workers) by taking a job in the semiconductor industry. The overall earnings growth of two-jobbers and three-jobbers is about the same over the ten-year period, but the two-jobbers have higher initial earnings.

Table 6.4
Semiconductor career paths, higher education men aged 35 to 54

	One job	Two jobs	Three jobs
Initial earnings[a]	$36,084	$22,893	$18,197
Earnings growth (annual)[b]	0.059	0.048	0.047
Simulated earnings (after ten years)	$65,207	$36,925	$29,068

Source: *Economic Turbulence* (Brown et al. 2006, tab. 6.1). Original calculations by authors from Census LEHD data.
Notes: Simulated 2001 final average earnings (2005 dollars). Career paths are for workers in all occupations in the semiconductor industry, so they include engineers as well as other occupations over the period 1992 to 2001. An employee is included in the data set if he has at least one job in the semiconductor industry over the period.
a. Mean initial earnings (2005 dollars, using the CPI-urban).
b. Net annualized earnings growth rate (in log points) across ten-year simulation.

Job changers experience lower earnings growth over the decade than the loyalist. The legendary job hoppers in the Silicon Valley, namely engineers who leave good jobs for an even better ones, are a much smaller group than the job changers shown here, who are leaving lousy jobs for slightly better ones

A survey of earnings of fab engineers in the mid-1990s show the returns to experience of fab engineers was falling (Brown and Campbell 2001). The companies were lowering maximum pay while increasing entry-level pay (in constant dollars). In interviews we learned that fabs liked having young engineers with knowledge of new technology, and they did not worry about losing older engineers. Over time, consequently, fabs were willing to increase wages of new hires without raising the wages of experienced engineers. Fast-changing technology plus an ample supply of new hires and low turnover allowed the companies to flatten engineers' career ladders with no adverse consequences, which is consistent with the ACS career paths in 2005 that showed low returns to experience for engineers after age 30.

These patterns are consistent with the way big semiconductor companies changed their employment practices to increase workforce flexibility, especially to reduce head count during downturns. The era of lifetime jobs with career development died in the 1990s; most workers must use mobility to improve their job prospects.

IBM provides a good example of how downsizing programs evolved over the 1980s into the 1990s. In 1983 IBM offered workers at five locations a voluntary early retirement program in which workers with twenty-five or more years experience would receive two years of pay over four years. IBM offered voluntary retirement programs again in 1986 and 1989.[19] Because these programs were voluntary for the general workforce, rather than for targeted job titles or divisions, the change in workforce usually did not turn out to be what the companies might have chosen: the better workers often opted to leave, and the weaker workers, without good job opportunities elsewhere, often stayed.

The deep recession in the early 1990s finally pushed IBM, DEC, and Motorola, once known for their employment security, to make layoffs.[20] The new approach to downsizing included voluntary programs for *targeted* workers. If workers did not accept the termination program, they could become subject to layoff, making the program less than voluntary. In 1991 and 1992 IBM selected workers eligible for termination, which included a bonus of up to a year's salary. Over 40,000 workers were "transitioned" out. Downsizing continued through 1993. By 1994 actual layoffs were occurring at IBM.[21]

With the dot.com bust in the early 2000s, massive rounds of layoffs by semiconductor companies occurred again. By the end of 2001 Motorola had laid off over 48,000 workers from its 2000 peak of 150,000 employees.[22] The volatile swings in demand meant that the idea of lifetime employment in the US semiconductor industry was a thing of the past, although selected workers still had excellent job ladders with long careers. In contrast to the United States, Japan electronics companies have maintained lifetime employment for regular workers and improved flexibility in headcount by significantly increasing the proportion of non-regular workers (Nakata and Miyazaki 2010). Chip and systems companies in the United States and Japan announced large layoffs both domestically and globally in 2009 as the recession deepened. In Japan lay-offs mostly affect nonregular workers without lifetime employment. For example all of the 4,500 workers targeted for domestic layoff by Toshiba in a January 2009 announcement were in "temporary jobs."[23]

The human resource management system at most US chip companies could now be characterized as a *high-innovation system* (Katz 1997; Brown 2006) that supports rapid innovation through using the mobile talent pool connected to informal global knowledge networks. Engineers are typically hired because their skills and knowledge are required for a specific technology or product being developed. The company wants engineers to remain at least for the tenure of the project. Once hired, the company signals to engineers their future with the company by assignments to follow-up projects, including development of engineers as managers and executives. Engineers can be let go, or they are encouraged to leave by being put on dead-end projects, such as maintenance of legacy technology. Additional formal training and "need to know" proprietary company knowledge are taught when required on the project. The mobility of engineers among companies under this system is seen as cost effective, since the company can hire required skills and does not have to retrain experienced workers, who usually command higher wages than new graduates.

This is a sharp contrast with the *high-commitment system* (Baron and Kreps 1999) that is still more typical at chip companies in Japan and the European Union. In the archetypal form of the high-commitment system, engineers are managed to elicit loyalty, high effort, and responsibility. This approach works well when knowledge is tacit, specific to the company, and cumulative or depreciating slowly. Much learning occurs on the job and experience is valued. In the high-commitment system the loss of an engineer who quits is seen as a net asset loss to the company. The company is able to plan for the skills required over time, since the company is in charge of the development of workers' skills and knowledge through job assignments, which determine on-the-job training, and through occasional formal classroom training. Engineers can be flexibly deployed across projects and can be quickly reassigned when needed, since they have been broadly trained and such movements are accepted in order to meet company needs.

Overall, the weak external environment and the internal need for engineers with the latest technical knowledge eventually forced US semiconductor companies to abandon the high-commitment system for the high-innovation system. Of course, this puts engineers, who are no longer retrained by their companies, at a disadvantage as they age, and the national data confirm that older semiconductor engineers are experiencing a troubling drop in real earnings and a decline in hours.

6.1.5 Analysis: The Outlook for US Engineers and Their Employers

Even during the industry's latest growth period before the onset of the 2008 recession, we found evidence of labor market problems, especially for older engineers who face rapid skill obsolescence and deteriorating job opportunities. In general, after a few years of working, experience becomes less valuable to employers than knowledge of new technology, and engineers face stagnant and even lower earnings as they age. We saw in our fieldwork that experienced engineers were often forced to work on mature technologies with stagnant earnings, rather than being allowed to learn and work on new technologies with rising earnings.

This issue is complex because US companies tend to want newly minted graduate engineers who have state-of-the art knowledge to work on projects for five to seven years. Then companies select and train engineers who have leadership potential to become program managers and higher level managers. This bifurcation creates a group of engineers who move into the managerial ranks and another group who see deteriorating job opportunities as they age. When companies claim they face a shortage of engineers, they usually mean that they face a shortage of young, relatively inexpensive engineers with the latest skills, even when they have a queue of experienced engineers who want retraining. US chip companies may be ignoring a vital resource by not adopting more active retraining efforts to complement their ongoing efforts to recruit fresh graduates.

Today's engineers must be in charge of their careers; they can no longer depend on the employer to provide them with the continual training they need to keep up their skills (Brown and Campbell 2001; Saxenian 2006; Cappelli 2008). In general, the well-educated semiconductor engineers who are employed worldwide by multinational companies (or high-tech start-ups) are known for their flexibility and ability to solve challenging problems and learn new technologies, and they take it for granted that the semiconductor industry is in continual crisis and change. Chip engineers even use these industry characteristics to their advantage in planning their careers by seeking jobs where they can learn about new technologies and new markets. What is new for the engineers and companies is both the quickly expanding market demand in developing countries, especially China and India, and the quickly expanding global supply of elite engineers from a variety of countries.

Both the supply of and demand for engineers with leading-edge knowledge have become more mobile and more global. US government policies that impact graduate education and immigration are a major force in shaping the high-tech labor supply.

6.2   US Engineering Graduate Education: Foreign Students

Graduate education plays an increasingly important role in the development of talent for the US semiconductor industry, and also for the diffusion of chip technology as some graduates return to their home countries, often after gaining work experience. Foreign nationals play an important role in US graduate engineering programs, where they were 60 percent of doctoral students and 50 percent of masters' students during 2000 to 2005.[24] Enrollment of foreign graduate students in engineering programs almost doubled from 1985 to 2003, when 60,000 were enrolled. In computer science, enrollment of foreign graduate students rose dramatically from 7,500 in 1985 to 24,000 in 2003.[25] Slightly more foreign national students were enrolled in master's programs than PhD programs in US engineering schools since the mid-1980s. However the number of foreign nationals in the PhD program continued to rise. By 2004 more foreign students were enrolled in engineering PhD programs than master's programs.[26]

The highest level of engineering education, the PhD, provides engineers with state-of-the-art knowledge plus the ability to conduct research and to stay abreast of the latest technology during their careers. Here we look at which countries are sending students to engineering PhD programs in the United States, since engineers with doctoral degrees (especially in EE) provide leadership in the semiconductor industry, from managing projects to running companies.

Figure 6.3 shows the annual engineering PhDs (not including computer science) awarded at US universities to students from five key Asian

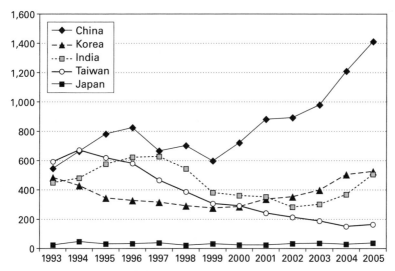

Figure 6.3
Engineering PhDs in the United States by country of origin, 1993 to 2005.
Source: National Science Foundation, Division of Science Resources Statistics,
Science and Engineering Doctorate Awards: 2002 (app. tab. 5), 2003 (app. tab.
11), 2004 (app. tab. 11), 2005 (app. tab. 11).

countries over a twelve-year period. In 2005 students from these five
countries received 42 percent of the engineering PhDs awarded to noncitizens, who in turn received 64 percent of engineering PhDs.

The figure makes clear that Chinese students received a large and
growing number of engineering PhDs. At the other extreme Japanese
students received few PhDs in the United States during the period, as
Japanese engineers obtained graduate training at home often through
programs set up by their companies with Japanese universities. Indian
students received a growing number of PhDs in the 1990s, and in 1997
received almost as many PhDs as Chinese students. However, the number of Indian engineers granted PhDs then fell while the number of Chinese PhD engineers soon began to rise sharply.

Taiwan, which relied on PhDs from US universities to develop its
semiconductor industry during the 1980s, began sending many fewer
students to the United States during the 1990s as university programs
and job opportunities improved at home. The number of PhDs awarded

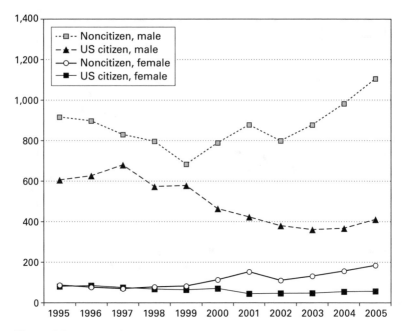

Figure 6.4
Electrical engineering PhDs by gender and citizenship status, 1995 to 2005.
Source: National Science Foundation, Division of Science Resources Statistics,
Science and Engineering Doctorate Awards: 2004 (app. tab. 3), 2005 (app.
tab. 3).

to Taiwanese students in the United States declined dramatically since
the mid-1990s, and Taiwanese experts in the semiconductor field have
worried about the impact this might have on the supply of engineers for
semiconductor research, since Taiwan's PhD education in engineering is
not as advanced as that in the United States. Korean students also
received decreasing numbers of PhDs through the late 1990s, although
the numbers started to increase beginning in 2002.

If we compare the number of US and noncitizen PhD graduates in electrical engineering (EE), we see that noncitizens garnered significantly
more diplomas than US citizens during the decade ending in 2005, and
most PhDs went to men (see figure 6.4). The year 1999 seems to be a
turning point, when the number of PhDs to noncitizen males began to
rise sharply as the number to citizen males fell. The same data for computer science (CS) PhDs shows similar, but muted, trends with less differ-

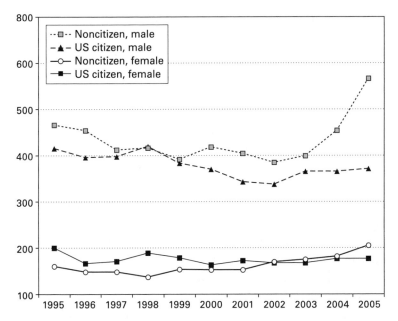

Figure 6.5
Computer science PhDs by gender and citizenship status, 1995 to 2005. Source: National Science Foundation, Division of Science Resources Statistics, *Science and Engineering Doctorate Awards*: 2004 (app. tab. 3), 2005 (app. tab. 3).

ence between citizens and noncitizens (figure 6.5), and with many fewer PhDs awarded in CS than in EE.

Graduate students enter the PhD program four to five years before the year the students receive their PhDs, which is shown here. A sharp increase in foreign graduate students began in the early 1990s just as the PC market and then the Internet were taking off. As the semiconductor industry prospered, job opportunities for engineers with BS degrees expanded rapidly and the relative return to graduate training for US citizens declined.

The earlier discussion of the returns to education noted that the premium for a BS in EE to pursue a graduate degree was low for domestic students. For foreign-born engineers with a BS in EE, the financial incentive to pursue a US graduate degree is much greater, since a US graduate degree opens the door to high-paid jobs both in the United States and at home. Our fieldwork found that advanced degree holders, especially with some US work experience, in semiconductor centers like Shanghai or Bangalore where they are project managers (and higher) are often paid similarly to their US counterparts while locally educated engineers are paid much less.

The wisdom of attracting bright hard-working students from abroad to graduate programs in the United States depends partly on whether these students stay and contribute their talents to the US economy or they return home, where they might still work for US companies or help build networks that favor US relationships. The NSF surveys graduating PhD engineers about their postgraduation plans to work in the United States or abroad. When surveyed in 2005 only about 60 percent of the foreign engineers had made plans (including a post-doc, industry job, or academic appointment) and, of those, 82 percent of the plans involved remaining in the United States. For new CS PhDs, two-thirds of the foreign engineers had postgraduation plans, and 83 percent of their plans involved staying in the United States. Unfortunately, no ongoing survey tracks what happens to these highly educated foreigners in the years after graduation, so we do not know how long they remain in the United States. However, we observe high-profile foreign engineers who were trained in the United States and then go on to executive positions, often as founders, in US companies or go on to executive positions, including founders, of companies in their home countries. Saxenian (2006) documents the process of foreign-born, US-educated engineers who return home to Taiwan, China, and India to start new companies. Wadhwa et al (2008) found that one-quarter of all engineering and technology companies established in the United States between 1995 and 2005 had at least one immigrant key founder.

Hidden discrimination against ethnic groups, who hit glass ceilings in many large US companies, has pushed many of them back to their home countries, where their opportunity to start new companies, especially in China, or to work for multinational companies, especially in India, provides them with superior careers over the alternative of stagnation in middle management in the United States. Others may strike out as entrepreneurs in the United States, where many have succeeded, A Duke study of technology companies that were established in the United States from 1995 to 2005 reported that a key founder was foreign born in 25 percent of the companies, and this percentage rose to 35 percent in the semiconductor industry. In 2005 these immigrant-founded companies employed 450,000 workers and had $52 billion in sales (Wadhwa et al. 2008).

Clearly, the United States has benefited from the global brain circulation that brings bright foreign students to the United States for advanced education followed by jobs. Many of them join a mobile global supply of high-tech workers and executives. No longer is the decision "stay or return"; many engineers now move easily between the United States and their home countries as well as other countries (Saxenian 2006). We expect more and more foreign engineers to return home as well as to become globally mobile after being educated and working in the United States. US immigration policies need to entice these highly talented foreign nationals to develop long-lasting ties to the US economy.

6.3   H-1B Visas

US visa and educational policies directly impact the supply of engineers, especially those with advanced degrees, to the domestic market. The H-1B visa program for temporary skilled workers is highly controversial, with companies lobbying hard to increase the number of visas, and with professional groups such as the IEEEUSA lobbying hard for better oversight of the program and against increasing the cap because of the harm caused to domestic engineers. Both groups favor increased permanent migration of engineers. Here we briefly evaluate the competing claims by analyzing the employment and earnings of H-1B visa holders over the 2001 to 2005 period.[27]

The H-1B visa is used by companies to hire a foreigner temporarily for a job that requires specialized knowledge and at least a bachelor's degree. H-1B visas are granted to companies (rather than workers) through a process that requires the company to submit an application with a job title, location, and intended wage rate or earnings at least as high as the prevailing wage. Once hired, the foreigner submits the certified application to obtain an H-1B visa. H-1B employees can work only for the sponsoring US employer, and only in the activities described in the application. The US employer may place the H1B visa worker with another employer if certain rules are followed.[28] A foreigner can work for a maximum of six continuous years on an H-1B visa (including one extension). With application fees and legal expenses, the initial cost to an employer ranges from $2,500 to $8,000 per application. H-1Bs are granted to a wide array of occupations, including those in engineering, medicine, law, social sciences, education, business specialties, and the arts, which places US chip companies in competition with other industries for the scarce visas.

Among the heaviest users of H-1B visas over the last decade have been India-based information technology (IT) services companies like Infosys and Wipro, which held six of the top ten places among firms receiving H-1B petition approvals in fiscal 2007.[29] Among them, the Indian IT firms had nearly 10,000 approvals of the 126,000 total. The one chip firm in the top ten, Intel, had only 369 approvals.

The Indian firms, bringing in mostly Indian nationals to provide software programming services to US customers, pay lower wages than US competitors that use the program (Hira 2004). Chip companies, which, as we show below, typically pay their H-1B engineers the same as equivalent citizen engineers, are in competition for the same pool of visas.

The current law limits the number of certified H-1B visas to 65,000 annually, although the limits were temporarily raised to 195,000 in October 2000 through September 2003 in response to business lobbying.[30] However, the actual number of H-1B visas granted is much higher, since only initial applications are included in the annual limitation (requests for extensions are not included), applications by universities and non-profit research institutions are not counted against the cap, and an additional 20,000 H-1B visas for foreigners with master's and PhD degrees from US universities are allowed. Even in 2003, before these exemptions for US graduates with advanced degrees were implemented, many H-1B visa holders had advanced degrees. Unfortunately, the data on the H-1B visas actually granted are not available.[31]

We analyzed data from the H-1B applications certified to the top ten US chip vendors during fiscal years 2001 through 2005 to see how H-1B visa holders were faring. On the application, companies can provide either a specific proposed pay rate or the minimum and maximum of the proposed pay range, and the top ten companies were equally divided between those stating a specific salary rate and those stating a minimum-maximum salary range.[32] The ten US chip companies had 14,035 H-1B visa applications certified during the five years. Two occupation groups represent most of their H-1B applications: electrical engineering (37 percent with average pay $77,560 or, where a range was specified, average minimum pay $66,944) and computer science (52 percent with average rate $78,537 or average minimum pay $75,685).[33] The high EE and CS pay indicates that these engineers in the chip industry are receiving a premium, which is consistent with the national earnings distributions in table 6.1.

We examined the applications by all other companies (called "other firms" here) for EE and CS jobs in 2005 in order to see if they used comparable rates and ranges, since H-1B visas might be functioning differently in different industries. Interestingly the other firms mostly specified an earnings rate in their H-1B applications for both EE and CS jobs. The rates used on EE applications by other firms have a lower mean and 10th percentile compared to the top chip firms; the rates used on CS applications by other firms have a considerably lower distribution compared to the top chip firms, which probably reflects the dependence of the IT outsourcing companies upon imported cheap programmers. The top chip companies accounted for 56 percent of all EE applications and only 5 percent of all CS applications.

We know from the OES data that firms paid EE/CS engineers $66,000 to $84,000 (overall average $74,000) during 2000 to 2005, which seems to be below the rates on the top US firms' H-1B applications. However, these earnings comparisons are not for engineers with similar experience and education, since the national data includes engineers with all education levels, and the H-1B visa holders must have at least a college degree and one-half had a graduate degree in 2003 (MS 29 percent, PhD 14 percent, professional degree 6 percent).[34] A government study (GAO 2003) shows that the EEs with H-1Bs are younger (32 years vs. 41 years; 62 percent under 35 years old vs. 28 percent) and much more likely to have graduate degrees (50 vs. 20 percent). Many semiconductor companies hired their H-1B visa engineers as graduates with advanced degrees from US universities, and in our fieldwork the foreign-born and national engineers were not distinguishable at the US companies, which treated them the same.

A government study (GAO 2003) compared median annual salaries of EEs aged 31 to 50 years old with H-1B visas and with US citizenship. H-1Bs with graduate degrees earned $77,000, and citizens earned $88,000. H-1Bs with less than a graduate degree earned $65,000, and citizens earned $70,000. For younger EEs (aged 18 to 30) without a graduate degree, however, H-1Bs earned more than citizens ($60,000 vs. $52,000). These data indicate that H-1B visa holders may be having a downward impact on the earnings of mature engineers but probably not on young engineering college graduates, which is consistent with the fab-level data and national data that indicate older engineers' experience is not highly valued.

To understand how US companies are using H-1B visas in their hiring, we examined the H-1B visa applications for the top three visa users in our sample of United States: top ten—IBM, Intel, and Motorola—over the five year period 2001 to 2005. We also examined data on the top ten non-US chip companies for comparison. However, foreign companies are more likely to use an L-1 visa (intracompany transfer) to bring in employees who have worked for the company abroad. The ten non-US firms had only 1,749 H-1B certifications during the period. Compared to US firms, more of the applications by non-US firms were for business and support jobs (15 percent) or for non-EE/CS engineering jobs (18 percent). Compared to US companies, the earnings stated by the non-US companies for EE/CS applications tended to be slightly higher on average and to be lower on average for the non-EE/CS jobs.[35]

IBM, the top user of H-1B visas in our sample, received 3,994 H-1B visa certifications during the five years. IBM's average minimum pay ($82,072) was considerably higher than the average minimum of the other companies. Since IBM has become more of a services company then a hardware company, we assume that many of these jobs are not chip related.

Intel received 2,696 H-1B visa certifications and applied for H-1B visas to fill jobs that varied across skill and experience. Overall their rates seemed to reflect the top ten averages.

Motorola received 2,520 H-1B visa certifications, and the average minimum earnings were 4 percent below the top ten average. Even so, the Motorola rates seem to be slightly higher than national EE/CS salaries.

The H-1B visas granted to these three companies jumped in 2004 and remained high, even as the national H-1B limitation dropped dramatically. The semiconductor companies seemed to be using the additional 20,000 H-1Bs available for foreigners with a graduate degree from US universities that went into effect in 2004. Over the five-year period, approximately 60 percent of the H-1B visas awarded to the top ten companies were awarded during the 2004 to 2005 period.

How important are H-1B visas to the companies in their hiring? To answer the question, we begin by estimating the relevant pool of workers for each company. In 2005 Intel employed approximately 99,900 people worldwide, with more than 50 percent located in the United States. Motorola employed 69,000 employees with 35 percent eligible for stock options, which indicates the number of nontemporary professional employees in the US. IBM employed 329,000 worldwide, and approximately 40 percent were eligible for the US retirement plan (at end of 2004, when the plan was discontinued).[36]

We roughly estimate[37] that in 2005, 2.6 percent of Intel's domestic employees were newly hired H-1B visa holders and 5.4 percent of Intel's domestic employees (and, of course, an even larger percentage of their engineers) were H-1B visa holders. Almost 3 percent of Motorola's domestic professionals were newly-hired H-1B visa holders by our estimate, and 8 percent of Motorola's domestic professionals were H-1B visa holders in 2005. Almost 1 percent of IBM's domestic workforce was newly hired H-1B visa holders, and 2.8 percent of their domestic workforce were H-1B visa holders in 2005.

The earnings listed on the H-1B applications made by the top ten US chip companies indicate that some of the H-1B visas were for high-level jobs that paid well over $100,000, as well as for low-level jobs that paid well under $50,000. These data, and the relatively small share of H-1B workers in these firms' total employment, indicate that semiconductor companies use H-1B visas strategically in hiring and managing their engineering talent. The data do not support the charge that H-1B visas are being used to keep semiconductor earnings low for domestic new hires, or that many higher paying jobs are going to foreigners at the expense of qualified experienced US engineers. Our analysis suggests that the concerns of semiconductor engineers might be more usefully directed at the labor market problems faced by mature engineers.

6.4   Lessons and Conclusions

The global brain circulation has strengthened the semiconductor industry as it has opened new opportunities for companies and workers to undertake activities worldwide, even as it has made any one country's future labor supply of high-tech engineers less certain. Being the leader in engineering graduate education puts the United States at the center of the global circulation, and US companies benefit from having easy access to the well-educated graduating engineers. European chip companies also participate in the global brain circulation through education and hiring flows, but Japan has kept itself relatively isolated.

The global brain circulation laid the foundation for multinational companies to offshore activities to lower cost countries (Crisis 4), and for developing countries to attract foreign-educated engineers back home to help develop the semiconductor industry (Crisis 8). Consumers in developing countries have benefited from the greater chip activity in these economies because more designs are aimed at their specific needs and price point.

The lesson for governments is that immigration, education, and technology policies interact in complex ways. In the United States, for example, a relative dependence on foreign graduate students may make the US supply of engineers vulnerable over time, especially because of cumbersome immigration policies and administrative delays that deter foreign students from staying. Although some companies use the H-1B visa system to hire low-cost foreign skilled workers, we do not find this to be the way that the semiconductor companies use these visas. Chip companies use H-1B visas to hire engineering students graduating with masters' and PhDs. A better program would be to let engineers with graduate degrees from US universities be automatically eligible for permanent residency. In doing this, however, US policy makers may also want to think about how to change the incentives in the current educational system, which provides high returns to graduate training for foreign students but not for US students.

The lesson for firms, especially those facing a tight labor market, is that they need to be aware of a variety of sources of talent, which include experienced engineers as well as new hires. Most US companies have initiated university outreach and internship programs to improve their access to prospective engineers from the global labor pool. They should also take a closer look at the talent they already have in-house and consider retraining programs for their older engineers.

The lesson for US engineers is that they are in charge of their own careers. We have seen in earlier chapters how the fortunes of companies rise and fall, and the employment relationship, especially at US-based firms, has become more tenuous. Workers must maintain their professional networks both to stay abreast of technology trends and to keep aware of employment options.

We think that part of the reason behind employers' fear of a labor shortage is their fear that engineering salaries will increase and further exacerbate cost pressures. The problem of low returns (Crisis 7) has plagued the industry as a whole, but the price of talent is not the root cause. We will see in the next chapter that return on investment varies widely across companies; the pattern is not related to how much companies pay for engineering talent, and integrated (fab-owning) companies, where labor accounts for a very small share of total costs, also suffer low returns on investment.

Crisis 7

Low Returns, High Risk

...the cost of building manufacturing sites, individual product design costs, and the short lifecycles of product all make it harder to get the return on investment. Therefore, the economic challenges need to be considered, too.
—Satoru Ito, President of Renesas Technology, March 2007[1]

Although the semiconductor industry has created enormous value for other industries and for society, chip companies have found it difficult to capture this value as net income. The industry's relatively low and volatile average rates of return reflect the growing costs of manufacturing and design (Crises 2 and 3) combined with competitive product markets that quickly push prices down. Few firms have been able to build sustainable competitive advantage that allows them to capture value above competitive rates, and the severe downturn that started in 2008 brought these weaknesses into sharp relief.

This chapter begins by documenting the return on assets (ROA) over the 1984 to 2005 period for the semiconductor industry and for a selected group of systems firms. We discuss the rising trend in the industry's R&D-to-sales ratio for various groups of firms, and the international alliances that have sprung up as one response to the crisis. Next we look at the chip firms with the best ROA performance over the past decade, and at the restructuring taking place among firms whose performance has been less than satisfactory. We conclude with a discussion of some of the strategic steps that chip firms have taken to enhance their value capture.

7.1   Measuring Value Capture

Semiconductor companies have relatively large R&D budgets, which are driven by the rising costs of designing increasingly complex chips (Crisis 3) and, for vertically integrated companies, by developing ever-more-demanding fabrication processes (Crisis 2). In order to pay for the escalating design and fabrication R&D costs, chip companies have had to improve their ability to capture value, especially in the increasingly important but fragmented and price-sensitive consumer markets (Crisis 4). Often the value is captured elsewhere in the value chain. For example, the two most valuable chips (the main controller and a video processor) in Apple's Video iPod released in 2005 earned combined gross profits of just $6.60 per unit for their two suppliers, while Apple's estimated gross profit was $80 (Linden et al. 2009).

To assess more precisely the chip industry's record of value capture, we look at return on assets (ROA), defined as income (net income after extraordinary items) divided by gross assets (equity minus liabilities).[2] Our focus is on the firm as a unit of production rather than a financial instrument, so we use ROA rather than return on equity (ROE).[3] In general, ROA indicates how profitable a company's assets are in generating income, while ROE shows how well a company uses its shareholders' investment.

We want to know if firms earn adequate returns to invest in long-term R&D, and to have an indicator of how efficiently capital is used. Although we cannot directly compare ROA to stock returns or bond yields, we use the five-year US Treasury bond as a benchmark of risk-free yield. For the period 1984 to 2005, the five-year bond interest rate averaged 6.5 percent. ROE, which excludes debt from its denominator, is greater than ROA and usually less than the long-maturity bond yield, so we would expect ROA to be below the bond yield as well. The trend of ROA compared to the bond yield provides a point of comparison for how well the companies are doing in value capture.

We analyzed the ROA of 149 public companies whose main products are integrated circuits, which includes 61 firms that own fabs (integrated firms; e.g., Intel, TI, and STMicroelectronics), 84 firms that are fabless (design only; e.g., Qualcomm, Broadcom, and Nvidia), and four firms that are foundries (contract fabrication only; e.g., TSMC and Char-tered).[4] We also looked at the ROA of 27 selected systems firms (e.g., IBM, Motorola, Dell, Nokia, Sony, and NEC), some of which also own semiconductor divisions that are not their primary source of revenue. For each group the combined annual net income of all companies in the group was divided by the year's combined gross assets, and then this an-nual ROA was averaged across a range of years. This approach shows the overall returns to a segment in the value chain, rather than the aver-age ROA of the firms. The standard deviation of these segment averages provides a measure of the ROA variability over time, which indicates the riskiness of the firm as an investment. The lower the standard deviation, the less variable is ROA over time, and the less risky is the investment.

Returns, both average level and riskiness, showed wide variation across firms and groups during 1984 to 2005 (see table 7.1). The right-hand column lists the largest number of firms in the sample in any single year. The semiconductor industry leader Intel took home the highest re-turn on assets with an average ROA of 13.1 percent over more than two decades. During the period Intel accounted for 28 percent of net sales of the chip companies (fabbed and fabless) in our sample[5] but only 23 per-cent of the R&D expenditures. We discuss R&D expenses below.

Although not in the semiconductor industry, Microsoft, the other near-monopolist in the PC value chain, performed even better (ROA 21.3 percent) and experienced less risk. Microsoft's standard deviation was only 30 percent of its average ROA compared to 60 percent for Intel.

Integrated firms excluding Intel and fabless firms did much worse than expected. The integrated firms earned the same average ROA as the fabless firms (2.7 percent), but with lower volatility (s.d. was 2.3 times average ROA for integrated firms compared to 3.8 for fabless). The higher volatility of fabless firms most likely reflects their smaller size and less-diversified product range.

The systems firms with their broader product portfolio would be expected to experience even milder fluctuation, which was the case (s.d. 1.2 times the average ROA), and the systems firms' ROA of 3.1 percent put them above the integrated firms without Intel. Among these sys-tems firms, the Japanese firms perform below the US and European firms. The large Japanese firms, including Matsushita, Sony, and six others,

Table 7.1
Average ROA for 1984 to 2005, selected firms

	Average ROA 1984–2005 (s.d.)	Maximum firms[a]
Microsoft	21.3% (6.5)	1
Five-year bond	6.5% (2.2)	—
Chip firms, including Intel	5.5% (6.4)	145
Intel	13.1% (7.8)	1
Fabbed (x-Intel)	2.7% (6.1)	60
Fabless	2.7% (10.3)	84
Foundries (pure-play)	11.0% (8.3)	4
Selected systems firms	3.1% (3.6)	27
Japan based	1.5% (1.6)	8
Other	4.3% (5.2)	19

Source: Authors' calculations based on Compustat data collected in September 2007.
Note: Standard deviation of ROA given in parentheses.
a. Maximum firms is the largest number of firms in the sample for any single year. Not all firms reported data in all years.

averaged 1.5 percent ROA for the period, while the nineteen large US and European firms, including IBM, Motorola, and Philips, averaged ROA almost three times higher, 4.3 percent. The volatility of the Japanese group (1.1 times ROA) was only slightly lower than for the others (1.2 times ROA), so that the greater return of non-Japanese firms was not offset by greater riskiness.

One of the newer and more successful links in the semiconductor supply chain, pure-play foundries, exhibited high ROA during the 1990 to 2005 period. Foundries can realize economies of scale from demand aggregation provided that they are able to keep their expensive fabs filled. The four foundries in our sample (TSMC, UMC, Chartered, and Tower) are the most mature foundries. Many other firms, especially in China, have entered the field in the past five years (see Crisis 2 and Crisis 8).

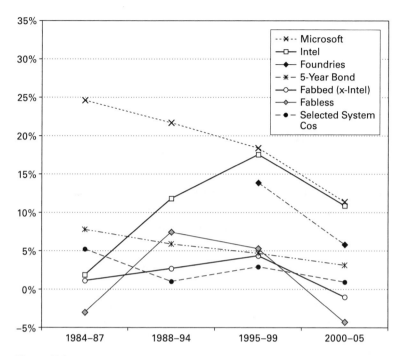

Figure 7.1
ROA in the electronics industry, 1984 to 2005. Source: Authors' calculations based on Compustat data collected in September 2007.

Doubtless the ROA is considerably lower at less-established foundries. The most aggressive foundry entrant, SMIC, has mostly incurred losses each year from its establishment in 2000 through 2008.

We must be cautious in comparing these point estimates across groups. The large standard deviations make the average ROA statistically indistinguishable across groups, and in most cases the ROA is statistically indistinguishable from a zero rate of return. Also the subgroups of chip companies represent all publicly held companies in the United States, while the systems firms are a nonrandom selection.

The average ROA for the twenty-two year period hides important business cycle variations. We calculated the average ROA for the semiconductor business cycles, which reached peaks in 1984, 1988, 1995, and 2000, by using the peak years as starting points for each subperiod (see figure 7.1).[6]

Figure 7.1 shows that Microsoft's highest ROA actually occurred during the 1980s, and that once the Internet took off in the mid-1990s, Microsoft and Intel profited almost equally in ROA terms. Although all groups suffered dramatic declines during the dot.com meltdown, the leaders Microsoft and Intel maintained ROA considerably above the Treasury bond rate.

Another interesting comparison is between chip firms and system companies. Both fabbed and fabless firms display lower ROA than the systems firms before 1988, and again after 1999, suggesting that the 1990s represented an especially favorable period for chip firms, when they benefited from rapid adoption of computers and networking equipment and a strong US economy on the demand side and a relatively predictable technology path for manufacturing and design. By the 2000s, the systems companies were once again earning higher average ROA than their chip suppliers.

The ROA of both fabbed and fabless companies became negative in the recession of the early 2000s, but the fabless companies suffered much more than the integrated firms, which generally have more product diversification. Over the four periods, these integrated firms (x-Intel) experienced less fluctuation in ROA than the fabless companies. We will examine this relationship more carefully below.

The foundries (especially the largest, TSMC and UMC) also suffered lowered ROA during the early 2000s recession, as their ROA dropped by over one-half from the late 1990s, with a rate of change similar to those of Intel and the fabless companies. Their average ROA, however, remained well above those of their fabbed and fabless customers. Although foundries run the risk of deep falloffs in orders if integrated firms pull back their orders to internal fabs in a downturn, their performance indicates that they were able to manage demand fluctuations during the business cycle without profits being overwhelmed by the depreciation on their expensive fabs.

An ongoing controversy in the semiconductor industry concerns the relative profitability of the fabbed and fabless models. Industry analysts have recently claimed that fabless companies earn higher gross profit and higher return on invested capital than their fabbed counterparts.[7] Table 7.1 showed that the fabbed (x-Intel) and fabless firms earned the same

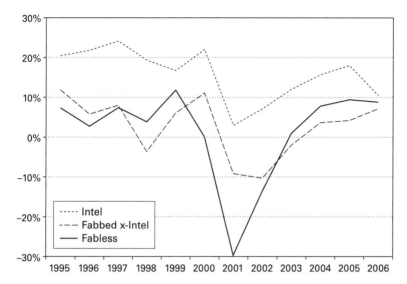

Figure 7.2
Annual ROA in the semiconductor industry, 1995 to 2006. Source: Authors' calculations based on Compustat data collected in September 2007.

ROA (2.7 percent) over the long term but that fabless firms experience greater volatility (higher standard deviation: 10.3 versus 6.1).

To further illuminate this relationship, figure 7.2 shows annual data from 1995 to 2006 for Intel, other fabbed (x-Intel), and fabless chip companies.[8] These data confirm that the ROA of fabbed and fabless firms are close on average, but that the fabless ROA is much more volatile. However, the annual data also reveal that the higher volatility was generated by the fabless sector's poor performance in the unusually severe dot.com downturn in 2001 and 2002. Possibly this volatility will be repeated during the economic crisis that began in 2008. Down the road, we expect the volatility of the younger and smaller fabless firms to decline as they grow and mature, and the volatility of the fabbed firms to decline with their growing reliance on foundries. Yet vicious swings in product prices will continue to plague chip firms. The ROA data do not point to either business model, fabbed or fabless, as an inherently stronger performer.

A striking feature of figure 7.2 is that all three lines, including that of Intel, appear to be converging in the last few years. Despite its powerful market position Intel found itself facing competitive pressure from its chief rival AMD, the consumerization of the PC market, and difficulty in diversifying away from its heavy dependence on computer processors into communications and other markets. Meanwhile the other large fabbed companies were raising the percentage of chips that they outsource to foundries, and leading fabless companies were becoming more involved with the development and mastery of process technology. These trends may well underlie the observed convergence in ROA.

We expect the steep recession underway in 2009 to have a differential impact across the segments and within segments, because the severe crisis in credit markets will affect companies based on their debt structure. Companies that rely less on external debt and can weather the current crisis without new external sources of financing will be better able to contend with volatile swings in their product markets.

7.2   The R&D Factor

Some of the differences in average returns across groups of firms can be understood by looking at the role of R&D expenses, which have been increasing as a share of revenues. Firms have joined a variety of research alliances and consortia to mitigate the impact.

7.2.1   Rising R&D Expenses

Figure 7.3 shows R&D expenses as a percentage of net sales calculated using the same aggregation method as our ROA data.[9] Intel's sharp drop in ROA in the 2000 to 2005 period corresponds to a noticeable rise in its R&D ratio, partly as a result of the slowing of sales growth. In all four subperiods Intel's R&D expenses increased in absolute terms, but only in the final subperiod did sales grow much more slowly than R&D.

Other chip companies, fabbed and fabless, saw dramatic increases in their R&D as a proportion of sales, both in the late-1990s boom and during the bust of the early 2000s. Integrated firms (x-Intel) saw their R&D-to-sales ratio grow from 10 percent in the early 1990s to 17 percent in 2006, as R&D grew by a factor of eight and sales grew by a factor of less than five. Fabless firms show a particularly large jump in their

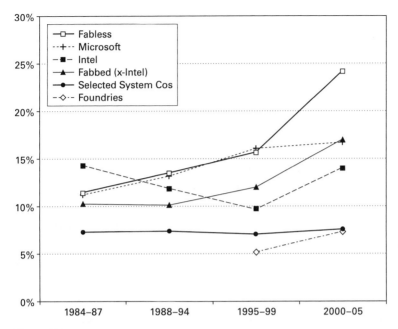

Figure 7.3
R&D expense to net sales, 1984 to 2005. Source: Authors' calculations based on Compustat data collected in September 2007.

2000 to 2005 R&D-to-sales ratio because the sharp sales drop in 2001 and 2002 was not accompanied by a commensurate cut in R&D. The annual data (not shown) indicate that the R&D-to-sales ratio for fabless firms rose from about 14 percent in the early 1990s to almost 23 percent in 2006.

The high-ROA foundry sector has, not unrelatedly, a relatively low R&D ratio. Although fabrication requires considerable capital expenditure, their engineering input per dollar of sales appears to be considerably less than that for chip design, as represented by the fabless companies. The fabbed companies (including Intel) fall between the foundries and the fabless companies, since they must undertake R&D for both fabrication and design.

The systems firms appear able to cut R&D as sales fall, and they kept their R&D a fairly steady proportion of sales (about 8 percent). Since much of systems R&D is product development with relatively short cycles that can quickly be cut in a downturn, they are better positioned to adjust their R&D than chip companies. A new desktop PC model based on an existing chassis can be designed in as little as two weeks (Dedrick and Kraemer 2008), while a derivative chip design requires several months.

Despite the rising R&D burden shown here, leading chip companies have been spending at least as much on stock buybacks. Lazonick (2008) documents that from 2000 through 2007 Intel and Texas Instruments, which had R&D-to-sales ratios of 14.4 and 16.3 percent respectively, had buyback-to-sales ratios of 15.8 and 17.7 percent (Lazonick 2008, tab. 7). We are not in a position to say whether these sizable stock repurchases are the result of excess cash on hand, a belief in the undervaluation of the shares, an attempt by insiders to raise the value of options, or any of several other explanations that have been proposed. They do suggest that industry leaders had the financial capacity to fund the additional R&D that the perpetuation of Moore's Law requires. Whether individual companies still have the incentive to participate in industry-critical basic research beyond their own medium-term development programs is an open question, especially during the major industry downturn taking hold in 2008.

7.2.2   An Industry Response: Alliances and Consortia

A few companies, including top ten firms like TI and AMD, are opting to step off the Moore's Law treadmill by ending their internal process development efforts. TI ended its process development for standard digital products as of the 0.032-micron generation in favor of working with foundries, while AMD became fabless by selling its entire manufacturing operation to a new joint venture called Global Foundries whose majority owner is an Abu Dhabi-based investment fund.[10]

Most other leading firms have opted to participate in international alliances to share the considerable cost of developing a new process generation. One development cost estimate for the 0.065-micron generation at a single firm was $1.5 billion, and costs have continued to rise with each node along the Moore's Law roadmap.[11] Many firms participate in multiple collaborative research projects with other firms as well as in bilateral projects with universities and government-subsidized labs.

One of the most significant interfirm alliances is IBM's Common Platform group (http://commonplatform.com/). It started in 2002 with IBM and Chartered Semiconductor, a foundry in Singapore. IBM had begun offering foundry services and wanted to align its 0.090-micron process with that of Chartered so that large IBM clients would have a second source for fabrication. In 2003 Infineon, a European company, joined the two partners to develop a 0.065-micron process in IBM's fab in New York state. Samsung, interested in offering foundry services as a sideline to its memory business, joined in 2004. The joint development partnership expanded in 2007 to include Freescale (the former Motorola semiconductor division) and Europe's STMicroelectronics, both of which had formerly been in a similar European alliance ("Crolles II") that had dissolved after Philips withdrew.

Japan's chip firms had historically taken a Japan-only path in joint research, for reasons such as language barriers and geographical distance. Beginning in 1996 the Japanese government funded a collaborative research program called the Association for Superadvanced Electronics Technologies (ASET, http://www.aset.or.jp) with an annual budget of roughly $70 million (Ham et al. 1998). ASET's budget declined after 2003 as completed projects were handed off to the participating firms to complete development. As of November 2008 the list of 34 participants is primarily Japanese but includes Intel, IBM Japan, and Samsung.[12]

In the face of the enormous challenges confronting the industry and a weakening international position, Japanese companies began to join research partnerships outside Japan. In 2001, Hitachi joined a collaborative program at Europe's leading microelectronics research center, the Belgium-based Interuniversities Microelectronics Center (IMEC, http://www2.imec.be) for developing generic processes and materials relevant to sub–0.1-micron processes in IMEC's 300-mm pilot fab. In 2002, Matsushita (now renamed Panasonic) joined IMEC for research related to the 0.065-process generation, and stayed for the 0.045-micron program in 2004, which included Intel and TI as well as the major European producers; TI and Samsung joined later. Matsushita, which became the first company in the world to produce 0.045-micron chips in 2007,[13] has stayed with IMEC for its sub–0.045-micron programs. It was joined by Japan's Elpida in 2007, along with Taiwanese and Korean chip companies.

In 2004, Matsushita (Panasonic) also joined the US-based International Sematech Manufacturing Initiative (ISMI), a subsidiary of SEMATECH that already included Europe's Infineon and Philips and Taiwan's TSMC among its members. ISMI is oriented toward near-term research such as increasing manufacturing productivity. In 2006, Japan's Renesas and NEC Electronics also joined.

In 2007, Panasonic became a full SEMATECH member, which involves participation in medium-term joint research programs such as the development of next-generation lithography infrastructure (Crisis 5). Other SEMATECH members include IBM, Intel, Infineon, Texas Instruments, Micron, and, as of October 2008, Taiwan's UMC.

As IBM's Common Platform partners set their sights on developing a 0.032-micron process in 2007, they were also joined by Japan's Toshiba and (in 2008) NEC, plus the manufacturing arm of AMD that was spun off as an independent foundry. The IBM Alliance now includes five of the world's top ten chip producers, all concentrating a portion of their basic process development in IBM's New York facilities.

These alliances, in which companies share the cost of precompetitive research that complements their in-house development, are helping to keep the industry on the Moore's Law trajectory. Development alliances can mitigate, but not eliminate, the negative drag on profit margins caused by the increase in process development costs for fab-owning firms.

7.3 Beating the Average

In this section we look more closely at chip firms that have created competitive advantage during the past two business cycles, and then look at how the weaker large firms have restructured in hopes of reversing their fortunes

7.3.1 High-Performing Chip Firms

We discussed in preceding chapters how semiconductor firms have pushed toward the physical limits of their technology to bring exponential performance improvements to businesses and consumers (Crises 2 and 5). Yet figure 7.1 showed that most of the chip and system firms in our sample have experienced relatively low ROA. There is a risk that disproportionate growth in R&D and capital investment requirements will drive more firms and investors away from the sector, despite the considerable societal value that has been created by the industry.

But the situation is not quite so dire at the individual firm level, as we see in table 7.2, which shows the highest performers (with an ROA higher than the 4.9 percent average five-year bond return) among the large (sales above $1 billion) fab-owning, fabless, and foundry firms in our sample for the period 1995 to 2006. The table also breaks out ROA for the two business-cycle subperiods, 1995 to 1999 and 2000 to 2006 so that the impact of the dot.com meltdown in 2000 and 2001 can be seen.

The list confirms that fab-ownership is not inherently good or bad for profits, since both fabbed (7 companies) and fabless (5 companies) firms are well represented. The list includes some of the leading fabbed (Intel and TI) and fabless (Qualcomm and Xilinx) companies, and also a number of lesser known medium-size companies from both the fabbed (mainly analog) and fabless sides of the industry. Overall, a higher proportion of integrated firms (11 percent) were high performers compared to fabless firms (6 percent).

Somewhat surprisingly, Intel is not the top performer but the fourth, after the Taiwan foundry TSMC that achieved similar ROA to Intel across the two subperiods. The two highest earners, Linear Technology and Maxim Integrated Products, are medium-size producers of analog chips. Unlike Intel, which derives most of its revenue from a small number of very large designs, Linear and Maxim produce a wide variety of low-cost chips that are nevertheless highly profitable. Analog chips don't require the cutting-edge CMOS processes developed by companies like Intel and TSMC, and the ability to use older, depreciated fab equipment is an important contributor to their profitability. Analog chips often have much longer life cycles than digital logic chips, which adds to their profitability. Analog Devices, Texas Instruments, and STMicroelectronics are the other sellers of analog chips on the list, although they also make other types of chips that are a larger proportion of their sales. Other analog suppliers, including National Semiconductor and Motorola/Freescale, were less successful over the period as a whole.

Table 7.2
Large chip firms with high earnings, 1995 to 2006

Type	Company name	1995–1999	2000–2006	1995–2006	Data availability in Compustat	Sales in most recent year (000s)
Fabbed	Linear Technology	21.38%	16.34%	18.44%	1988–2006	$1,093.0
Fabbed	Maxim	22.33%	15.65%	18.43%	1988–2006	$1,858.9
Foundry	TSMC (Taiwan)	20.00%	13.80%	16.38%	1995–2006	$9,739.4
Fabbed	Intel	20.42%	12.55%	15.83%	1988–2006	$35,382.0
Fabless	Altera	13.97%	12.08%	12.87%	1988–2006	$1,285.5
Fabbed	Microchip Tech.	11.78%	10.31%	10.92%	1991–2006	$1,039.7
Fabless	Xilinx	15.58%	6.36%	10.20%	1989–2006	$1,842.7
Fabbed	Texas Instruments	8.42%	11.34%	10.12%	1988–2006	$14,195.0
Fabbed	Analog Devices	9.46%	9.34%	9.39%	1988–2006	$2,573.2
Fabless	ATI (Canada)	21.15%	-0.12%	6.97%	1997–2005	$2,222.5
Fabless	Qualcomm	3.54%	9.39%	6.95%	1991–2006	$7,526.0
Fabbed	STMicro. (Europe)	9.00%	4.58%	6.42%	1993–2006	$9,854.0
Fabless[a]	SanDisk	7.99%	4.83%	6.15%	1994–2006	$3,257.5

Foundry	UMC (Taiwan)	5.71%	5.95%	5.90%	1998–2006	$3,436.8
Low-risk asset	Five-year Treasury bond	5.90%	4.25%	4.94%	1995–2006	

Source: Authors' calculations based on Compustat data collected in September 2007.

Notes: Companies without a geographic designation are US-based. The criteria for inclusion in the list were (1) ROA higher than the average for five-year treasury bonds from 1995 to 2006, (2) data available for most of the period, and (3) the most recent sales figure greater than US$1 billion.

a. SanDisk is part owner of fabs through a joint venture with Toshiba.

Looking at subperiod performance, those worst affected by the 2001 downturn (measured by percentage drop in ROA between the two subperiods) were ATI (−101 percent), Xilinx (−59 percent), STMicro (−49 percent), SanDisk (−40 percent), and Intel (−39 percent). Again, no obvious relative strength of the fabbed (Intel and STMicro) or fabless (ATI and Xilinx) model is evident.

Turning to system firms, we asked a similar question about whether ownership of chip manufacturing made any noticeable difference. Table 7.3 lists high-performing firms from our selected sample of systems companies. One of the striking features of the list is that only one Japanese company (Canon) out of the eight performed better than a Treasury bond over the twelve-year period.

As for chip manufacturing, IBM owns fabs, Philips did until 2006, and Hewlett-Packard did until 1999. Nokia and Cisco design some of their own chips on a fabless basis. Of these high-performing firms only Dell has in fact no internal chip development program. However other fab-owning system companies, including Motorola and the major Japanese chip-and-system firms, performed worse than the average.

Our data suggest that internal chip capability does not handicap a system firm, but a much more careful investigation would be required to establish it empirically. However, investors seem to think systems firms and chip production would perform better independently, as most integrated systems firms outside Japan have now spun off their chip divisions as part of a wave of restructuring.

7.3.2 Spin-offs and Private Equity Buy-Outs

A response adopted by many of the chip firms that aren't on the high-performance list is restructuring. These transformative episodes have occurred regularly in the industry's past with varying levels of success. In the European chip industry, for example, STMicroelectronics, Europe's largest chip company, was created in 1987 from the merger of Italy's SGS Microelettronica and the semiconductor division of France's Thomson. STMicroelectronics has grown to be one of the top ten chip companies during the 2000s.

The chip sector of the United Kingdom began restructuring at around the same time as SGS and Thomson but failed to produce an industry

Table 7.3
Large system firms with high earnings, 1995 to 2006

Company name	1995–1999	2000–2006	1995–2006	Years used	Sales in most recent year (000s)
Dell	17.46%	13.56%	15.33%	1988–2005	$55,908.0
Nokia (Europe)	13.50%	15.50%	14.67%	1993–2006	$54,592.0
Cisco Systems	19.55%	8.87%	13.32%	1989–2006	$28,484.0
IBM	7.07%	7.61%	7.39%	1988–2006	$91,424.0
Philips (Europe)	8.20%	6.04%	6.94%	1988–2006	$35,600.2
Hewlett-Packard	9.55%	4.21%	6.44%	1988–2006	$91,658.0
Canon (Japan)	3.35%	7.84%	5.97%	1988–2006	$34,930.7
Five-year Treasury bond	5.90%	4.25%	4.94%	1995–2006	

Source: Authors' calculations based on Compustat data collected in September 2007.
Notes: Companies without a geographic designation are US-based. The criteria for inclusion in the list were (1) ROA higher than 4.9 percent, the average for five-year treasury bonds from 1995 to 2006, (2) data available for most of the period, and (3) the most recent sales figure greater than US$10 billion.

leader. In 1987 the then-largest UK chip firm, Plessey, combined with another UK firm, Ferranti Semiconductors, and then with the Marconi Devices division of the General Electric Company Ltd. in 1990, but the amalgamated operation failed to thrive and was sold to a Canadian chip firm, Mitel, in 1998. According to an industry analyst, the company never "really had the government support. They...found it difficult to plug into the European collaborative research programs...because the UK government wouldn't chip in."[14] Although the United Kingdom still has small domestic chip firms and multinational subsidiaries, it has no major domestic chip firm.

Over the 1995 to 2006 period many of the largest chip firms were separated from deep-pocketed parent companies, some having been bought out by private equity partners with unknown appetites for the large investments needed to stay competitive in this industry. The spin-off of chip divisions began because of the electronics boom of the late 1990s. Vertically integrated system firms could see that the cost of staying in the chip business would soar, requiring major commitment of capital and engineering resources. Chip divisions were often not separate profit-and-loss centers, and investors came to believe that they should be cut loose to take advantage of the attractive terms then available for initial public offerings (IPOs) in the US stock market.

Spin-offs that occurred before the crash of 2001 include Agilent (spun off from Hewlett-Packard; IPO in 1999), Infineon (spun off from Siemens; IPO in 1999), Intersil (spun off from Harris Corp; IPO in 2000), and Agere (spun off from Lucent; IPO in 2001). After a hiatus the practice resumed, with Freescale (spun off from Motorola; IPO in 2004), Spansion (spun off from AMD and Fujitsu; IPO in 2005), Qimonda (Infineon's memory division spun off through a 2006 IPO), and NXP (spun off from Philips in 2006 to private investors).

Asian electronics firms have pursued the same type of restructuring. The memory operations of Hitachi and NEC were combined in 1999 to form Elpida Memory. Mitsubishi's memory operation was added in 2003, and Elpida was listed on the Tokyo Stock Exchange in 2004. NEC's non-memory chip division was spun off as NEC Electronics in 2002 but remains majority-owned by NEC Corporation. Fujitsu followed suit with Fujitsu Microelectronics in 2008. The non-memory chip divisions of Hitachi and Mitsubishi were combined in 2003 to form Renesas Technology, which is still held by the parent companies as a joint venture. In Korea, LG's chip division was taken over by Hyundai in 1999, with the resulting company spun off from the Hyundai Group as Hynix Semiconductor in 2001. Hynix sold its non-memory division to private equity investors in 2004 under the name MagnaChip Semiconductor.

Restructuring in Japan occurs differently than elsewhere. Japanese electronics groups have retained close ties to their chip divisions, while European companies and governments have mostly allowed market forces to determine the fate of chip firms. When the German industrial conglomerate Siemens spun off its chip division (now called Infineon) and the Netherlands' Philips did likewise (now called NXP), both parents retained only a minority share in the new businesses. In sharp contrast, Japan's Renesas is still owned by its parent companies, Hitachi and Mitsubishi. NEC and Fujitsu also continue to own their spun-off chip divisions. Only Elpida, the Japanese memory joint venture announced in 1999, has become mostly independent via its 2004 stock flotation.

The latest twist to this spin-off activity is the participation of private equity firms, which were awash in cash during the real estate bubble of the 2000s.[15] Some observers think it is time for marketers and financial wizards to steer the industry in more profitable directions that build on the efficiencies that the spin-offs are expected to impose on the newly independent chip divisions. Large cash balances held by some chip companies and their relatively low stock valuations also made them attractive targets.[16] Other industry observers attribute these buyouts to the maturation of the industry, namely slower growth. Figure 7.4 shows how, over the last quarter century, the peak revenue growth of each industry cycle is on a slow downward trend. Future revenue growth after the current downturn is expected to be even slower as the pursuit of Moore's Law becomes more difficult. If the industry's technical progress were to slow considerably from its current pace, the industry would no longer be able to drive down prices while raising performance, which in the past was the key to new and expanding market opportunities.[17] At that point a new business model, based on new applications of existing technology, will be needed.

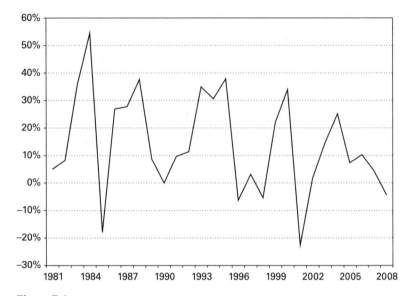

Figure 7.4
Semiconductor industry revenue, annual growth rate, 1981 to 2008. Source: Market research data and authors' calculations.

Private equity deals are not unknown in the chip industry. In the late 1990s, some of the same investment organizations active today performed buyouts of low-end chip producers. In 1997, private investors acquired the commodity-chip side (renamed Fairchild Semiconductor) of National Semiconductor and a mid-tier integrated firm named Zilog for about $500 million each. In 1999, similar deals involved the semiconductor unit (renamed Intersil) of Harris Corporation for $600 million and the commodity-chip side (renamed ON Semiconductor) of Motorola's semiconductor business for $1.6 billion.

The industry's next round of buyouts, which began in 2004, involved more money and higher profile targets. The first action took place in Korea, where the non-memory businesses of troubled memory producer Hynix Semiconductor was taken private (renamed MagnaChip) by a group of US-based investors for $800 million The next year, different investors conducted a similar deal with the semiconductor division of Agilent (itself a spin-off from Hewlett-Packard) and named it Avago in a deal worth $2.7 billion. This was just a warm-up for two major deals in

2006 involving top-tier chip firms. First, the same investors that acquired Agilent/Avago (KKR and Silver Lake) acquired a majority share of Philips Semiconductors, now known as NXP, for $10 billion. One month later, different investors took Freescale, Motorola's chip spin-off, private for $17.6 billion. Freescale, the third-largest US chip firm, far from being a distressed property in need of a turnaround, had already returned from losses to profits.

This surge of activity raises the question of what these investors, who loaded up the balance sheets of the acquired companies with new debt, expect to do with the assets they now control. The insiders at the acquired firms were quick to state that the buyout gives them flexibility that a public listing denied them. NXP's CEO, Frans Van Houten, said that the new owners' strategy was "buy and build."[18] A Freescale executive described his company as "a platform for participating in the consolidation of the industry" through acquisitions.[19] However the new owners of NXP and Freescale have already had to swallow losses, taking write-downs of their investments of 15 and 25 percent respectively in early 2008.[20] The severe credit crisis that began later that year further clouded the future and will limit the zeal of the private equity owners for investing in new capacity and in the research needed to keep the companies' technology moving forward.

7.4   Linking Value Creation to Value Capture

As the crises related to low returns have unfolded, the basis for capturing value in the industry has been changing. The strategic management literature offers volumes of advice on turning innovation into profits.[21] Here we confine ourselves to reviewing the main issues with an emphasis on changes that have occurred since the 1980s.

We focus on three sources of firm competitive advantage: firm capabilities, product-level barriers to imitation, and relations with other firms.

7.4.1   Firm Capabilities
A sustainable competitive advantage can be based on capabilities of the firm that are hard for competitors to reproduce. In recent years the most

important capabilities have been shifting from manufacturing to design and software.

Before the 1990s the "real men have fabs" approach described in Crisis 2 was the dominant path to profit, since excellence in manufacturing was necessary to keeping performance high and/or costs low. While this is still true in some markets such as memory, the path to profitability has changed in other markets.

One of the chief factors that has devalued the benefits of owning efficient manufacturing capacity is the success of foundries. As discussed in Crisis 2, the rising cost of building new fabs has driven more and more companies to embrace fabless and fab-lite business models in which all, or at least some, manufacturing is outsourced, especially for non-memory chips. This has diminished the importance of fab ownership in using process know-how as a competitive tool. Fabless companies have access to process knowledge by employing experienced production engineers who interact with the foundries (sometimes in residence) to prevent or fix problems. This way process knowledge can still provide a competitive advantage to fabless firms over rivals. For analog chips, fab ownership and tight integration of design and manufacturing are still critical for suppliers, like the high-performing firms Linear Technology and Maxim Integrated Products.

Other capabilities that have increased in importance are system-level knowledge and software. As discussed in Crisis 3, the system-level integration of chip design has shifted more of the application development from the system customer to the chip supplier. System customers increasingly expect their main chip providers to supply a platform complete with a schematic diagram for a sample printed circuit layout, basic software applications, and a software development kit. At the same time convergence has forced both chip and systems firms to become multispecialized as networking, multimedia, and computing increasingly coexist in a tightly integrated system. To master the diverse domains of the digital convergence requires the ability to integrate software and hardware within the personnel and organizational routines of a company, which cannot easily be duplicated by other companies.

However, developing application knowledge is necessary but not sufficient to gaining competitive advantage. For chip firms the other elements, particularly knowledge about the needs of end users, must usually come from a systems customer. STMicroelectronics, for example, has had an alliance with Finland's Nokia since Nokia entered its period of rapid growth in the 1990s. STMicro received advance notice of Nokia's requirements and planned its product roadmap accordingly.[22] The alliance kept it one of the top chip suppliers to the cell phone market even though it didn't make the most valuable chip in a phone, the baseband processor, which Nokia sourced mainly from Texas Instruments. Nokia's alliance with STMicro endured on an almost exclusive basis for over a decade—several lifetimes in the chip industry—until Nokia's announcement of a multisourcing initiative in 2008 after having sold its in-house chip design team to STMicro.[23]

Chip companies prosper by developing chips that customers want, and too often we see technology developed in the absence of viable systems applications or business models (Chesbrough and Rosenbloom 2002). SOC development by many Japanese companies falls in this category despite the integration of chip and systems groups within the same firm.

Part of the problem for chip firms is that brand awareness, a common path to market leadership in many industries, has found limited application in the chip industry. Intel with its "Intel Inside" campaign is an exception that reflects its near-monopoly position. Other chip companies have failed to create similar awareness. For example, most people have no idea who supplies the chips in their cell phones, yet about half of those chips (including most of those in Nokia-brand phones) come from one company: Texas Instruments.[24]

7.4.2 Product-Level Barriers

Even without branding, sustainable competitive advantage can be established at the product level by making necessary features of the product difficult for competitors to imitate.[25] Classic means of achieving this are through intellectual property protection, such as patents or trade secrets, and through control of industry standards.

The chip industry greatly increased its patenting activity beginning in the 1980s (Hall and Ziedonis 2001). Much of this was defensive patenting used to fend off lawsuits, and surveys suggest that patents are not the most important means of protecting chip firms' intellectual property (Levin et al. 1987; Cohen, Nelson, and Walsh 2000).

Standards, which apply to every piece of electronics from a mini-USB plug to a Blu-Ray disc player, are a potential source of competitive advantage. Firms throughout the electronics industry strive to influence and control standards. Government or industry bodies can attempt to set de jure standards, such as those applicable to telecommunications. Regulated standards can still be privately owned, as in the Korean government's adoption and licensing of Qualcomm's proprietary CDMA. De facto standards set by the market may evolve as a result of widespread adoption, especially when one customer's usage is affected by the usage of others, termed network effects, as was the case with the initial uptake of the http protocol and html code that enabled the World Wide Web in the early 1990s.

Intel's control of a de facto standard, established by a fortuitous deal with IBM followed by years of hard, and often bitter, battles to establish and maintain its position, has given it tremendous bargaining power with its customers. In order to stay ahead of any competitors, especially AMD, Intel relied on the execution of several strategies to defend its franchise. One strategy was breakneck innovation enabled by relentless shifts from one process generation to the next, combined with the development of processors whose introduction they carefully timed. Intel has set the industry's pace for new process introduction since the 1990s.

Many standards are set formally within industry, and sometimes government-run, groups. Firms participating in these groups compete to advance their own intellectual property as the basis for the standard. Success usually involves some form of compulsory licensing at "reasonable" royalty rates, and the standard-owning firm's experience with the technology may give them an added advantage over rivals pursued alternative technologies.

Large chip firms regularly participate in standards committees, but small, focused firms can still do so successfully. For example, Silicon Image, a small fabless firm with 2006 revenues of about $300 million, contributed to High-Definition Multimedia Interface (HDMI), a key interface protocol for high-resolution digital media, alongside electronics industry giants Hitachi, Matsushita, Philips, Sony, Thomson, and Toshiba. Silicon Image, which also operates several of the global equipment test centers for HDMI compliance, became the leading vendor of HDMI chips.

7.4.3   Relations in the Value Chain

Innovations require complementary products, technologies, and services to compete successfully (Teece 1986). Chip firms are particularly dependent on their downstream system customers in order for their products to reach consumers. Maintaining market power within this relationship is one of the key ways chip firms capture value, and this is often achieved through patent and standards strategies, which make imitation difficult or raise the cost of rivals through licensing fees. The key issue is how to develop a chip with unique properties that are valued by users of the end product.

One strategy is to create an ecosystem that favors the company's chips, and a prime example of this is Qualcomm, one of the high-performing companies discussed earlier. Qualcomm was founded in 1985 to develop a wireless protocol and soon settled on code division multiple access (CDMA) technology, which had great potential in the developing cell phone market. However, CDMA lacked the broad support of rival technologies, and Qualcomm recognized the need to foster a favorable environment. This involved becoming involved in downstream businesses, most notably handsets. It exited the handset business in 1999 after its technology was well established, and it did not want to compete with its customers.

In the early years, to build acceptance for CDMA, which faced resistance because of doubts about its technical feasibility, Qualcomm also worked with carriers and government agencies.[26] One of the earliest and most important of Qualcomm's alliances was with the Korean government, which entered a Joint Development Agreement with Qualcomm in 1991. Qualcomm was actively involved during the following years of development with Korean carriers and manufacturers while the technology and the CDMA chip sets that ran it were refined. Korean CDMA service was rolled out on a large scale in 1996, when the technology was just beginning to take root in the United States. Although CDMA has not achieved the global adoption of the dominant cellular standard, Europe's GSM, by late 2008 CDMA and its successor technologies were in use by nearly 475 million cellular subscribers worldwide, of whom nearly one-third are in North America.[27]

The strategic relationship between Qualcomm and the carriers gave the chip company a strong bargaining position vis-à-vis the manufacturers of handsets and base stations. Although the chip company must maintain good relationships with the system manufacturers to avoid being shut out of future business opportunities, it may exert some bargaining power over the system house when it can offer a chip that has been tightly tailored to the specific functionality requirements of a carrier.

Qualcomm also builds the ecosystem for its technology by developing software that will be attractive to consumers. In 2000 it introduced a suite of "Wireless Internet LaunchPad" applications for which its chips carried built-in support. The following year it added a middleware package called BREW (binary runtime environment for wireless), which permitted greater phone customization for its customers while working with a variety of operating systems. Over fifteen years Qualcomm's ROA averaged 7 percent while its revenues grew from $90 million in 1991 to $7.5 billion in 2006.

However, most chip companies face formidable obstacles in gaining sustainable market power vis-à-vis their systems customers who own valuable brand names and can play off current chip suppliers against their rivals. Apple, for example, displaced PortalPlayer, the primary supplier of controller chips for its iPods, when it went with a more-integrated chip from Samsung in its second-generation iPod Nano, introduced in September 2006. PortalPlayer, a start-up, had not yet diversified its customer base and was acquired by Nvidia in November 2006.

7.5   Lessons and Conclusions

The chip industry's crisis of low returns with high risk is still unfolding. Chip companies, as a whole, have long had a difficult time capturing value commensurate with the enormous value they've created for the electronics industry, other industries, and consumers. But now a variety of factors, including rising costs, competitive pricing, and rising R&D

expenses relative to sales are combining to narrow the window of opportunity available for chip companies to charge prices adequate to recoup their large investment costs.

High-performing chip companies have used a variety of responses to improve their ROA, including accelerating R&D investment to gain a performance advantage (e.g., Intel), building megafabs to lower costs (e.g., Samsung), pursuing niche markets (e.g., Linear Technology), championing standards (e.g., Qualcomm), building enduring alliances with high-growth customers (e.g., STMicroelectronics), being first to market (e.g., ATI), and developing expensive-to-imitate application-specific platforms of software and hardware that add value for system firms (e.g., Texas Instruments).

Meanwhile a strategy of organizational and financial restructuring has created a new set of possibilities. Many chip divisions that were once part of large, integrated enterprises are now forced to go it alone. For some, such as Renesas, it seems to have given access to new customers and new sources of finance. For others, such as Infineon and Freescale, it seems to have simply cut off the cross-subsidies from systems divisions that had sustained them in the past.

Private equity has taken several big chip firms away from the short-term demands of Wall Street, but the credit meltdown in early 2008 has amplified existing questions about the willingness of large, private investors to support the investments needed to move the industry forward. During the latest round of industry restructuring, financial managers have taken over the reins of numerous chip companies that in previous years were run by engineers. This potentially shifts the focus from value creation to value capture, but it remains to be seen whether that focus will be on short-term or long-term profitability. Our guess is that the problem for the semiconductor industry will become how to innovate and create value, while the problem of how to make a profit will recede once the industry emerges from the latest recession into a new growth cycle, at least for the firms that survive.

The 2008 economic downturn makes risk-taking investment even more difficult than usual. Consumers have gone from being the drivers of the business cycle to being its casualties, which greatly increases the uncertainty for chip firms about product markets.

Countries whose governments are willing to support local firms in facing the large and rising investments required, as well as the risks, have an opportunity to develop their competitive advantage in the industry. We have observed global competitive advantage shift when firms with help from their government made a sustained investment commitment, as happened with Japan in the 1980s, Taiwan and Korea in the 1990s, and China in the 2000s.

One dire possibility for the chip industry is that the commitment of current market leaders to R&D, especially the basic research needed to extend the industry's impressive record of technical progress, is being weakened just as chip firms in industrializing economies are preparing to claim a bigger share of the industry. Global competitive advantage could be preparing for another seismic shift, a possibility we explore in Crisis 8.

Crisis 8
New Global Competition

For more than 50 years, world leadership in technology and innovation has been the foundation of American strategies for economic growth, improved productivity, a better standard of living, and national security. US leadership, however, is not a birthright. Other countries have recognized the strategic importance of leadership in the semiconductor industry and are becoming formidable competitors.

—George Scalise, president, Semiconductor Industry Association (SIA), January 2006[1]

Even as most semiconductor companies struggled to raise profitability and survive demand swings, companies and industry analysts in developed economies were raising warning flags about the potential loss of industry leadership to newcomers Taiwan, China, and India. We have come full circle back to our first crisis in a new guise—fear of loss of competitive advantage to new Asian rivals. Although the rise of chip industries in these countries owes much to foreign investment by industry leaders and to the experience of local engineers in these multinational companies, these rapidly developing countries are now home to local companies with considerable semiconductor capabilities.

Here we look at two popular theories about why competitive advantage is shifting. One says that as chip manufacturing has moved to Asia (see Crisis 2), R&D will inevitably be drawn there, which we call the "manufacturing-pull" hypothesis. A corollary is that the offshoring of R&D undermines the domestic engineering labor market and weakens technological innovation at home.

The second theory, which we call "large-market pull," says that the booming economies of China and India, with their rapidly growing, potentially vast product markets fueled by technology that was offshored by current industry leaders, will produce national champions who become world leaders, much as Korea's Samsung eventually became the envy of Japan's consumer electronics giants. A corollary is that the series of crises reshaping the industry will shift competitive advantage in favor of firms based in developing countries: competition for the global supply of engineers (Crisis 6), continual escalation of fabrication and design costs (Crises 2 and 3), and cost pressures in the new consumer markets (Crisis 4) favor firms with direct access to low-cost engineers, cheaper land, lower taxes, and fewer environmental regulations.

In addition chip firms like Freescale in the United States and NXP in Europe are increasingly being cut off from deep-pocketed parent companies (Motorola and Philips respectively) even as the industry's investment requirements spiral upward. Faced with high risk and low returns (Crisis 7), the current market leaders may be less willing and able to shoulder the ongoing high R&D expenditures, leaving the door open for new entrants with access to subsidies from governments or other product divisions to charge in. Some also fear that a slowdown in the pace of technological change for some segments of the chip industry will allow companies in developing economies to catch up and become industry leaders on the strength of lower costs.

In this chapter we start by examining the manufacturing-pull hypothesis, which turns out to have limited applicability in the chip industry. Then we explore how the engineering talent pools and university systems in the United States, Japan, Taiwan, China, and India contribute to the potential global competitive advantage of high-tech firms in these countries. This leads to a more detailed analysis of the capabilities of the chip industries of Taiwan, China, and India, after which we discuss the industry leaders' responses. We conclude with an evaluation of the popular theories that predict a shift of global competitive advantage toward developing countries, and find that for the most part they do not seem to be supported by the facts.

8.1 The Manufacturing-Pull Theory

The manufacturing-pull theory is based on the assumption that R&D follows manufacturing, so research and development in leading-edge technology is eventually pulled offshore by manufacturing.

There are two primary types of R&D in the chip industry: process development and chip design. The validity of the manufacturing-pull hypothesis is different in the two cases, and so it plays out differently in the integrated and in the fabless-foundry segments of the industry.

8.1.1   Process R&D

Process development is one of the most critical and advanced activities of a chip manufacturer, and the costs have escalated with each generation. As a rule, process R&D will to some extent follow fab location in line with the manufacturing-pull hypothesis. As shown in Crisis 2 (rising fabrication costs), the majority of large-scale fabrication on 300-mm wafers is located in Asia. This means that more process development will also be

Table 8.1
Top ten fab equipment suppliers, 2007

2006 rank	Company	Headquarters country	2007 revenue (US$ millions)	Market share
1	Applied Materials	United States	$6,787.5	15.0%
2	Tokyo Electron	Japan	$5,362.0	11.8%
3	ASML	Netherlands	$4,609.1	10.2%
4	KLA-Tencor	United States	$2,325.9	5.1%
5	Lam Research	United States	$2,244.9	5.0%
6	Nikon	Japan	$1,805.8	4.0%
7	Advantest	Japan	$1,607.5	3.6%
8	Novellus Systems	United States	$1,199.8	2.7%
9	Dainippon Screen	Japan	$1,195.5	2.6%
10	ASM International	Netherlands	$1,023.0	2.3%
	Others		$17,116.7	37.8%
	Total		$45,277.7	100.0%

Source: Revenue and share data are from "Gartner says worldwide semiconductor manufacturing equipment sales grew 6 percent in 2007," Gartner Press Release, April 3, 2008.

done there, but other factors will keep significant process R&D activity elsewhere.

One factor is the role of equipment firms, since process development is shared between chip manufacturers (integrated or foundry) and equipment suppliers, which are based mainly in the United States, Japan, and Europe. Semiconductor equipment emerged as a separate specialty in the 1970s and was a $45 billion industry in 2007 (table 8.1), nearly one-sixth the size of the semiconductor industry overall. Furthermore equipment companies are R&D intensive and are responsible for overcoming some of the chip industry's fundamental challenges. Their combined R&D spending is about one-quarter of that of the chip manufacturers (Hutcheson 2005).

Table 8.1 shows the location of the top ten suppliers of fab equipment in 2007; together the top ten accounted for 62 percent of global equipment sales. While these companies undertake important development work at their customers' sites, their primary research labs are located near their headquarters in the United States, Japan, and Europe.

Another factor that runs counter to the manufacturing-pull effect is the growing use of process development alliances (discussed in Crisis 7), such as IMEC in Europe, IBM's New York–based Common Platform Alliance, and Japan's ASET. These alliances are in the home country or region of the main participants and help keep process development activities homebound. A recent study of patenting by US semiconductor firms found that fewer than one-fifth of their US patents applied for between 1994 and 2003 listed a non-US inventor, with the share increasing only by a couple percentage points over the period (Macher et al. 2007).

There is growing evidence, however, that even leading producers are giving up development of leading-edge processes to Asian foundry partners. In the most significant example, TI announced that it would no longer develop digital process technology in-house beginning with the 0.032-micron generation. Instead TI will partner with foundry leaders TSMC and UMC to develop process technology for use in its own fabs as well as those of the foundries.[2]

8.1.2   Design R&D

The manufacturing-pull effect is even weaker with respect to chip design. Consider, for example, the fabless-foundry sector. Foundries, primarily in Taiwan, have taken over a growing proportion of chip manufacturing, but as discussed in Crisis 2, the largest concentration of successful fabless companies is still in the United States, with Taiwan's fabless sector a notable but still-distant second. It is debatable whether the strength of the Taiwanese fabless sector owes more to the presence of foundries or to that of numerous systems companies.

Some chip design by US companies is moving offshore, at times for cost-based reasons (Crisis 4) but almost never because of the fab's location. This can be seen most clearly in the case of India, which as of 2008 remained unsuccessful in enticing a fab to be built there. Specialized skills are another important reason that US semiconductor companies acquire or set up design centers overseas, particularly in Europe. Britain, for example, has developed expertise in consumer multimedia, and Scandinavian countries are noted for their skills in wireless network technology. US firms have often acquired small European companies to obtain both application know-how and a team of pretrained engineers. Neither skill-driven nor cost-driven offshore design investment is normally associated with the location of manufacturing.

Markets also exert a big attraction for design centers, and the United States has benefited from being the largest end-user market. Many foreign companies maintain a Silicon Valley or other US design center to be closer to US customers as well as to take advantage of the high skills available there. Toshiba, for example, has a network of three ASIC design centers in the United States.[3] Even foreign start-ups may need to have a US design team to work with US customers or to access leading-edge analog design skills. Ralink, a Taiwanese fabless company that started in analog chips and branched out to mixed analog and digital chip sets for WiFi networking, had a 20-person R&D group in California to complement its 100-person team in Taiwan.[4]

We see little indication that the shift in manufacturing is adversely affecting US leadership in chip design. What's actually occurring is that the rest of the world is beginning to catch up in design capability as well as constituting a growing share of chip product markets.

Next we examine the "large-market pull" theory that powerful new lead firms, sometimes known as "national champions," will emerge in industrializing Asia and overtake the current industry leaders. Because engineering talent is a critical determinant of the capability of a semiconductor company, our first step is a comparison of semiconductor engineering capabilities across key Asian countries.

8.2   Engineer Capabilities across Countries

Engineers in China and India, and to a lesser extent Taiwan, are younger with less experience and less education than the engineers in the United States and Japan, so direct comparisons of engineers across countries can be misleading. In India and China, technicians with a two-year degree are often classified as engineers, and this is not usually the case in the United States and Japan. India and China have relatively little graduate training available in semiconductor engineering, and most of what is available is not comparable to the graduate programs in the United States and Japan. Taiwan is an intermediate case, with undergraduate and master's engineering programs comparable to those in the United States and Japan, but PhD programs are still catching up.

8.2.1   Comparing Engineers

Bearing in mind these differences across countries, we present rough estimates for engineer salaries in table 8.2. We also include other indicators of the environment for the semiconductor industry that reflect the process for deciding where to locate activities: the value of fabs constructed, the number of active chip designers, and an index of intellectual property protection for these countries.

The salary figures suggest that engineers in the United States and Japan earn much higher pay compared to most Asian engineers. These data are imprecise and have high variance; they are intended as a general guide only. The salaries are for engineers with at least five years of experience in the United States and for engineers approximately 40 years old in Japan. Japanese engineers typically exit the union at about the age of 40 and begin to experience greater salary increases, while US engineers typically see their salary trajectory level out in their 40s and salaries may even fall in their 50s, as we saw in Crisis 6. As they age, Japanese engineers catch up to US engineers. Semiconductor engineers in the other

Table 8.2
Estimates for selected countries

	Annual salaries for EE/CS engineers, 2004	Value of fabs constructed, by country of ownership, 1995–2006	Number of chip designers, 2005	Intellectual property rights, 2008 (10 = high)
United States	$82,000	$74 billion	45,000	7.9
Japan	$60,000	$66 billion	—[a]	8.2
Taiwan	$30,000	$72 billion	14,000	6.4
India	$15,000	$0	7,000	5.2
China	$12,000	$26 billion	5,000	4.4

Sources: US salary from 2004 BLS Occupational Employment Statistics website (average for electronics and software engineers in NAICS 3344); Japan salary (average for circuit designer and embedded software engineers aged 40 years old) from Intelligence Corporation's data on job offers in 2003; Taiwan salary information from March 2005 interview with US executive in Taiwan; China and India salaries estimated based on a combination of interviews, business literature, and online job offerings; value of fabs (when fully equipped) from Strategic Marketing Associates (www.scfab.com), reported in "Chipmaking in the United States," *Semiconductor International*, August 1, 2006; number of chip designers in United States from iSuppli as reported in "Another lure of outsourcing: Job expertise," *WSJ.com*, April 12, 2004; number of chip designers in Taiwan from interview with Taiwan government consultant to industry, March 2005; number of chip designers in India and China from author estimates based on conflicting published sources and discussions with industry analysts in 2005; intellectual property protection rights index from IPRI 2008 Report, http://www.internationalpropertyrightsindex.org/. All numbers are rounded to reflect lack of precision.
a. We have been unable to obtain an estimate for the number of chip designers in Japan.

countries are younger and less experienced, and the salaries for China and India are for engineers with one to three years of experience.

At least part of the pay gap reflects productivity differences. An engineer with a BS and three years of experience in India or China does not have the valuable skills of an engineer with a master's degree and five to fifteen years of experience in the United States or Japan. In fact engineers with a master's from a US institution and five or more years of experience who returned to India to work for a US company had earnings comparable to those in the United States, in part because housing and child-schooling costs for returnees to Bangalore are almost as high as in the United States.[5] For lower skilled engineers the costs of coordinating offshore projects, discussed in Crisis 4, contribute to maintaining the wage gap.

As the semiconductor industry booms in China and India, wages are reportedly rising rapidly. In our interviews at semiconductor design firms in India, we were repeatedly told that earnings of domestically trained Indian engineers have been doubling in their first five years on the job. Senior managers with foreign experience are paid a large premium, since these managers are critical in implementing new technology and projects.

The second column in table 8.2, the value of fab construction from 1995 to 2006, gives an indication of this part of the value chain in each country. China, at $26 billion, has made significant inroads since its early public–private joint ventures with Japan's NEC in the mid-1990s. India, in sharp contrast, has yet to see a single commercial-scale fab constructed, although several have been proposed.

The rightmost column of table 8.2 shows the strength of intellectual property rights. IP protection is an important consideration in deciding what engineering activities to undertake in other countries. The rating covers all industries, so weak scores in the table may be driven by lapses in specific sectors such as pharmaceuticals, trademark goods, or recorded media, which would not be relevant to the semiconductor industry.

We also estimated the number of chip designers, a group critical to developing a national semiconductor industry. The number of chip designers is imprecise because there is no universal definition of "chip designer" and reported estimates can vary widely. To be consistent, we tried to include logic and physical designers, but not include embedded

Table 8.3
EDA industry revenue by consuming region, 2007 (US$ millions)

Region	EDA consumption	Share of world total
North America	$2,658.3	46%
Japan	$1,175.7	20%
Western Europe	$1,079.1	19%
Rest of world	$856.2	15%

Source: Calculated from quarterly EDAC.org press releases.

software programmers, which is a different discipline even though designers and programmers often work side by side.

Some sources estimate 400 chip designers are being added each year in both India and China. We think this number is inflated, possibly by the inclusion of embedded software programmers.[6] One chip industry executive claimed that the number of "qualified IC designers" in China in 2004 was only 500, a number that seems too restrictive based on other information sources.[7] Moreover the numbers for China and India have undoubtedly been growing faster than the numbers for the other countries. Overall, non–Japan Asia has a considerable number of chip design engineers.

A less impressive picture is indicated by data on regional sales of EDA (electronic design automation) software and services as reported by the EDA Consortium (table 8.3). EDA software is a critical input in IC design and is licensed per each engineer who will have access to it. Sales to the "rest of world" region, which is predominantly Asia outside of Japan, are only about one-third the level of North America, which has close to one-half of world total. Japan and Western Europe are each about one-fifth of the world total.

These data sometimes reflect headquarters' location rather than the location of offshore engineering centers, but they may give a more accurate picture than designer headcount of where the leading-edge design is being done. Access to EDA tools for designs that use older process technology is often available through universities or software piracy, which mostly impacts the "rest of world" category.[8] On the other hand, the

Table 8.4
Higher education, selected countries

	2005 ARWU universities in top 500	Universities in top 50 technology listings, 2007	Engineering bachelor's degrees granted, 2003
United States	168	27	130,000
Japan	34	4	100,000
Taiwan	5	1	44,000
South Korea	8	1	80,000
China	13	3	350,000
India	3	1	110,000

Source: Academic Ranking of World Universities (ARWU) values tabulated by authors from ARWU 2005 edition, accessible at http://ed.sjtu.edu.cn/ranking .htm. Universities in top 50 technology listings were averaged from data in the 2007 ARWU engineering field ranking and the Times Higher Education Survey's top 50 universities for technology (http://uniranks.unifiedself.com/2007technology .html). Engineering bachelor's degrees for the United States, Japan, and South Korea were tabulated by authors for "engineering" and "math/computer science" from appendix table 2–38, "Science and engineering indicators 2008," National Science Foundation; China and India from appendix "USA–China–India" in "Framing the engineering outsourcing debate," Gary Gereffi and Vivek Wadhwa, et al., Engineering Management Program, Duke University, 2005; and Taiwan from Taiwan Ministry of Education (http://english.moe.gov.tw/ct.asp?xItem =4095&ctNode=816&mp=1), "2005 educational statistical indicators/skills man-power cultivation."

values for North America and the other leading regions are understated because some EDA software is written in-house by large companies such as IBM and Toshiba.

8.2.2 Comparing Higher Education
The capability of chip engineers depends on the quality of domestic higher education and, in the case of new entrants, the number of engineers sent to the United States and elsewhere for graduate training. The United States leads the world in higher education, as table 8.4 shows.

Of the top five hundred universities, as assessed in the 2005 Academic Ranking of World Universities (ARWU) from Shanghai JiaoTong University's Institute of Higher Education, 168 are in the United States and 34 in Japan. By far the largest concentration in industrializing Asia is China's 13 universities. A more-focused count of the top fifty engineering colleges, for which we combined rankings from the ARWU and the Times Higher Education Survey, lists 27 colleges in the United States, 4 in Japan, 3 in China, and 1 each in Taiwan, South Korea, and India. These rankings indicate that the United States is a strong leader in engineering education, and that China is beginning to rival Japan in the number of world-class engineering colleges.

If we look at engineer BS graduation rates by country for 2003, we see that China and India produce many engineering bachelor's degree holders, and most of them graduate from low-ranked colleges because so few top schools are located there. China's large number of engineering graduates should also be put in perspective by its much greater need, relative to India, for engineers to staff its many factories; by 2005 China was producing about 15 percent of global electronics output.[9] Although China's graduation numbers indicate political and social commitment to advancing technical education, how long it will take the new programs to develop high-quality teaching for high-tech engineers is an open question.

Graduates from US universities, according to our interviews, are better trained than chip engineers in China and India, especially on software and equipment and in teamwork on projects. For example, undergraduate students in India and China usually do not have the opportunity to work on automated chip design (EDA) tools, while EE students in the United States do. According to the consulting firm McKinsey, only 10 percent of Chinese and 25 percent of Indian engineering graduates are likely to be suitable for employment by US multinationals (McKinsey Global Institute 2005).[10]

Graduate training in the United States provides an important source of technology capability in Asia when foreign students return home. As we saw in Crisis 6 (figure 6.3), US universities have attracted large numbers of foreign students to their graduate engineering programs. In 2005, 63 percent of 6,404 engineering PhDs were granted to noncitizen students,

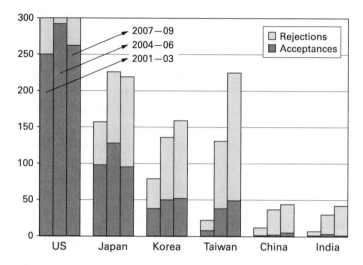

Figure 8.1
ISSCC acceptances and rejections by country, 2001 to 2009. US markers are truncated to improve the scale for other countries. Source: Tabulated from unpublished ISSCC data.

and 31 percent went to students from China (1,422 PhDs), Korea (525 PhDs), India (505 PhDs), and Taiwan (164 PhDs). Foreigners earned even more of the PhD degrees in electrical engineering (69 percent).[11]

Foreign-born US-educated engineers can help develop the semiconductor industry in their home countries through two routes—returning to work in their home country or starting a new company in the United States with activities in the home country. Both paths are used by a small but influential number of engineers from India and China.[12] Although the lifetime return rates for engineers is not known, at the time of graduation 80 to 85 percent of noncitizen PhD graduates planned on remaining in the United States to work in 2005.[13] However, only 60 percent of the noncitizen graduates, compared to 70 percent of citizen graduates, had made job plans, and this indicates some trouble in acquiring a visa to work in the United States

One measure of the capability of semiconductor design engineers, both in the universities and in companies, is the submission of papers to the International Solid-State Circuits Conference (ISSCC), which is IEEE's global forum for presentation of advances in chip design. In figure 8.1

the acceptances and rejections are aggregated in three-year periods to smooth transitory changes, and US rejections are truncated to preserve a useful scale for the other countries. This measure suggests that design capability in Asian countries has been improving. Over the 2001 to 2009 period total submissions from South Korea, China, India, and especially Taiwan increased noticeably. The absolute number of acceptances rose in Taiwan, China, and Korea. We expect that acceptances from India and China will increase in the near future as the quality of their university engineering programs improves.

8.3   The Large-Market Pull Theory

Having provided some comparative background data, we now consider the evidence for the emergence of leading global firms in China and India, two countries that have successfully used their large markets to attract foreign technology. We examine the evidence that they are successfully leveraging this technological opportunity to create globally competitive firms of their own. As a point of comparison we start with Taiwan which, despite its small size, has proved to be a fertile ground for a wide variety of semiconductor firms. We omit South Korea, whose chip industry is dominated, perhaps too much so, by a single company, Samsung, which is already a formidable chip competitor. Korea's other top ten chip firm, Hynix, is more narrowly focused on memory chips. The rest of Korea's chip industry consists of two small foundries and a few dozen small fabless companies, only two with annual sales above $100 million by 2007 (compared to twenty in Taiwan and seven in China).[14]

8.3.1   Taiwan

After the United States and Japan, Taiwan has the third most mature and developed semiconductor industry. According to Taiwan's Ministry of Economic Affairs, Taiwan ranked third (behind the United States and Japan) in semiconductor-related patent grants in 2005 from the US Patent and Trademark Office.[15] This is not surprising because the foundry model originated in Taiwan in 1987, three of the top ten foundries are located there, and Taiwan has the world's second-largest concentration of fabless companies after the United States.

Table 8.5
Taiwan's semiconductor industry value, 2007

Firm type	Output value (US$ billions)	Growth rate over 2006
Foundry	$13.5	1.2%
Fabless and design services	$12.2	23.6%
Fab-owning	$8.7	−9.8%
Packaging	$6.9	8.2%
Testing	$3.1	10.7%

Source: IEK-ITIS data reported in Vanguard International Semiconductor 2007 Annual Report (http://www.vis.com.tw/annualreport/2007/english/pdf/en/) and converted to US dollars at 0.03044267 $US:$NT.

Table 8.5 shows the 2007 revenue of Taiwan's domestic semiconductor firms by firm type. While most major chip-producing countries have large integrated producers that undertake all stages of production, Taiwanese companies have embraced the disaggregated business model, and only a handful of companies undertake multiple parts of the value chain.

The largest category is the foundry sector (discussed in Crisis 2) at $13.5 billion total for 2007, followed by fabless design, including design services, at $12.2 billion. Independent providers of chip packaging and testing services account for another $10 billion. Traditional integrated (fab-owning) chip companies had less than $9 billion in revenue, about half of which was attributable to the island's DRAM manufacturers.

The development of Taiwan's semiconductor industry is indicative of the island's symbiotic relationship with chip firms in developed countries. Beginning in the late 1970s, development was driven by government initiatives, the return of US-educated and trained engineers, and licenses of older chip technology from RCA, and, later, Philips (Saxenian 2002, 2006).

Taiwan's foundry and, especially, memory fabs have continued to use alliances and joint ventures with leading chip firms. The foundries experimented during the late 1990s with hybrid models. US-based fabless firms such as ATI and Xilinx co-invested with UMC in building fabs so that they would be assured capacity, but the operations were merged back into UMC in 1999 to give UMC better control over its capacity.[16] Although many fabless-foundry relationships are at arm's length, the leading fabless companies, as discussed in Crisis 5, need to work with foundries during the process development cycle in order to build the necessary knowledge and design libraries to design a successful chip.

In memory chips, the entry of Taiwanese firms was facilitated by a series of alliances. The first of these was a 1989 joint venture between Acer, Taiwan's leading computer brand, and Texas Instruments (TI), which was able to sell the output under its own brand. This arrangement originally kept production and market risk at an acceptable level for Acer. Volume production began in 1992 with a relatively mature product and process. In 1997 Acer was buying only 7 percent of the joint venture's production,[17] and TI exited the DRAM market in 1998. the following year the fab was acquired by TSMC.

In the meantime more Taiwan companies rolled the dice on DRAM with a series of subcontracting deals (the foreign partner supplied a prior-generation design and process and also handled the marketing of the output) and joint ventures (the foreign partner also contributed capital). Subcontracting agreements include those of Nan Ya with Japan's Oki in 1994, and Winbond with Toshiba in 1995. Joint ventures included Powerchip, between Umax and Mitsubishi Electric (1996), and ProMOS, between Mosel-Vitelic and Germany's Siemens (1997). Some of the Taiwan partners, such as Nan Ya and Umax, had no prior semiconductor experience, but the engineering labor pool in Taiwan had enough skilled fab engineers that the new companies were able to enter production successfully with sufficient help from the foreign partner during start-up. Taiwan's memory producers continue to compete using a combination of internal skills and foreign alliances, which have shifted with the restructuring of chip companies in Europe and Japan (Crisis 7).

The Taiwanese chip design sector is dominated by local firms, with only a few multinational design subsidiaries. Taiwanese companies have embraced the fabless model, and Taiwan is second to the United States in fabless firms by revenue. Over fifty fabless companies were listed on the

Table 8.6
Top ten Taiwanese fabless firms, 2007

Company	2007 revenue (US$ millions)	Growth rate over 2006
MediaTek	$2,472.60	52%
NovaTek	$1,110.99	15%
Himax	$918.21	23%
Phison	$622.91	63%
Realtek	$483.09	27%
VIA	$450.34	−32%
Etron	$406.49	26%
Sunplus	$283.33	−46%
Elite	$210.64	18%
SiS	$200.25	−17%

Source: Global Semiconductor Alliance.

Taiwan Stock Exchange as of December 2007, compared with about eighty publicly listed US fabless companies.[18] The top ten Taiwan fabless firms for 2007 are shown in table 8.6.

One advantage for Taiwan's fabless firms is the availability of an important local market for their chips: many Taiwanese systems companies design, assemble, and procure components for computers, communication equipment, and consumer electronics for world-famous brands, including Hewlett-Packard, Nokia, and Sony. For example, in 2007, over 90 million of the 107 million notebook computers manufactured worldwide were made to order for brand-name vendors by Taiwanese companies, mostly in Chinese factories.[19] In 1999, 62 percent of Taiwan's chip design revenue came from local sales, but this declined to 40 percent by 2006 as the China market grew in importance.[20]

The importance of sales to local and mainland firms is double-edged. On the one hand, geographic and cultural proximity to their customers has allowed local chip firms to develop a deep understanding of their market requirements. On the other hand, these customers are primarily targeting the low-end of the markets in which they operate, and this has perhaps made it harder for Taiwan's fabless firms to target high-end innovation instead of their current expertise in cost-down, fast-follower design (Breznitz 2005). Taiwan's design teams were praised in our interviews for their execution, which is a vital trait in an industry where time to market is often the difference between profit and loss.

Another potential problem for Taiwan's design sector is the island's relative withdrawal from the US branch of the global brain circulation. Taiwan depended on graduate training in the United States in the early stage of development of its semiconductor industry. Since the mid-1990s the number of Taiwanese receiving PhDs in engineering has declined steadily, and today few Taiwanese engineers are obtaining graduate training in the United States (see Crisis 6, figure 6.3). Although PhD education has improved in Taiwan, we heard in our interviews in Taiwan some concern about the declining numbers of returnees from the United States. Past returnees brought with them both graduate training and work experience that imparted management skills as well as practical knowledge.

Taiwan's government has instituted several programs to improve the local design sector, including a plan to train several thousand new design engineers in Taiwan's universities, the creation of an exchange where local chip design houses can license reusable functional blocks, and an incubator where early-stage start-ups can share infrastructure and services.[21] For example, the government began a renewed effort (Si-Soft) in 2001 to improve local chip design capabilities. As part of the program, the faculty teaching chip design more than doubled from 200 in 2001 to more than 400 by 2005.[22] Another initiative aims to attract chip design subsidiaries of major semiconductor companies, with early takers including Sony and Broadcom (a major US fabless company). Following a model that Taiwan has used successfully in other segments of the electronics industry, a government research institute created the SoC Technology Center (STC) in 2000 to design functional blocks that can be licensed to local companies (see Crisis 3). By 2005 the STC had over 200 engineers, most of whom have a master's degree or better.[23]

For the Taiwanese semiconductor industry, China presents both a challenge and an opportunity. The challenge comes from competition in the foundry and fabless sectors, especially for low-cost designs using older technologies, and from competition for engineers, many of whom have been drawn to work in China's booming chip sector and bring with them their knowledge of advanced technology in design and manufacturing. The opportunity comes from the ability to partner with Chinese companies elsewhere in the value chain so that Taiwanese chip companies can gain access to the rapidly growing mainland market. Political issues have been constraining the opportunities for Taiwanese companies to develop partnerships and markets in China, particularly with regard to advanced manufacturing. Currently Taiwan-born engineers, including returnees from the United States, are an important ingredient in the technology development that is occurring in China, in much the same way that the United States played a role in the earlier development of Taiwan.

8.3.2 China

China appears to be following the Taiwan pattern of industry development: government sponsorship, access to local system firms such as Haier, Huawei, and TCL that are increasingly engaged in global markets, and active involvement of expatriates returning from the United States and experienced engineers relocating from Taiwan (Saxenian 2002, 2006). China's potential in the chip sector is considerable. In 2007 roughly one-third of the world's semiconductors by value were consumed in Chinese factories, but so far local design and manufacturing accounts for only a small fraction of the total.[24]

China's chip fabrication sector has its origins in technology transfers and joint ventures that the government fostered in the 1990s between domestic firms and foreign partners such as Alcatel, Lucent, and NEC. These projects showed the viability of high-volume chip production in China.

The most ambitious Chinese fabrication operation to date is Semiconductor Manufacturing International Corp. (SMIC), which was founded in 2000 by Richard Chang, a Taiwanese native with US graduate degrees and twenty years' experience at Texas Instruments followed by a brief stint as head of a small foundry in Taiwan. Drawn in part by tax benefits offered by the Shanghai government, Chang marshaled global investors and major customers for the creation of a foundry running a 0.250-micron process on 8-inch wafers, which was then the most advanced in China.

The company continued to upgrade and expand through a series of technology agreements with customers that include Texas Instruments, Toshiba, Infineon, Elpida, and Fujitsu. Its fourth fab was China's first 300-mm facility, which began production in 2004 in Beijing. SMIC was able to quickly learn and implement process technology to produce 0.180-micron chips on 300-mm wafers in less than a year, primarily through luring top engineers from TSMC and using TSMC's proprietary operational and technical materials, such as "detailed process flows . . . including process target and equipment type."[25] TSMC sued SMIC in 2003 for theft of intellectual property. The dispute was settled in early 2005 with an agreement for SMIC to pay TSMC $175 million over six years,[26] but in 2006 TSMC renewed the suit, alleging breach of the agreement.[27]

In 2004 SMIC raised more than $1 billion through an initial public offering on stock exchanges in Hong Kong and New York, but it has not all been smooth sailing. SMIC incurred annual net losses from 2005 through 2007. The losses continued in the first three quarters of 2008 as the global credit crisis deepened, and a government-connected firm, Datang Telecom Technology, agreed to invest $172 million in SMIC for a 16.6 percent ownership share.[28]

Nevertheless, SMIC's implementation of its ambitious plans made it the world's third biggest foundry, after TSMC and UMC, and SMIC has entered into agreements with municipal governments elsewhere in China (Wuhan, Chengdu, and Shenzhen) to build and manage additional fabs. Following SMIC's example, other Chinese chip entrants have taken the foundry path (table 8.7). However, SMIC's 2007 revenues are larger than the combined revenues of the other nine Chinese foundries, whose prospects are modest compared to the headline-grabbing predictions of the early 2000s.[29] But there is no question that chip fabrication is firmly established in China and will gradually expand. Although China's fabs pose a growing low-cost challenge to the Taiwan foundries, from the perspective of leading chip firms in the United States and elsewhere, they add welcome competition to the market for wafer processing.

Table 8.7
China foundry service providers, 2007

Company	Year entered production	Location(s)	2007 revenue (US$ millions)
SMIC	2001	Shanghai, Tianjin, and Beijing	$1,465
HuaHong-NEC	1999	Shanghai	$319
Hejian	2003	Suzhou	$259
Grace	2003	Shanghai	$202
Shougang-NEC	1994	Beijing	$185
TSMC	2004	Shanghai	$176
ASMC	1995	Shanghai	$156
CSMC	1984	Wuxi	$143
Shanghai BCD	2001	Shanghai	$100
Shanghai Belling[a]	1991	Shanghai	$52

Source: Revenue data from "China's impact on the semiconductor industry, 2008 update," *PricewaterhouseCoopers*.
a. Some products are sold under their own brands.

In little more than a decade, Chinese chip firms have developed considerable fabrication capability. As of 2006 Chinese fabrication was predominantly on 200-mm wafers with processes from 0.350 down to 0.110 micron, a generation or more behind the leading edge.[30] However, a small but growing fraction of output that year was on 300-mm wafers (4 percent) and near-leading-edge 0.090-micron process (2.5 percent), despite barriers erected by the US and Taiwan governments to restrict China's access to the industry's most advanced technology.[31]

Multinationals own little fabrication capacity in China, apart from residual shares in some of the foundries from when they were set up as joint ventures. The multinationals, such as NEC and Motorola, which went early to China to begin negotiations for semiconductor fabrication in the 1990s, found it hard going. The Chinese government continually changed the requirements, such as conditions for technology transfer and joint ventures, and their timelines slipped as the required investment rose.[32] Motorola was unable to sustain their cell phone market leadership in China in the early 2000s; they pulled back their plans for fabrication and sold their fab, which had yet to be built out, to SMIC in 2003.[33] NEC's joint-venture fabs with Shougang and HuaHong both opened, but they suffered from management conflicts and continued to use trailing-edge technology.[34] Like Motorola, NEC received no long-term advantage in penetrating the Chinese consumer electronics market from its technology transfer.

An exception to the trailing-edge fabrication role taken by multinationals is a memory joint venture in Wuxi that was started by Hynix Semiconductor and STMicroelectronics in 2006 to produce 200-mm wafers with feature sizes down to 0.080 micron. Months after the start of volume production, a 300-mm production line was added in the same building. The rapid and successful start of production was attributed to the employment of 500 Korean engineers during the early phase, which suggests that China suffers a shortage of experienced fab engineers that may constrain the expansion of capacity.[35]

In 2007 Intel, which has chip assembly and test plants in both coastal and western China, announced that it would build a 300-mm fab in the northern city of Dalian. The fab would initially produce chip sets that could be made with trailing-edge process technology. Production isn't expected to begin before 2010.[36]

Multinationals have invested heavily in China in chip packaging and testing plants, and they own about one-third of capacity. This includes major chip companies like Intel, Samsung, AMD, and Toshiba, as well as leading packaging service providers, including Korea's Amkor, Taiwan's ASE, and Singapore's STATSChipPAC. A number of Chinese firms are also active in the sector. The share of world package and test capacity located in China is between 10 and 20 percent.[37]

Chip design in China has made formidable progress on the strength of local initiative backed in some cases by capital and technology from overseas. As we observed in Crisis 4, US-based chip companies have opened far fewer design centers in China than in India. Their concern with the difficulty of enforcing intellectual property rights is often mentioned in interviews and press reports. Foreign firms are often reluctant to bring lawsuits for fear of displeasing the authorities and because they are unlikely to win in Chinese courts, but at least two US companies have sued Chinese rivals in export markets for intellectual property violations.[38]

Chinese chip design is at an early stage, and a few successful firms, all of which have adopted the fabless model, are progressing rapidly. Chinese authorities claim the existence of hundreds of fabless firms, but most of these are small, inexperienced firms making use of the generous subsidies that are available to start-ups.[39] The Global Semiconductor Alliance has identified 161 public and private fabless firms (excluding design services providers) in mainland China plus 7 in Hong Kong, of which 6 are publicly listed.[40]

If we look at China's ten largest fabless firms in 2007 (table 8.8), we see that their recent performance has been mixed.[41] Fabless companies targeting the communications sector, such as HiSilicon (a spin-off of China's Huawei telecommunications equipment powerhouse), Spreadtrum, and Datang (also connected to an equipment firm), saw healthy growth. Hong Kong-based Solomon Systech, which specializes in driver chips for low-end displays and was spun out from Motorola in 1999, has seen its revenue decline in recent years. Other consumer chip firms, like Actions (media player chips), and Vimicro (PC camera image processors), both of which had IPOs on NASDAQ in 2005, saw a decline in revenue in 2007. Actions was spun out in 2001 from a Taiwanese company that withdrew from China, while Vimicro was founded by returnees with experience as Silicon Valley entrepreneurs and with earlier experience at IBM, Hewlett-Packard, and Intel. Spreadtrum was also founded by returnees.

Government procurement plays an important role for other firms in the list. One of the earliest and largest applications for chips in China is the relatively unsophisticated circuits used in smart cards. Huahong, CEC Huada, and others are primarily involved in the smart card chip market, which includes applications in telecommunications, banking, and identity cards where state-run entities are major customers.

In terms of process technology, which is one measure of sophistication, most Chinese chip design is still a generation or two behind fabless companies in the rest of the world. In China in 2006, 0.250 micron and

Table 8.8
China's top ten fabless semiconductor companies, 2007

2007 rank	Company	HQ city	Year established	2007 revenue (US$ millions)	Change from 2006
1	HiSilicon	Shenzhen	1991	$170	50%
2	Solomon Systech	Hong Kong	1999	$165	−35%
3	Spreadtrum	Shanghai	2001	$145	249%
4	Datang Microelectronics	Beijing	1996	$142	23%
5	Actions	Zhuhai	2001	$115	−32%
6	China Resources Semico	Wuxi	2000	$112	6%
7	Silan	Hangzhou	1997	$108	5%
8	Vimicro	Beijing	1999	$93	−27%
9	Huahong IC	Shanghai	1998	$90	9%
10	CEC Huada	Beijing	1986	$74	9%

Source: Revenue data from "China's impact on the semiconductor industry, 2008 update," *PricewaterhouseCoopers*, except for Solomon Systech from Global Semiconductor Alliance.

0.180 micron were considered mainstream, with a few companies reaching 0.130 micron.[42] Globally 0.090 micron was considered mainstream, and the leading edge had moved to 0.065 micron.[43]

There is evidence that China's fabless firms will upgrade rapidly. Obukhova (2007) surveyed IC design firms in Shanghai to study their technological capability and their ability to upgrade their technology between 2002 and 2004 and found considerable improvement over the period.[44] The technology level of each design firm was ranked between 1 and 10 (global leading edge), with each level representing approximately a year of technological progress. In 2004 the median capability was a full level higher than in 2002, when only one firm ranked level 8 or higher, and over a quarter ranked at level 2 or lower.[45] However, the 2004 the technology capability of these firms was not high by global standards: the median was level 6, and approximately 10 percent of firms were at level 2 or below, and the same proportion were at level 8 or higher. Obukhova's work also shows the importance of the state's procurement in supporting local firms to upgrade technology.

In general, China's fabless firms have the opportunity to supply lagging-edge technology chips for low-end niches of the large domestic market. This is made possible by the large number of local systems firms, with whom the local fabless firms can interact directly, much as occurs in Taiwan. Local design firms are trying to use their expertise and the revenues gained from the large local market, including state procurement, to design products for the global marketplace. Besides procurement, the Chinese government has taken many steps in support of chip design firms, some of the largest of which are state-owned. Measures include tax reductions, venture investing, incubators in seven major cities, and special government projects.[46] A value-added tax preference for domestically designed chips was phased out under US pressure in 2005.[47] A 2007 corporate income tax law introduced a range of preferences for IC design start-ups and ended discrimination between domestic and foreign-invested enterprises.[48]

China's government has also tried to promote domestic firms by backing national product standards, many of which have direct impact on foreign chip firms. One prominent example was a mandatory encryption standard (known by the acronym "WAPI") for all wireless networking equipment to be sold in China that was announced in December 2003. The proprietary technology required cooperation with one of two dozen authorized Chinese companies. While China claimed WAPI was needed for national security, US firms such as Intel and Broadcom claimed that the licensing procedure forced disclosure of sensitive information. The dispute escalated to the government-to-government level and was finally resolved in an April 2004 meeting of the US–China Joint Commission on Trade, at which China backed down from the requirement.[49]

Other national standards, such as "AVS" for video compression and "TDSCDMA" for third-generation cellular service have met with less resistance from foreign firms, but as of mid-2008 have had little impact in

China or elsewhere. The government has vigorously supported these standards but has not imposed them on the market. Nevertheless, they demonstrate the government's determination to create a stronger intellectual property position for its firms and force foreign chip companies to invest resources in case the technology takes hold. Chinese firms will undoubtedly become more innovative in the years to come, but it's more likely to be the product of growing capabilities rather than the result of official policy.

China has been helped along its technology trajectory by the return of Chinese nationals with overseas education and work experience, and China is working to attract more high-tech returnees with a range of specially-targeted incentives and infrastructure (Saxenian 2002, 2006). The returnees provide valuable management experience and connectivity to global networks that tend to accelerate the pace at which China's chip sector can develop.[50] The government maintains statistics on student returnees. In 2003 it was reported that of 580,000 students who had gone abroad since 1978, one-quarter (or 150,000) had returned.[51] These returnees had started 5,000 businesses, including over 2,000 IT companies in Beijing's Zhongguancun Science Park (one-sixth of the Park's total).[52]

One factor that favors the development of local high-tech start-ups, including many fabless firms, is that engineers prefer to work for domestic companies rather than multinationals—virtually the opposite of what interviews revealed in India. Many young Chinese engineers, especially returnees, want to take the risk working for an emerging company that may result in great wealth. China's ability to continue to push along the technology curve will depend on the continual flow of highly educated and employer-trained returnees, as well as the government's ability to keep the state-run economy growing rapidly. In the current global recession China's high-tech sector may survive better than those in other countries because of government stabilization policies, which translate into purchases and subsidies. The current global recession may provide China with a period to improve global competitive advantage.

8.3.3 India

India presents a very different picture than China in the semiconductor industry. India faces benign neglect by the government, a lack of manufacturing for chips and systems, and weaker levels of brain circulation with its US-based expatriates (Saxenian 2002). Unlike Taiwan and China, India has no high-volume chip manufacturing. Only one fab proposal was submitted in response to the government's February 2007 announcement of its long-awaited fab subsidy program, and that project appears to be stalled as of November 2008.[53] India poses significant challenges for fabrication facilities that need reliable water, electricity, and transport infrastructure to keep a $3 billion chip factory running smoothly.

India's chip strength to date lies in design, and there were some 120 chip design organizations in India by 2005, generating an estimated revenue of $583 million.[54] This had grown to $766 million by 2007.[55]

But there is little evidence that India is leveraging its vast market potential to create national champions in the semiconductor industry. Most of India's chip design is taking place in foreign subsidiaries, including those of the top US and European chip companies (see Crisis 4). In Bangalore, where the majority of India's design centers are located, about two-thirds of the engineers are at multinational subsidiaries.[56] They are able to provide end-to-end solutions that incorporate in-house proprietary IP and cover the entire design flow. India's large software companies, such as Wipro (the largest with over 2,000 chip designers), Tata, and Sasken, have also developed sophisticated IC design capabilities.

Foreign chip companies have been attracted to India by Indian engineers' knowledge of English and the successful Indian software sector, which took off following the relaxation of government policies in the mid-1980s (Dossani 2005). Many of the early Indian investments by chip companies were software focused and involved writing the microcode that becomes part of the chip. Over time the Indian affiliates have taken on a bigger role that can extend to complete chip designs from specification to physical layout.

Multinationals' hiring of semiconductor engineers, who prefer working for MNCs rather than small local firms, may slow the diffusion of technology to local firms, although it lays the foundation for the potential creation of local companies if managers from multinationals decide to start their own firms. So far multinationals in India have had few instances where employees leave to start their own companies. Although we heard of at least two cases of this occurring during interviews in Bangalore in 2005, as of mid-2008 there is only one established domestic fabless companies in India, Moschip (2007 revenue $6 million), which was founded in 1999 by two returnees with decades of US experience.[57] A few other companies, such as Ittiam, are implementing product-oriented business models, but most domestic chip companies are providing design services to multinationals. Design services is generally a low profit business because the customer, who owns the key intellectual property, is able to capture most of the value created.

Outside of the large design services companies Wipro, Tata, and Sasken, local design services companies vary in their capabilities. Many use a time-and-materials pricing method, which allocates specific tasks to be carried out within set time lines and is easy to execute, according to an India Semiconductor Association (ISA) study.[58] These companies tend to develop simple subsystems based on customer specifications.

In contrast to China, Indian engineers, according to our fieldwork, prefer multinationals and large services companies over entrepreneurial start-ups because engineers and their family members do not tend toward taking risks and their Hindu values constrain pursuing and displaying wealth.[59] This is more similar to Japan, where there are very few fabless start-ups (Crisis 1), than to China, with its vibrant start-up sector. However, we also heard that the possibility of leaving a multinational to start a company is slowly becoming more acceptable among Indians engineers, whose personal motivation is often given as helping India develop rather accumulating personal wealth.[60]

The US subsidiaries are highly dependent on returnees with overseas advanced degrees and work experience to develop new projects in India because most domestically trained engineers lack the knowledge of the technology being transferred, lack the management skills required, and also lack knowledge of the entire product cycle. As in China the quality of engineering graduates is highly variable with only a small proportion graduating from the elite technical universities (Dossani 2007). This is exacerbated in India by the fact that most engineering students want to study computer science rather than electronics because of the booming, well-publicized market for India's software and related services. Many are not aware of the job opportunities in semiconductors, and graduate education in electronics engineering is still at an early stage of development. The very low wages paid to professors, the lack of expensive and ever-changing EDA tools, and the difficulty and expense in getting sample chips fabricated are just some of India's challenges in developing world-class graduate education.

In addition India has not attracted returnees to the extent that China has, so the flow of returnees with advanced design knowledge and experience is low. The low flow of new domestic graduates and returnees into the EE labor supply, coupled with the need for at least three to five years of experience to be a fully productive chip designer, has prevented the supply of design engineers from keeping up with the fast-growing demand. As a result wages for chip designers have been rising rapidly, both at entry level and during the first five years. As mentioned above, salaries after five years of experience are double the entry-level salary.

In addition to a tight labor market, design firms in India are coping with many of the same infrastructure problems in transportation, housing, and electricity that have made companies reluctant to build an Indian fab. The lack of a stable energy supply and lack of office space means that foreign subsidiaries must make substantial investments to provide both offices and reliable electricity. The small, pothole-filled roads are gridlocked in Bangalore, the country's primary city for high-tech, and employees spend long hours in commuting from affordable housing. In addition high-tech companies are spread out over the city, and commuting between companies, or even between company locations, is time-consuming. The housing stock has not kept up with growth, and housing prices and rents have been rising rapidly. Many employees are faced with the choice of living in inadequate housing or living far from work. The housing and schooling problems are especially severe for the returnees from the United States, who want to replicate the quality of housing and schools their families experienced in the United States. In Bangalore we were told by several executives that their cost of living was almost as high in Bangalore as in the United States because of the high cost of housing and international schools.[61]

The shortage of engineering talent and weak infrastructure is constraining how fast the semiconductor design industry, both for foreign subsidiaries and local companies, can grow in India, especially in Bangalore. Some companies have been moving operations to areas in India that are not as expensive as Bangalore and have better infrastructure. However, the talent shortages still remain, especially for experienced engineers with advanced degrees.

8.4   Industry Leader Responses

The strategic responses of the leading chip companies to the growth of semiconductor capabilities in Asia range from cooperation to competition. The key question facing the current industry leaders is whether the new Asian rivals represent synergistic complements or competitive substitutes. The numerous complementarities have given rise to extensive cooperation, and the leading firms have also repositioned themselves for direct competition with the new, low-cost rivals.

Chip companies from the developed countries have repeatedly entered cooperative technology alliances with firms from industrializing economies. This has been especially true in China, where the phenomenal growth of the local market has given the government considerable leverage to exchange technology transfer for market access. Foreign cooperation was also an essential element in the early stages of fabrication in Taiwan and design in India. Complementarities include the provision by Taiwan's foundries of critical manufacturing infrastructure for the US-dominated fabless chip sector, and DRAM joint ventures in China and Taiwan that have spread the considerable risk of building memory fabs. India's design outsourcing companies provide a resource for reducing project costs to meet consumer-friendly price points, while reserving in-house engineers for more critical core tasks.

Another type of response is foreign direct investment in the industrializing economies for fabs (e.g., the Hynix-ST memory fab in China), design (discussed in Crisis 4), and software development. These investments dull some of the low-cost edge of local competitors by directly employing local engineers. Moreover multinational subsidiaries are often able to attract better engineers than local rivals because of their prestige and by paying slightly higher salaries, which may in turn drive up costs for local rivals.

Many leading firms also make a direct competitive response, in which they develop low-cost variants of their products to compete with offerings from chip companies in Taiwan or China. In 2008 Intel announced that it would immediately use its newest, 0.045-micron process to make small "atom" processors for low-cost subnotebooks rather than using it only for adding more features to its high-end processors as was the case with earlier new processes.[62]

This market repositioning for direct competition with low-cost rivals is often entwined with cooperative and direct investment strategies. Design subsidiaries in India, for example, frequently work on low-cost variant products for developing-country markets. A typical example of this is Texas Instruments' "LoCosto" highly integrated cell phone chip for low-end handsets introduced in 2006. The bulk of the design engineering was done in India, and manufacturing was consigned to Taiwanese foundries rather than TI's own fabs.[63]

Whether local firms in China and India complement or compete with incumbents from developed countries, their participation in global value chains has been an important step in the necessary integration of the Chinese and Indian economies into the global system. This global integration supports the rapid growth of their potentially large markets, which in turn improves the prospects of local firms as well as multinationals. How quickly local companies in China or India can move up the technology curve and develop competitive advantage in global markets remains to be seen. China and India will play an increasingly important role in high-tech industries, both as markets and suppliers.

8.5 Lessons and Conclusions

New Asian competitors continue to join the global semiconductor industry, posing a challenge to the competitive advantage of the leading companies. Although a number of countries, such as Singapore and Malaysia, have launched domestic semiconductor industries (Mathews and Cho 2000), the recent entrants that loom the largest in terms of production, design, or multinational investment are Taiwan, China, and India. Their success has sparked fears that innovative activity will gradually be relocated from advanced countries like the United States and Japan to these dynamic upstarts.

New opportunities also beckon, such as potential markets with more than a billion new consumers for digital products. Firms can build competitive advantage by successfully bridging the gaps of technology and regional needs that separate world markets. Chip workers, especially those with personal networks that extend to other countries, have a chance to play a valuable role in helping the industry's global brain circulation function smoothly.

The fear that offshore manufacturing will pull development and design activities abroad and result in US losing leadership in innovation does not seem to have occurred. Leading chip companies have successfully integrated their value chain activities across global locations. The manufacturing-pull theory of shifting advantage in innovation is not straightforward. Manufacturing-pull may occur for process innovation but not in design. Even process innovation involves a variety of players, many with deep roots in their home region, including equipment manufacturers and government labs as well as the leading chip companies. For these reasons we don't think that the manufacturing-pull theory has much application in chip process innovation.

Manufacturing-pull is even less apparent for design. Geographic separation of fabrication and design activities appears to be viable even for leading-edge chip companies, and perhaps preferable for companies using mature technologies. As Crisis 2 showed, the rise of Taiwan-dominated foundries allowed the US-dominated fabless sector to become the fastest growing segment in the semiconductor industry. Crisis 5, the increasing need to link design and fabrication, led many analysts to anticipate that integrated chip companies would gain competitive advantage over fabless companies, yet we did not see this happen, and the US fabless sector has continued to thrive.

However, as R&D in process becomes too expensive to be undertaken by single companies except for the largest, such as Intel and TSMC, and by alliances with a strong technology leader, such as the IBM Common Platform Alliance, we think that few companies or alliances will develop process technology past 0.032-micron technology. This may result in increasing the market power of companies with leading-edge process, and may lead once again to process capability driving global competitive advantage, as it did in the industry's earlier decades before the Japanese success in DRAM. Although industry- or government-sponsored consortia devoted to process R&D, such as SEMATECH (United States) and SELETE and ASET (Japan) may become more important in the future, their efforts in the past have been constrained by the unwillingness of leading companies to join with rivals in efforts that would require sharing bleeding-edge process knowledge.[64] Companies seem more willing to partner with universities in undertaking basic research, often funded by the government.[65]

The large-market pull theory that the rapidly growing markets in China and India will provide their domestic suppliers with a competitive advantage, which they can then use in global markets to become world leaders, is also not straightforward. Although we have seen in Japan that the presence of a strong domestic market can help local firms in their early days, producing for the local market may constrain expansion to global markets over time.

Although a large and growing share of the global chip industry's resources and user markets are located in Taiwan, China, and India, the potential of these countries to become a global semiconductor leader is less imposing when we focus more closely on what local firms are doing.

In fabrication, India is still a nonstarter, while Taiwan and China are dominated by foundries. A foundry is unlikely to turn into an integrated chip company because it would risk losing its customers as it turns itself into their rival. The switch from services to product development and marketing would also require the organization to bridge a knowledge divide. So far history suggests that companies are much more likely to go from selling chips to selling manufacturing services than the reverse.

The situation in design is more mixed. Fabless companies based in Taiwan and China are primarily targeting low-end markets for now, yet those are some of the fastest growing opportunities in the global electronics industry, as cell phones and low-end computers become a part of everyday life around the globe. However, local companies do not necessarily have an advantage over multinationals in developing domestic markets, except in the important case of government procurement, which provides a significant part of domestic demand in China's state-run economy.

Chip firms in Taiwan, China, and elsewhere will most likely upgrade over time as the first waves of engineers and managers develop deeper experience and target more sophisticated markets in search of profits. Crisis 1 showed how the fortunes of national chip industries can rise and fall over time, and future shifts of fortune are to be expected in favor of Asia or perhaps elsewhere. The Russian government, for example, has begun to take a serious interest in updating its microelectronics sector, which could ignite fresh fears.[66]

The rise to prominence of developing country firms won't be easy or fast. Leading firms are more than just teams of engineers. They are complex organizations with a history of experience inventing technology, developing products, and taking them to market. Their intellectual property and embedded knowledge cannot be replicated simply by filing a certain number of patents. Learning is required, and this takes time and experience. Korea's Samsung Electronics provides an example of the learning curve involved. Samsung entered the chip industry in the 1970s making low-end products for consumer goods like early digital watches. After deciding in 1981 to compete in the advanced memory chip market, it started by licensing outdated product and process technology from US and Japanese firms. Samsung took ten years of steady effort and government subsidies to catch up to the leading edge in memory. Our analysis suggests that firms from industrializing Asia are moving up the technology curve and may present challenges to industry leaders in a ten- to twenty-year time frame.

We conclude by considering the impact on global competitive advantage of the worldwide financial crisis that began in the United States in 2008. Countries and companies must weather the resulting recession, and emerging companies without established market niches may find it especially difficult. Overall, we expect the developed world to be able to withstand the crisis better than the developing world, with the notable exception of highly leveraged companies such as those taken private in a recent wave of buyouts (Crisis 7). We also expect that India will be affected more than China, whose government controls the currency and quickly implemented a major stimulus package. In the developed world we expect that mergers and spinouts will be part of company survival strategies, for example, AMD's spin-off of its fabs to a joint-venture majority owned by an Abu Dhabi investment company.

But the recession could also erode the foundations of long-run global competitive advantage for established firms, especially in the United States. One of these foundations is the role that universities play by partnering with semiconductor companies in cooperative R&D programs such as those administered by the Semiconductor Research Corporation (http://www.src.org/), a non-profit founded by industry in 1982.

A survey of 249 R&D-intensive companies headquartered in the United States and Western Europe found that half of the R&D effort in developed nations is for new science, and the type of science undertaken is most influenced by the ease of collaboration with nearby universities (Thursby and Thursby 2006). These results underscore the importance of government and educational policies that preserve the excellence of research universities and accessibility by foreign students.

Recession-induced cutbacks in either government or private sector funding of US university-based research, while other countries increase their funding, could change the national leadership positions for university education and research and eventually affect US global competitive advantage. The global brain circulation is another foundation of competitive advantage that is at risk in the United States. Educational immigration restrictions in response to the recession would be harmful to the US educational system, while allowing developing countries a chance to keep their best students at home and entice experienced expatriates to return.

Finally, the recession may reduce the willingness and ability of industry leaders to conduct the necessary long-term R&D to maintain a technological advantage. If current leaders shed experienced engineers without regard to preserving organizational memory and long-term research initiatives in response to short-term necessities, then Asian newcomers may find it easier to catch up.

Overall, the threats to current market leaders lie within their own organizations and national economies as much as in industrializing Asia. The strategies undertaken by companies as well as the policies of their by governments will determine global competitive advantage over time.

Conclusion
The Way Ahead

The eight crises analyzed in this book are interconnected and recurring, so understanding any one crisis relies upon understanding the ongoing dynamics of the related crises. For example, Crisis 8 (new global competition) is a new version of Crisis 1 (loss of competitive advantage) and is exacerbated by competition for the global labor supply of engineers (Crisis 6). Crisis 7 (low returns with high risk) is exacerbated by the squeeze on prices (Crisis 4) and the technological limits to Moore's Law (Crises 5). Higher fabrication and design costs (Crises 2 and 3) add to the price pressure (Crisis 4) and elicit new levels of industry outcry as technology advances.

Finding solutions to one crisis can ameliorate or aggravate others. For example, tapping into new pools of skilled labor in lower cost locations (Crisis 4) can help reduce the cost for new chip designs (Crisis 3) while it raises US concerns about the engineering labor market (Crisis 6) and about loss of industry leadership (Crisis 8). A new lithography fix (Crisis 5) may come with a high price tag that further drives up the cost of leading-edge fabs (Crisis 2).

In this chapter we review how the eight crises have affected countries, firms, workers, and consumers to date; then we discuss how the crises continue to unfold. We conclude by suggesting overarching lessons other industries might draw from the experience of the semiconductor industry.

Impact of Crises

Table 9.1 summarizes the impacts that the eight crises have had on participants in the industry at various levels.

Table 9.1
Impacts of eight crises in the semiconductor industry

	Countries	Firms	Worker	Consumer
Crisis 1 Loss of competitive advantage	National fortunes rise and fall	Shifted advantage from US memory producers in the 1980s	Fortunes of workers rise and fall with their companies	Focus on business customers; PC era
Crisis 2 Rising cost of fabrication	Favors countries willing to subsidize	Created opening for fabless firms in the 1990s	Growing automation; higher skill requirements	Customers continue to benefit from lower prices
Crisis 3 Rising cost of design	Limits entry points	Favors incumbents	Designers with deep submicron knowledge highly valued	Higher integration makes smaller electronics, better reliability
Crisis 4 Consumer price squeeze	Speeds diffusion of design know-how to countries with lots of young engineers	Firms expected by investors to have a China and/or India strategy	Implicit competition between low-end engineers in advanced countries and young engineers in followers	Consumer markets important, especially telecom products
Crises 5 Limits to Moore's Law	Limits entry points; favors incumbents	Requires more communication between fab and designers	New mentality required as engineers no longer "throw product over the wall"	Should not see any change

Crisis 6 Finding talent	Governments can influence domestic industry by education policies	Firms need to choose a recruiting strategy to compete for the best talent	Older engineers under pressure; engineers must manage own career	Consumers in developing countries getting more access to digital world
Crisis 7 Low returns, high risk	Favors countries willing to subsidize	Restructuring	Decreased job security	Consumer markets push business cycle
Crisis 8 New global competition	New entrants making a big impact	Competition more global	Global brain circulation	Developing markets begin to catch up

At the country level, the dominant experience has been a shuffling of national advantage as firm-level sources of competitive advantage have shifted. When the memory market favored manufacturing excellence that produced high yields, Japanese companies surpassed the US-based pioneers, and then were surpassed in their turn by Korean rivals who developed even greater manufacturing efficiency. The infant industries in both Japan and Korea were supported by their governments in important ways. Later, when wafer fabrication became readily available from Taiwan-based foundries, Taiwan benefited from the runaway success of TSMC, in which the government was a major investor. Taiwan also benefited from the successful creation of local fabless firms because its financial infrastructure, among other factors, was close to the Silicon Valley model that had spawned the most successful fabless chip firms. Finally, the combination of high growth in emerging economies and the drive to lower costs led major chip companies to invest in design centers and other operations in China and India. This greatly shortened the industry development cycle for those countries, especially for China, where government policies that included subsidies, preferences, and procurement, helped along the rapid progress of the semiconductor industry.

At the level of individual firms, some crises have favored incumbents, particularly those that raised barriers to entry, such as the rising costs of fabrication and design. However, most crises have challenged incumbent firms, especially the majority of incumbents who are unable to stay at the forefront of the technology frontier. Even when a crisis was expected to provide competitive advantage to large integrated firms, such as when the looming limits to Moore's Law required more communication between the fab and designers, the fabless-foundry model found ways to remain competitive by incorporating the required information flow into standard procedures. The rise of new lower-cost global competitors and the growing importance of price-sensitive consumer markets have both put downward pressures on the return on investment for most firms. During each downturn the most vulnerable firms often undergo radical restructuring. Meanwhile the global brain circulation requires firms to cast their recruitment net ever wider to take advantage of new national pools of engineering talent worldwide. The global brain circulation offers opportunities to workers and firms as well as threats of an ever-increasingly mobile and competitive labor supply.

Engineers, who create new technology and then turn it into reality, have been buffeted by these waves of change. The industry as a whole has grown, which has minimized the disruption to overall employment and helped individuals make necessary transitions. Engineers trained in the key technologies, such as physical design for the next-generation process, find themselves in high demand, but their knowledge depreciates rapidly. As we showed in Crisis 6, US engineers over 50 years old face diminished prospects as companies favor young graduates who have been trained in cutting-edge techniques, possibly depriving the firms as well as the engineers of valuable opportunities. The global brain circulation expands opportunities worldwide in both education and employment. However, engineers in the leading nations feel threatened by the increased mobility and competition that goes with the global brain circulation.

Meanwhile consumers, who ultimately determine the successes and failures of nations and firms, are largely unconcerned with the challenges facing other industry participants. They have experienced a long series of benefits from the relentless competition. Chips have continued to get smaller, cheaper, and faster, and this has brought increasingly sophisticated devices at falling prices to consumers in the developed world and allowed millions of consumers in emerging markets to buy inexpensive electronic devices and join global information and communication networks.

Industry Response Modes and Strategies

We have seen how the semiconductor industry as a whole has overcome a series of crises as it has maintained a trajectory of exponential improvements in chip performance. In almost no case, however, is a crisis ever solved permanently.

Of course, the industry does not take steps as a unified group; actions are taken by individual firms. For the purposes of this discussion, however, we focus on the dominant response modes and strategic actions that defined the industry's approach to each crisis.

Although the industry addresses crises as they arise, these fixes often make the problem manageable for only a short period of time before the crisis reappears, perhaps with new characteristics. This should not be surprising. The industry has always had to deal with global movements of workers, capital, and information; rapid technological change with escalating costs; and shifting markets. Pressure from these ongoing changes strains existing business models, and periodic elevation of the problem to "crisis" status helps focus the attention of industry leaders on the need for immediate response.

Here we look at how each crisis played out by classifying the industry response along two dimensions. *Response mode* is the type of response used to address the crisis: either an incremental improvement within the current technology or organization ("incremental"), or a break-through technology or new business model that was not anticipated ("radical"). *Strategy* is the type of actions used in addressing the crisis: new positioning in the market ("positioning"); offshoring of value chain activities ("offshoring"); cooperation through standards or collaboration through alliances ("cooperation"); and restructuring of industry or reorganization of firms ("restructuring"). Table 9.2 summarizes the response mode and strategy for each crisis.

Response Modes

In Crisis 1 (loss of competitive advantage to Japan), US companies took radical steps, including in many cases exiting the market. Some companies followed a strategy of market repositioning toward logic chips, out of which emerged the booming, Intel-led market for personal computer (PC) chips. When Japan faced a loss of leadership to the United States and Korea, its firms were constrained in their response by macroeconomic and institutional factors. The leadership crisis has reappeared in a new guise as Crisis 8, with Taiwan and China posing the "threat" to industry leaders.

In Crisis 2 (rising cost of chip fabrication), the response was an unanticipated new business model built around the creation of contract-only wafer fabrication in Taiwan. The industry's strategies included offshoring of fabrication and a new type of chip company, the design-only fabless start-up. The problem of elevated fab costs will not go away,

Table 9.2
Ongoing crises in semiconductor industry

Crisis	Description	Response mode	Strategy
Crisis 1	Loss of competitive advantage	Radical	Positioning
Crisis 2	Rising cost of fabrication	Radical	Offshoring; restructuring
Crisis 3	Rising cost of design	Incremental	Cooperation; restructuring
Crisis 4	Consumer price squeeze	Incremental	Offshoring; positioning
Crises 5	Limits to Moore's Law	Incremental	Cooperation
Crisis 6	Finding talent	Incremental	Offshoring
Crisis 7	Low returns, high risk	Radical	Restructuring; cooperation
Crisis 8	New global competition	Incremental	Cooperation; positioning

however, with an escalating cost for each new process generation and wafer size, which has not stopped industry leaders from pushing for a transition to sub–0.022-micron process technology and larger (450-mm) wafers.

In Crisis 3 (rising cost of chip design), the industry took incremental steps to make system-on-a-chip (SOC) cost effective: expanding design reuse by setting standards; expanding design libraries provided by EDA companies and foundries; and creating the design core industry. This approach requires a strategy of cooperation and collaboration by companies, as well as a reorganization of the design flow to ensure that the licensed parts of the design are well-integrated and function as anticipated. Despite the supportive efforts of industry consortia, the independent design core business model has not proved very successful. Design cores are too important to the industry's future to be abandoned. However, the majority of cores will probably be offered by foundries, EDA companies, and design services companies, each with complementary products and services to sell, rather than by specialist core providers, most of whom lack the resources to offer the required assurance and support for the cores' reliability. Meanwhile a major proportion of design costs for leading-edge chips are now for software programming, which makes weak gains in software productivity one of the chip industry's looming crises.

In Crisis 4 (consumer price squeeze), companies have pursued an incremental approach of accelerated offshoring to lower cost regions. Company strategies include offshoring some operations and developing new markets for consumer products, especially wireless products in developed countries and low-cost computing platforms in developing countries. The price-sensitive consumer market is now a fact of life for the chip industry, and most chip firms seeking high volumes have adapted or quit.

In Crisis 5 (limits to Moore's Law), chip companies have mostly pursued evolutionary approaches to the challenges of designing for and fabricating ever-smaller linewidths. These include extensions of optical lithography infrastructure on the process side and new EDA tools that incorporate more fab-level feedback on the design side. This ad hoc approach required cooperation and collaboration of chip firms, foundries, EDA companies, and other elements of the design chain, and has proved successful so far because the cooperation is vertical (buyer to supplier) rather than horizontal (among competing firms). The industry's evolutionary approach may be inadequate, however, as the pressure to find new fabrication technologies and to closely integrate design and fabrication activities moves forward.

In Crisis 6 (finding talent), companies responded by expanding their global brain circulation. US companies lobbied to increase the number of visas for skilled foreign workers and sent some of their foreign-born workers back to their native countries to manage offshored projects there. The existence of a talent shortage is still debated in the developed countries. In the United States, companies favor recent graduates over experienced engineers, while engineers claim that companies are using young skilled foreign engineers to keep wages low. The chip industry's problems are unlikely to be resolved by policy changes because the US visa debate is driven by the software and services industries, which rely on importing low-wage foreign workers, while the semiconductor industry relies more on hiring foreign students as they graduate with advanced engineering degrees from US universities. Offering permanent residency to these graduates would go a long way toward resolving the controversy in the semiconductor industry. We hope that the industry downturn that began in 2008 does not lead to measures that interfere with the global brain circulation that is vital for US universities and the chip industry. Foreign-born engineers play an important role in starting technology firms in the United States and in providing critical networks across countries for the industry.

In Crisis 7 (low returns with high risk), companies are restructuring with the spin-out of chip operations into joint or private ventures. The old and new chip companies are struggling to increase the linkage between the value they create and the value they capture. However, the end of cross-subsidies within the firm and higher debt loads make this difficult. As a result cost-cutting is one of the dominant strategies. The newly independent or private chip companies have not had time to show whether they can prosper, or to what extent they will maintain the necessary investment in research and development in both process and products. For most large fab-owning firms, R&D consortia form a part of the cost-control strategy.

Finally, Crisis 8 (new global competition) presents the new rendition of potential loss of competitive advantage to China, Taiwan, and possibly India. This time around, the chip industry has been able to draw on its extensive experience with globalization for an incremental response. Leading chip companies have adopted cooperative strategies where feasible, such as the use of Chinese foundries and Indian design services. Some companies have also repositioned themselves in selected low-cost markets to counter new rival start-ups from Taiwan and China, while they still continue to pursue their existing high-end opportunities. The competitiveness issue is bound to take on greater prominence over the next decade and beyond, as at least a few Asian chip start-ups stake out a place in global markets.

The pattern in table 9.2 suggests that companies' response modes and strategies are independent of each other. Incremental responses have been made using all four of the strategy types, while radical responses have involved all the strategies except cooperation.

As the predominance of the incremental response mode makes clear, the industry will use evolutionary methods built on current practices as long as possible in responding to a crisis, perhaps because engineers are very clever at solving problems in an ad hoc way. Breakthrough or revolutionary approaches involve more cost, risk, and uncertainty because, by definition, they involve doing something new.

Strategies

We now take a closer look at the four types of strategies used by the industry.

Positioning, which companies have used effectively to compete with the challenge from new competitors and to cope with consumerization, is the highest risk strategy, since it involves applying corporate competencies to new market areas. In the case of the response to Japan, it was the shift from memory chips to processors. In the case of consumerization, it was the expansion from high-price corporate markets to low-price, high-volume consumer markets. These shifts require an entrepreneurial approach as the company copes with new technical trade-offs and a new customer base.

Offshoring, which was another element of the response to consumerization and to the rising costs of design and fabrication, requires companies to steer among a number of obstacles. Any moves need to be made as nonthreatening as possible to domestic employees to avoid undermining morale, and local managers familiar with both offshore and headquarters cultures must be in place, with project managers capable of handling global complexity. This strategy entails hidden costs that go beyond the obvious growing pains of the initial setup for a new offshore engineering center, or the absorption of an acquisition. Among the persistent costs are cultural misunderstandings, the need to codify all specifications, extra monitoring, and coordination across time zones.

Cooperation, which the industry has used in response to design complexity, manufacturing–design interaction, and low return on investment has proved the most difficult to implement. Cooperative strategies suffer from the inherent difficulty of getting rival firms to trust each other and truly cooperate, and can even affect buyer–supplier collaboration when there is fear of knowledge spillovers. Firms in the fabless design chain, for example, were slow to share sensitive data needed to facilitate design for manufacturing. Broad cooperative efforts, such as standard-setting committees, suffer from the added burden of firms positioning themselves for competitive advantage and bureaucratic slowness in a fast-changing environment. This has been particularly noticeable in the efforts to create standards for licensing and evaluating design cores. Cooperation between major chip firms and local firms in Asia, such as the use of design services in India or Taiwan, has had a better record of success because of the less-equal status of the parties involved. Collaborative R&D alliances between equal firms also appears to be achieving at least some of its desired results as the R&D costs become exorbitant for any firm acting alone.

Restructuring in various forms has been the industry's approach to the rising cost of fabrication and design, as well as the perennial low return on investment. The results here are also mixed. The fabless-foundry model (Crisis 2) has been a huge success for the industry, but the creation of a separate design core sector (Crisis 3) has failed to produce all the hoped-for benefits. In the case of the latest round of financial restructuring, we do not know the ultimate impact of the private equity buyouts (Crisis 7) that swept the industry before the financial implosion and credit crunch that started in 2007. We have concerns about possible spillover effects on the industry's overall level of innovation, since these private equity companies seek a high return on investment.

The Road Ahead

Having analyzed the industry's evolution over more than two decades, we now turn toward the future, in which new waves of change are certain to wash over the industry.

The semiconductor industry is facing greater technological uncertainty than ever as CMOS technology runs into both physical and economic barriers that no amount of engineering can fix. Although we have adopted the convention of discussing linewidths in terms of microns (millionth of a meter) for consistency, the industry converted a number of years ago to thinking in terms of nanometers (billionth of a meter). Thus the 0.065-micron process generation is usually called the 65 nanometer, or 65 nm.

The end of the road for CMOS processes is currently expected to occur at linewidths of 16 or 6 nm. The end must come eventually because CMOS structures are in danger of running foul of the laws of physics. Waiting in the wings are exotic nanotechnologies such as carbon nanotubes, quantum dots, and spintronics, each of which still requires considerable research and development before knowing its suitability for volume production. Any of these technologies will need well over a decade to make it from the lab to the factory.

We are not willing to predict if a radical new technology will keep Moore's Law alive, but it is clear that many companies must begin to think beyond Moore's Law. The industry already acknowledges a design productivity gap, where design has not been able to take full advantage of the enormous growth in available transistors. We also observe a "consumer gap," where consumers have not been able to keep up with the vast increase in functionality of many devices. Much of the industry's contribution to global society will be through producing simple low-cost products for poor populations, as well as finding clever ways to design and produce products that business and consumers in the developed economies will value. To do this, firms must concurrently develop new technology and the new product markets that can use it. Even if the chip industry does not stay on the Moore's Law trajectory, chip firms can continue to reduce the cost per transistor through improving design productivity and taking advantage of fab economies of scale, which will enable lower prices while providing firms an adequate return on investment.

In pushing ahead on developing technological breakthroughs, universities are playing an important role. In 2005, the US chip industry, which has long funded joint research with universities through the nonprofit Semiconductor Research Corporation, launched the Nanoelectronics Research Initiative (NRI, http://nri.src.org) to prove the feasibility of one or more post-CMOS technologies by 2020.

Although many of the NRI research projects receive government support, industry participants have expressed frustration that the US government is not doing more to support the industry's huge R&D burden. The tone has become increasingly desperate. In September 2008 Craig Barrett, then chairman of Intel, sounded almost resigned: "When you look at the agricultural subsidies and the bailouts and the earmarks it is hard to believe the government can't come up with $1 billion to fund innovation. We as a country have chosen not to compete."[1]

The willingness of the US government to support innovation changed dramatically in the wake of the global financial crisis and deep recession that began in 2008. The Obama administration's $787 billion stimulus package included funding for a wide array of programs to support the technology sector, such as funding of science and engineering research and business-university partnerships across many agencies, including funding to NSF for grants to improve engineering facilities that conduct basic research; incentives for college science and engineering majors to become K–12 teachers, and funding for wireless broadband infrastructure. We cannot estimate how much of the stimulus funding will actually reach the chip industry, because funding for research and development was focused on clean energy and health care, which use integrated circuits to varying degrees.

The question to be asked about the industry ten years from now is not so much "What will it be making?" as "Who will be making it?" The trend toward megafabs, which require enormous throughput to realize their economies of scale, unquestionably pushes further consolidation. We expect integrated firms to continue their shift in manufacturing toward the foundries, and many eventually to become fabless. We also expect firms to continue their consolidation either through mergers and acquisition, especially among the Japanese companies, and through even more tight-knit alliances, such as the IBM process alliance and a Japanese common fab. A handful of second-tier firms are likely to vanish as they fail to find a safe niche as markets shift.

At the national level, Japan is likely to undergo further restructuring, at least at the level of resource sharing in the form of a common fab, although a common foundry was studied and rejected prior to the round of Japanese investment in 300-mm fabs in the early 2000s. Europe may retain STMicroelectronics as a major producer, but any other companies there will be of modest size. Taiwan's memory firms will not survive in their current independent state. China will become a larger version of Taiwan with a presence mainly in the fabless and foundry segments. India, which gives little sign of upgrading its infrastructure or bureaucratic efficiency, will probably remain tied to design.

The semiconductor industry has spread around the world, especially in Asia, as governments and investors in new countries have developed a taste for the high-tech risks and rewards in the industry. Japan, Korea, Taiwan, Singapore, Malaysia, and China have each taken the plunge with varying degrees of success. However, apart from Asian pioneer Japan, they did so during a particularly stable phase of the industry's development, during which the CMOS process was dominant and each process node offered predictable benefits to designers and acceptable cost increments to fab owners. As technological challenges mount and annual sales growth settles into the single digits, new entry becomes exceedingly difficult.

Governments will continue to play a role. During this deep recession, governments have expanded their role with additional infusions into research and development and financial arrangements for company consolidation and restructuring. Earlier, government planning and support was an element in each of the Asian cases, starting with Japan (Fransman 1990; Mathews and Cho 2000). Mechanisms of government support varied between countries but included trade preferences, subsidies, tax incentives, higher education programs, infrastructure assistance, and direct investment. New countries may build competitive advantage in a similar way, as politicians and technocrats continue to value a presence in the chip industry. Russia had announced some ambitious plans prior to the inception of the 2008 global financial crisis, and Brazil, the world's other large emerging economy, is also developing its chip capabilities. As the competitive pressures—and consumer benefits—of the semiconductor industry spread to every corner of the globe, the prediction in which we are most confident is that change is the only constant.

Lessons Learned

In this book we have shown how, for more than two decades, the chip industry has found ways to deal with crises as they have arisen. Industry participants relied on incremental fixes in the short term, which allowed longer term organizational and technological changes to be developed in a cost-effective manner. US semiconductor companies have fared better than their Japanese and European rivals over this period. There have been various winners and losers in each of the regions as some companies made strategic missteps (e.g., National Semiconductor, an industry leader in the early 1980s) while others made winning strategic moves (e.g., Texas Instruments and STMicroelectronics).

Four major lessons emerge from our study of the crises faced by the chip industry, and we think these lessons apply broadly to high-technology industries.

1. *Crises are a fact of life in industries with rapid technological change.* The rapid introduction of new technology leads to points where old business models break down or where new applications bring forth new market leaders. The endless crises aren't necessarily bad for the industry as a whole because they usually foster innovation, even as they create winners and losers.

2. *There's no one "best" answer to a crisis.* No strategy or response mode will be right in every circumstance, and each crisis can potentially be surmounted by any of several approaches. A crisis sets up the opportunity for a firm to build a new global competitive advantage, and this entices firms to stay in the race and to develop new ideas and markets.

3. *Technology must go hand in hand with a business model.* Competitive advantage requires any plan for value creation (innovation) be created with a plan for value capture (business model). Creating a new technology does not guarantee that a firm will be able to develop an adequate product market and recoup its investment. Companies must develop their marketing capabilities as much as their technical capabilities in order to develop products that customers value and to provide the company with bargaining power with its value chain partners.

4. *Supporting institutions are vital for a sector's growth.* Financial infrastructure, universities, the global brain circulation, and overall economic vitality are critical elements of how US companies have stayed on top of the semiconductor industry. The commitment of Asian governments, particularly Japan, Taiwan, and China, to support the creation

and growth of a domestic semiconductor industry poses both opportunities and challenges to other countries vying for leadership. Especially during a global financial crisis that tests the ability of companies without deep reserves to stay afloat—and this includes many smaller and private companies—the activities by governments to provide emergency loans, tax breaks, and other subsidies are important in determining what companies survive under what structure globally.

The semiconductor industry is the engine of the knowledge economy, and the industry's ability to overcome continual crises has propelled the world economy into an era of ubiquitous computing. New industries, such as green energy technologies, could do worse than to emulate its strategy and structure. By the studying the chip industry's past, we hope they may be fortunate enough to repeat its successes and avoid its speed bumps.

Notes

Introduction

1. There are a number of good books covering the industry's earlier history, including Braun and MacDonald (1978), Borrus (1988), Henderson (1989), Tilton (1971), and Flamm (1996).

2. Mark LaPedus, "ITRS chip roadmap returns to three-year cycle," *Silicon Strategies*, January 21, 2004.

3. The Competitive Semiconductor Manufacturing program is a multidisciplinary study of the semiconductor industry established in 1991 by a grant from the Alfred P. Sloan Foundation with additional support from the semiconductor industry. Further details are available at http://microlab.berkeley.edu/csm/ and http://irle.berkeley.edu/worktech/online.html.

Crisis 1

1. Reported in Stuart Auerbach and Peter Behr, "Japan to seek cancellation of tariffs; US sees chip war as threat to defense," *Washington Post*, April 7, 1987, p. E1.

2. Reported in Young (1992, p. 269).

3. Jane Erwin, "Achieving total customer satisfaction through Six Sigma," *Quality Digest*, July 1998.

4. Private discussions with industry participants, October 2008.

5. Semico Research estimate reported in John Day, "Sector to return to double-digit growth," *Electronic Buyers' News*, April 10, 2000.

6. http://www.usdoj.gov/atr/public/testimony/hhi.htm; an industry in which a single firm holding a 42 percent share would be near the lower bound of the Justice Department's threshold for "concentrated."

7. Russ Arensman, "Big blue silicon," *Electronic Business*, November 2001.

8. Russ Arensman, "Nimble giant," *My-ESM*, November 1, 2005.

9. Jeff Chappell, "Flash: Moore's law and then some," *Electronic News*, July 12, 2005.

10. Josephine Lien and Steve Shen, "Commentary: Is consolidation a remedy to Taiwan's DRAM problems?" *DigiTimes*, October 28, 2008.

11. Josephine Lien and Jessie Shen, "Elpida CEO to visit ProMOS and Winbond for partnership talk," *DigiTimes*, April 13, 2009.

12. Chuma and Hashimoto (2008) provide a different analysis of the decline of Japan's DRAM business that focuses on the companies' organizational constraints to responding adequately to the increasing complexities of technology and markets.

13. We are grateful to Robert Leachman for helpful discussions on this point.

14. "Teenagers help start belated PC boom in Japan," Reuters, August 16, 1995.

15. We are grateful to David Hodges for elucidating this point for us.

16. We are grateful to YasuhiroTakada, CTO at THine Electronics, for bringing this term to our attention.

17. Based on Semiconductor Industry Association data (see https://www.sia-online .org/downloads/shares.pdf, accessed in March 2008).

18. This section draws from our work with Eiichi Yamaguchi on "The role of Japanese start-ups in high-tech innovation", ITEC Policy Brief, Doshisha University, March 2005.

19. Calculated by the authors based on the listing by *Electronic Business*, http:// www.edn.com/article/CA630171.html?partner=eb.

20. Calculated from National Science Foundation Science and Engineering Indicators, 2004, tab. 4–5.

21. Calculated from 2003 data from Japan's Statistics Bureau downloaded in March 2005 from http://www.stat.go.jp/data/kagaku/2003np/index.htm.

22. Based on field interviews in the United States and Japan in 2004 to 2006.

23. Calculated from data provided by the Fabless Semiconductor Association.

24. Study Group of the Creation and Development of Start-ups, Final Report: Creation and Development of Start-ups for Innovation in the Japanese Economy, April 2008. Available at http://www.meti.go.jp/english/report/data/Startups _Finalreport.pdf.

25. Ministry of Economy, Trade, and Industry data accessed via the Venture Enterprise Corporation (http://www.vec.or.jp/). Also see the Study Group Final Report 2008 (op cit) for comparison of venture capital investment in Japan, the United States, and Europe.

26. Personal communication, November 2008.

27. "Silicon Strategies' 60 emerging start-ups," *Silicon Strategies*, April 6, 2004.

28. http://www.doingbusiness.org.

29. Elizabeth Tchii and Lisa Wang, "Taipei sends lifeline to chip sector," *Taipei Times*, November 11, 2008, p. 12, and Dylan McGrath, "Datang to acquire 17% stake in SMIC," *EE Times*, November 10, 2008.

Crisis 2

1. "Pico frontier," *EE Times*, December 30, 1996.

2. "Chip makers gripe bitterly, but litho costs keep soaring," *Semiconductor Business News*, July 1999; lithography accounts for one-third of semiconductor manufacturing costs (Silicon Valley Group Form 10-K for fiscal year ended September 30, 1998).

3. Mark LaPedus, "Sematech: 450-mm is progressing," *EE Times*, July 10, 2008.

4. G. Dan Hutcheson, CEO of market research firm VLSI Research, cited in David Lammers, "Consumer era gives birth to 'gigafabs'," *EE Times*, October 31, 2005.

5. Christian Gregor Dieseldorff, "Flash Fabs costing $7 billion and more roar with capacities never seen," SEMI feature article, April 3, 2007. Available at http://www.semi.org/en/marketinfo/FabDatabase/P041386.

6. LaPedus, *EE Times* (as cited at note 4).

7. SEMI, Equipment Suppliers' Productivity Working Group 450 mm Economic Findings and Conclusions. 2008.

8. For positive cost simulation, see Scotten W. Jones, "A simulation study of the cost and economics of 450 mm wafers," *Semiconductor International*, August 8, 2005.

9. Goldman Sachs estimates reported in Ann Steffora Mutschler, "Leveraging shorter product lifecycles for new collaboration opportunities," *Electronic News*, July 19, 2007.

10. G. Dan Hutcheson, "The R&D crisis," VLSI Research doc 600201, January 28, 2005. https://www.vlsiresearch.com/public/600201_r&d_crisis.pdf.

11. Claire Sung and Esther Lam, "Siltronic: 12-inch wafer will take time to become mainstream," *DigiTimes*, September 4, 2007.

12. Colleen Taylor, "Outsourcing held 43.5 percent share of 2006 chip packaging market," *Electronic News*, June 29, 2007.

13. "Outsourced semiconductor assembly and test: Preparing for the next boom cycle, 2006–2008," *Chip Scale Review*, April 2005.

14. Based on data from EDAC.org quarterly press releases, 2007 EDA industry revenue totaled $5.77 billion, of which about 30 percent was derived from design services, design module licensing (see Crisis 3), and circuit board layout software. The remaining $4 billion was specifically for chip design software.

15. Bob Johnstone, "Chips and sushi," *Far Eastern Economic Review*, July 20, 1989, pp. 51–53.

16. Martin Marshall, Larry Waller, and Howard Wolff, "For optimal VLSI design efforts, Mead and Conway have fused device fabrication and system-level architecture," *Electronics*, October 20, 1981. Available at http://ai.eecs.umich.edu/people/conway/Awards/Electronics/ElectAchiev.html.

17. "It's a pure play foundry world," *Electronic News*, August 11, 2005.

18. "TSMC sues SMIC," *Electronic News*, December 22, 2003.

19. Mark LaPedus, "Updated: TI tips details on IC-production efforts," *EE Times*, February 20, 2007.

20. Data reported by Semico Research Corp, reported in "System houses remain weak link for silicon foundries," *Silicon Strategies*, May 11, 2004.

21. See "More changes ahead for foundries, industry," *Electronic News*, December 4, 2003, for a similar analysis.

22. The well-known quote is generally attributed to Jerry Sanders III, then-CEO of AMD ("Only real men have fabs," *The Register*, February 25, 1999), but we have been unable to identify the exact date when it was said.

23. Data supplied by Global Semiconductor Alliance.

24. Michael Kanellos, "Soaring costs of chipmaking recast industry," *CNET* .com, January 22, 2003; Laura Peters, "300 mm fabs need to be more competitive," *Semiconductor International*, April 1, 2007.

25. "UMC buys SiS subsidiary SiS Microelectronics," *DigiTimes.com*, February 26, 2004.

26. J. Robert Lineback, "UMC to merge joint ventures, speeding capacity expansion in foundry arena," *Semiconductor Business News*, June 14, 1999.

27. Data from Global Semiconductor Alliance.

28. Mark LaPedus, "Samsung buys CMOS image sensor firm," *EE Times*, October 31, 2007.

29. Data from Global Semiconductor Alliance.

30. These historical data come from our colleagues Leachman and Leachman (2004). Because older fabs use a range of wafer sizes and linewidths, the underlying data have been normalized using a capacity metric based on the number of functions, where a function is one memory bit or one logic gate.

31. Based on the Leachman data.

32. David Lammers, "Analysis: Samsung fab deal ends drought for Austin," *EE Times*, April 14, 2006.

33. Rob Leachman generously helped us to calculate the share of capacity located offshore. The Leachman data do not include ownership shares for jointly owned fabs. We divided such fabs by the number of regions (2 or 3) involved in ownership to estimate the US share. As much as 10 percent of US-owned capacity was in joint-venture fabs in 2001, but those fabs were spread across all regions,

so our estimation error is not likely to be more than 1 or 2 percent up or down from the figures in the table.

34. Rob Leachman, personal communication, May 2005.

35. Authors' calculations based on data in Howell et al. (2003, app. 2). Labor costs for 200-mm fabs are 8 percent in Taiwan and 3 percent in China.

36. TSMC, which accounts for about half the foundry industry, had one 150-mm, one 300-mm, and five-and-a-half 200-mm fabs outside the United States in 2005. These fabs have various rated capacities, but we can approximate employment by calculating 750 workers per plant, which works out to 5,625. Doubling that to approximate the entire foundry sector brings us to 11,250.

37. Fabless Semiconductor Association, "Global fabless fundings and financials report, Q4 2005."

Crisis 3

1. Rich Wawrzyniak, "SOC trends in the year 2000," *Electronic News*, January 3, 2000.

2. Bryan Lewis, "SOC market is set for years of growth in the mainstream," *Gartner*, October 17, 2005.

3. Bill Roberts, "Compound complexity—and how to manage it," *Electronic Business*, September 2004.

4. Synopsys estimate reported in Mark LaPedus, "Costs cast ICs into Darwinian struggle," *EE Times*, March 30, 2007.

5. Charles DiLisio, "Can You Continue to Profit by Moore's Law?" FSA Fabless Forum, March 2003. The model assumes 50 percent cost of goods and 25 percent overhead (SG&A) with a 20 percent operating profit target, which leaves 5 percent for design cost.

6. Jerry Fiddler, chairman of Wind River Systems, cited in "Keynoter says chip value is in its intellectual property," *EE Times*, June 14, 2002.

7. Jack Ganssle, "A million lines of code," *Embedded.com*, January 14, 2008. The exponential growth rate for software schedules is 1.35, so the schedule for a million lines of code is 22 times that for 10,000 lines.

8. International Business Strategies data cited in Amir Ben-Artzi, "GSA contends fabless is more," *EE Times*, May 5, 2008.

9. Based on Global Semiconductor Alliance data.

10. "SOC-Mobinet, R&D and education in SoC design," presentation by Hannu Tenhunen at International Symposium on System-on-Chip 2004, Tampere, Finland, on November 16–18, 2004, accessible at www.cs.tut.fi/soc/Tenhunen04.pdf as of April 19, 2005.

11. Lance Pickup and Scott Tyson, "Hot Chips? . . . Not!" *Chip Design Magazine*, August–September 2004.

12. Richard Goering, "Low-power IC design techniques may perturb the entire flow," *EE Times*, May 7, 2007.

13. Aart J. de Geus, "The technomics of design and manufacturing," presentation at Industry Strategy Symposium, Half Moon Bay, CA, January 13–16, 2008.

14. Ann Steffora Mutschler, "Semiconductor IP continues growth path, Semico reports," *Electronic News*, March 26, 2008.

15. Industry analysts Bryan Lewis, cited in Peter Clarke, "IP99: Panel raises pay-to-evaluate IP issue," *EE Times*, November 1, 1999.

16. The Wikipedia entry at http://en.wikipedia.org/wiki/Vendors_of_semiconductor _IP_cores lists approximately 80 as of November 2008.

17. SPIRIT stands for "Structure for Packaging, Integrating, and Re-using IP within Tool flows."

18. Ron Wilson, "VSIA RIP: IP consortium winds down operations," *EDN.com*, July 9, 2007.

19. John Cooley, "The 2007 DeepChip Verification Census." Available at http:// www.deepchip.com/posts/dvcon07.html.

20. See, for example, Serge Leef of Mentor Graphics quoted in Ann Steffora Mutschler, "Embedded microprocessor design requires system-level approach," *Electronic News*, October 27, 2006, and Ron Wilson, "Is IP reuse, rather that an ESL, the next level of abstraction for SoC design?" EDN Practical Chip Design blog, June 4, 2007 (http://www.edn.com/blog/1690000169/post/670010267 .html).

Crisis 4

1. Charles DiLisio, "Can you continue to profit by Moore's Law?," *FSA Fabless Forum*, March 2003. Available at http://www.dside.com/articles/index.html.

2. Matthew Yi, "Intel switches gears with purchases," *San Francisco Chronicle*, September 29, 2002.

3. "Facing computer slowdown, Intel hopes new consumer devices will boost growth," *Wall Street Journal Interactive*, January 2, 2001. The StrongARM processor architecture used in the digital audio player was created under a license from ARM.

4. "Intel's new network ICs target enterprise-class applications," *Electronic Buyers' News*, May 1, 2000. Intel's "IXP" networking chips also use the Strong-ARM architecture.

5. "ADI-Intel DSP core appears ready for prime time," *Electronic Buyers' News*, December 1, 2000.

6. Dean Takahashi, "Intel: A lesson in how NOT to diversify," *Electronic Business*, August 2006.

7. Jeff Chappell, "Flash: Moore's law and then some," *Electronic News*, July 12, 2005.

8. China's impact on the semiconductor industry: 2006/Update, Pricewater-houseCoopers, 2007, p. 7.

9. Charles DiLisio, "Au revoir, system-on-chip," *Buyside*, May 2004, pp. 19–20.

10. "Outsourcing trend proves: Complex by design," *EE Times*, January 31, 2005.

11. iSuppli data reported in "Silicon Valley semiconductor industry retains dominant role, says iSuppli," *DigiTimes*, August 30, 2007.

12. "Mean wages edge closer to six-figure mark," *EE Times*, August 25, 2004.

13. Interview, November 2005.

14. Email communications with Indian chip designer, June 2005.

15. Interview, May 2004.

16. Interview, December 2004.

17. The following description is based on a compilation of published accounts and the corporate website.

18. S. Swarn, "TI's Indian DSP integrates control functions," *Nikkei Electronics Asia*, July 1998.

19. "SIA pushes steps to better IP protection in China," *Electronic News*, November 17, 2004.

20. Yoshiko Hara, "Japan taps into 'glocalization'," *EE Times*, June 19, 2006.

21. Interview, April 1998.

22. Interview, August 2004.

23. William Quigley, managing director at Clearstone Venture Partners (Menlo Park, CA), quoted in "Venture capitalist explains new rules for IC startups," *EE Times*, January 16. 2003.

24. "Designs for digital audio, auto electronics," *Nikkei Electronics Asia*, October 2002.

25. "Complex chips reignite demand for design services," *EE Times*, October 11, 2004.

26. Interview, April 2004.

27. See, for example, "The perfect storm brews offshore," *Electronic Business*, March 2004, accessible at www.reed-electronics.com/eb-mag/toc/03%2D01%2D2004/.

28. "It's an outsourced world, EEs acknowledge," *EE Times*, August 27, 2004.

29. Alex Zaharov-Reutt, "OLPC '$100' laptop costs USD $175 + $1," www.itwire.com.au, April 28, 2007.

Crisis 5

1. Mark LaPedus, "Industry socked by next-gen litho woes," *EE Times*, March 5, 2007.

2. "Chip makers gripe bitterly, but litho costs keep soaring," *Semiconductor Business News* (http://www.semibiznews.com/), July 1999.

3. The only remaining US lithography supplier, Ultratech, based in San Jose, makes trailing-edge tools capable of fabricating feature sizes of 0.75 micron or larger. Many advanced chips can still incorporate such relatively large features for part of their manufacturing process.

4. "Semiconductor lithography market hits record in 2006, says The Information Network," *DigiTimes.com*, January 26, 2007.

5. Bill Roberts, "The 5 most enduring principles," *Electronic Business*, November 2005. See also Henderson (1995).

6. Jim Wiley, "Future challenges in computational lithography," *Solid State Technology*, May 2006.

7. Aaron Hand, "Double patterning drives computational upgrades," *Semiconductor International*, February 25, 2008.

8. Jack Robertson, "Chip makers gripe bitterly, but litho costs keep soaring," *Semiconductor Business News*, July 1999.

9. David Baldwin, "Taiwan foundries move to first-tier fabrication," *Nikkei Electronics Asia*, April 2000.

10. Marc A. Fischetti, "Solid state," *IEEE Spectrum*, January 1984, pp. 58–63.

11. Mark LaPedus, "Litho for 32-nm remains a question mark," *EE Times*, February 20, 2006.

12. Mark LaPedus, "Japan's ASET group discloses EUV tool for 35-nm processes," *Semiconductor Business News*, March 6, 2002.

13. David Lammers, "Intel: 'EUV facts don't add up' for 22 nm in 2011," *Semiconductor International*, April 22, 2008.

14. Bill Spencer, Linda Wilson, and Robert Doering, "The semiconductor technology roadmap," *Future Fab International*, January 12, 2005. Available at http://www.future-fab.com/documents.asp?d_id=3004.

15. The latest version of the International Technology Roadmap for Semiconductors can be accessed at http://public.itrs.net.

16. Mark LaPedus, "Nikon brings immersion into production," *EE Times*, February 16, 2006.

17. Phil Hester, senior VP and chief technology officer at AMD, quoted in Ed Sperling, "Inside AMD," *Electronic News*, June 16, 2006.

18. Thomas Blaesi, vice president of marketing and business development, SIGMA-C GmbH, quoted in Laura Peters, "DFM: Worlds collide, then cooperate," *Semiconductor International*, June 1, 2005.

19. EDA analyst Gary Smith, quoted in Richard Goering, "Designers gravitate toward RTL signoff," *EE Times*, August 11, 2003.

20. Ted Vucurevich, CTO of Cadence Design Systems in Richard Goering, "Hope seen for taming IC process variability at next design node," *EE Times*, April 17, 2006.

21. David Lammers, "For Intel, DFM means keeping variability in check," *EE Times*, September 25, 2006.

22. Laura Peters, "DFM: Worlds collide, then cooperate," *Semiconductor International*, June 1, 2005.

23. Christoph Hammerschmidt, "Chip alliances will gain importance, predicts Ziebart" *Electronics Supply and Manufacturing*, June 1, 2007.

24. Peter Clarke, "IMEC fleshes out DFM research project, declares it open," *Silicon Strategies*, October 12, 2004.

25. Jeff Chappell, "IMEC: Learn to live with process variation," *Electronic News*, October 13, 2004.

26. Richard Goering, "Variability upends designers' plans," *EE Times*, November 21, 2005.

27. Richard Goering, "Electronic system-level design tools come up short," *EE Times*, February 13, 2006.

28. Ron Wilson, "Does 65-nm design require DFM tools?" *EDN*, February 2, 2007.

29. See, for example, David Manners, "Fabless companies need Fab links, say conference speakers," *Electronics Weekly*, May 2, 2006; and David Lammers, "For Intel, DFM means keeping variability in check," *EE Times*, September 25, 2006.

30. Michael Smayling of Applied Materials, quoted in Dylan McGrath, "Robust process models needed for DFM, according to panel," *EE Times*, July 13, 2005.

31. Ron Wilson, "Qualcomm plots fabless strategy for 45 nm," *EDN*, November 21, 2006.

32. Mark LaPedus, "Fabless Qualcomm zooms to next node," *EE Times*, November 27, 2006.

33. "TSMC to get more involved in design, packaging, says report," *Silicon Strategies*, November 20, 2003.

34. Mark LaPedus, "IP providers cast wary eye on TSMC," *EE Time*, April 23, 2007.

Crisis 6

1. As quoted in "Overcoming America's semiconductor workforce crisis" *Design News* December 14, 2006.

2. Committee on Prospering in the Global Economy of the 21st Century, *An Agenda for American Science and Technology*, National Academy of Sciences, National Academy of Engineering, Institute of Medicine, Washington: National Academies Press, 2007, pp. 31–32.

3. See, for example, Richard B. Freeman (2003, 2005), Task Force on the Future of American Innovation (2005), National Research Council (2000, 2001), and William Butz et al. (2004).

4. The Bureau of Labor Statistics' Occupational Employment Statistics data (obtained online at www.bls.gov/oes/home.htm) provide a large sample collected from establishments that report detailed occupational characteristics. However, comparison of data across years is not exact, since OES is designed for cross-sectional comparisons and not for comparisons across time because of changes in the occupational, industrial, and geographical classification systems; changes in the way data are collected; changes in the survey reference period; and changes in mean wage estimation methodology, as well as permanent features of the methodology. More details can be found at http://www.bls.gov/oes/oes_ques .htm#Ques28. Also educational characteristics are not given.

5. For detailed analysis of career paths and comparisons with other industries, see Brown et al. (2006).

6. For the semiconductor industry, we use the North American Industry Classification System (NAICS 3344), "Semiconductor and other electronic component manufacturing," which includes relatively low-value components such as resistors and connectors. The most relevant subcategory, "Semiconductor and related device manufacturing" (NAICS 334413), accounted for 39 percent of employees (and 45 percent of nonproduction workers) in the 3,344 category in 2003, but occupation-specific data are not available at this level of industry detail. Source: US Census Bureau, "Statistics for industry groups and industries: 2003," *Annual Survey of Manufactures*, April 2005.

7. Here we exclude techs, drafters, and computer support occupations. Only occupations with at least 5,000 employees in the semiconductor industry are shown. For example, computer programmers are not shown; there were 3,310 semiconductor programmers in 2000 (average earnings $74,627) and 1,900 in 2005 (average earnings $74,370).

8. Comparison of 2000 and 2005 is not exact because SIC 367 was used in 2000 for the industry code and NAICS 334400 was used in 2005. The biggest drop in semiconductor engineering jobs occurred in the "electrical and electronic engineering technicians" subcategory (-62 percent), which reflects the sensitivity of employment in manufacturing jobs during the recession.

9. Data were provided by Ron Hira. BLS redefined occupations beginning with the 2000 survey covering 1999, but there is no evidence that the redefinition has contributed to the post-bubble unemployment rise. See also "It's cold out there," *IEEE Spectrum*, July 2003.

10. The analysis using 2005 ACS data extends the analysis using 2000, 2002, and 2004 ACS data in Brown and Linden (2006), which also looked at workers with less than a college degree. The results represented here for 2005 are consistent with the results from the earlier years, with older engineers doing even worse in 2005 than in previous years.

11. The American Community Survey (ACS) (http://www.census.gov/acs/www/), which is a relatively new household survey that began in 1996 in order to update the Census between decennial surveys, provides detailed occupation and industry characteristics as well as education, so it is much better suited for our labor market analysis. However, the sample size is not adequate for detailed analysis until 2002 and later years. For a more detailed comparison of the OES and ACS data, see Brown and Linden (2006).

12. Age-earnings profiles by education were calculated using the ACS for a sample of workers age 21 to 65, in industry code 339 ("electronic components and products," comparable to NAICS 3344 and 3346), in a set of occupation codes ("selected electrical and electronic, software, and other engineering occupations and selected managerial occupations"). We used several different samples of occupation codes in order to test for sensitivity of age-earning profiles to the definition of semiconductor engineer occupations. In the results presented here, we included SOC 172070, 172061, 151021, 151030, 151081, 172131, 172110, 172041, 119041, 113021, 111021, 112020, 113051, and 113061. When we restricted the sample to fewer occupation codes, the age-earnings profiles remained mostly stable, with the earnings of the top 10 percent increasing for older groups with the inclusion of more managerial occupations. BS includes college graduates who do not have a higher degree; MS/PhD includes workers with a master's or PhD degree. Workers with professional degrees (e.g., MD, DDS, LLB, JD, DVM) are excluded.

13. Earnings for *n* percent represents the earnings where *n* percent of observations are below this value and (100 – *n*) percent of observations are above this value. Earnings for those at 50 percent represents the median.

14. At 3 percent growth rate, the BS earnings would be $85,00 at age 40; at 3 percent growth rate, the MS/PhD earnings would be $109,000 at age 40.

15. We assume that the graduate student receives a fellowship that covers tuition and living expenses, which we assume offsets the discounting of the salary stream of the BS for the three years.

16. According to an executive in an American design services company in India, the ratio of a five-year engineer to a new hire will typically be more than 2 to 1 in India (interview, November 2005), compared with only 1.3 to 1 in the United States.

17. This material is taken from the Sloan Census project that produced the book *Economic Turbulence* by Brown et al. (2006) and related papers (see www.economicturbulence.com). See book chapter 5 for an overview of firms' job ladders and chapter 6 for an overview of workers' career paths in the semiconductor and four other industries (software, finance, trucking, and retail food).

18. The career paths are shown for modal groups, namely the largest groups of workers who have one, two, or three jobs, with at least one job in a semiconductor establishment during the decade. For those with two jobs, the modal group had a first job outside the semiconductor industry and the second job in it. For those with three jobs, the first two are outside semiconductors, and the last one in the industry.

19. http://www.allianceibm.org/news/jobactions.htm.

20. Some of the observations about specific firms here likely reflect divisions of these large, complex firms beyond their production of semiconductors. We think that the patterns discussed reflect the impact of globalization across high-tech firms.

21. http://www.allianceibm.org/news/jobactions.htm.

22. http://www.bizjournals.com/austin/stories/2001/12/17/daily22.html.

23. Daisuke Wakabayashi, "Stung by chip-unit losses, Toshiba to slash costs," *WSJ.com*, January 30, 2009.

24. See Engineering Trends, Report 1005B, October 2005, online at http://www.engtrends.com/IEE/1005B.php. Note that engineering does not include computer science, which is shown separately.

25. National Science Foundation, Science and Engineering Indicators 2006, online at http://www.nsf.gov/statistics/seind06/c2/fig02-05.htm, with link to source data.

26. Engineering Trends, Report (cited at note 23).

27. This section draws from Brown and Linden (2008), which provides detailed data on the employment and salaries of H-1B visa holders at semiconductor companies.

28. GAO (2003) http://www.gao.gov/new.items/d03883.pdf.

29. Marianne Kolbasuk McGee, "Who got H-1B visas petitions approved last year?" *InformationWeek*, April 2, 2008.

30. http://www.uscis.gov/graphics/howdoi/h1b.htm.

31. USCIS Report, "Characteristics of specialty occupations workers (H-1B): Fiscal year 2003," http://www.uscis.gov/graphics/aboutus/repsstudies/h1b/FY03H1BFnlCharRprt.pdf.

32. See US Department of Labor, http://www.flcdatacenter.com/CaseH1B.aspx.

33. The other applications at Intel, IBM, and Motorola were primarily for other engineering jobs (8 percent with average pay $79,806, or average minimum pay $65,425).

34. USCIS Report, "Characteristics of specialty occupations workers (H-1B): Fiscal year 2003."

35. Motorola spun off its chip operations as an independent company, Freescale, in 2004, and we include the applications made by Freescale with Motorola's applications.

36. These employment figures are from the company's 10-K reports: Intel at http://finance.yahoo.com/q/sec?s=INTC, Motorola at http://finance.yahoo.com/q/sec?s=MOT, and IBM at http://finance.yahoo.com/q/sec?s=IBM.

37. These estimates assume that these three companies used the granted H-1B visas to hire new domestic workers in 2005, and that H-1B visa holders worked for five years.

Crisis 7

1. Interview with Mike Green, *Electronic News*, March 2, 2007

2. ROA was calculated with data from Standard and Poor's Compustat (http://www.compustat.com) North America database. The data were gathered prior to a restatement of earnings by some companies because of underreported expenses for stock options. We have evaluated one other measurement, return on investment (same as ROA but excluding short-term liabilities from the denominator). The results, not reported here, are qualitatively similar to those we report but lower in levels because of the larger denominators. Refinements of the income measure used, for interest expense, minority interest, and other components of net income, also do not make a meaningful difference.

3. ROE = (net income after preferred stock dividends)/(average stockholder equity excluding preferred shares). ROE does not include equity capital gains. We are grateful to Roger Craine for his helpful discussions about measurements of return on investment, and regret we could not implement all his suggestions in this chapter.

4. These are the firms in SIC code 3674 that were available in Compustat for at least two years of the period under study, with some additions and deletions based on additional research.

5. Intel as a percent of our sample excludes firms that produce systems as well as chips. Using market research datafor all companies that sell chips, we calculate that Intel's share of all chip sales from 1984 to 2005 was 14 percent.

6. ROA (calculated by dividing the sum of annual net income by the sum of gross assets within each group) was averaged across four periods, each of which starts at a peak of growth in the semiconductor industry business cycle. Other definitions of return on investment and other divisions into subperiods yield similar results.

7. The gross profit result is from an iSuppli report, summarized in "Fabless firms outpace IDMs in costs, gross margins," *EE Times*, March 16, 2005; the ROIC result (11.4 vs. 9 percent from 1991 to 2002) is from Morgan Stanley in Ron Wilson and Crista Souza, "Future of semiconductor fab ownership debated," *EBN* (formerly Electronic Buyers' News), October 10, 2003.

8. The data include 2006 because none of these categories had significant missing data points in 2006, which was not the case for the "Selected Systems Companies" in figure 7.1.

9. As with ROA, the combined annual R&D expenses for each segment was divided by the year's combined net sales, and then this R&D-to-sales ratio was averaged across years.

10. Don Clark and William M. Bulkeley, "AMD to spin off manufacturing to new venture," *WSJ.com*, October 7, 2008.

11. Goldman Sachs estimate reported in Ann Steffora Mutschler, "Leveraging shorter product lifecycles for new collaboration opportunities," *Electronic News*, July 19, 2007.

12. http://www.aset.or.jp/english/e-outline/member_companies.html, list as of November 1, 2008; accessed November 14, 2008.

13. Mark LaPedus, "Matsushita enters 45-nm production," *EE Times*, June 19, 2007.

14. Jim Eastlake, director of semiconductor research at Dataquest Europe, cited in "GEC Plessey Semiconductors put on the block," *EE Times*, July 11, 1997.

15. Tennille Tracy, "Private-equity firms raked in record amounts last year," *Wall Street Journal*, January 11, 2007, p. C6.

16. Chris Kraeuter, "Why private money likes chips," *Forbes.com*, September 15, 2006.

17. CEO of Micron cited in Mark LaPedus, "CEO interview: Micron's Steve Appleton," *EE Times*, February 22, 2007 and Woodward Yang, a Harvard engineering professor in Brian Fuller, "'Tech overshoot' under fire," *EE Times*, October 2, 2006.

18. "Q&A: Philips Semi's CEO," *redherring.com*, August 4, 2006.

19. Paul Grimme, senior vice president and general manager of Freescale Semiconductor's Transportation and Standard Products Group, cited in "Private equity firm hungry for more IC makers," *Control Engineering*, March 22, 2007.

20. Edward Evans, "KKR fund writes down stakes in NXP, ProSiebenSat.1 (Update6)," *Bloomberg News*, February 29, 2008, and Emily Thornton, Peter Burrows, and Roger O. Crockett, "When a buyout goes bad," *BusinessWeek .com*, April 3, 2008.

21. See, for example, Porter (1985), Teece (1986), Christensen (1997), Gawer and Cusumano (2002), Chesbrough (2003), and Moore (2005).

22. Interview at STMicroelectronics Grenoble, June 2001.

23. Junko Yoshida, "Nokia disdains Samsung's 'flower-to-flower' design strategy," *EE Times*, October 24, 2008.

24. Geoffrey James, "Unmixed signals," *Electronic Business*, May 2005.

25. Rumelt (1987) provides a general discussion of such "isolating mechanisms," defined as "impediments to the immediate ex post imitative dissipation of entrepreneurial rents" (p. 145).

26. The following description is based on publicly available sources.

27. Based on data from http://cdg.org/worldwide/index.asp accessed November 23, 2008.

Crisis 8

1. SIA Press Release, http://www.sia-online.org/pre_release.cfm?ID=392.

2. Ann Steffora Mutschler, "Partnering to make room for maximum value-add" (interview with Dr. Hans Stork, CTO and senior VP of silicon technology development at Texas Instruments), *Electronic News*, July 27, 2007.

3. http://toshiba.com/taec/adinfo/socworld/design_eda.html, accessed November 16, 2008. The three centers are located in San Diego, CA, Boston, MA, and Minneapolis, MN.

4. Chris Hall, "Competing in wireless LAN: Q&A with Ralink EVP Rick Jeng," *DigiTimes*, February 23, 2006.

5. Interviews at US subsidiaries in Bangalore, Nov 2005.

6. For India: "Designs on the future," *IT People*, February 10, 2003; for China: "China's impact on the semiconductor industry," *PriceWaterhouseCoopers*, December 2004, p. 7. Available at http://www.pwc.com/Extweb/pwcpublications .nsf/docid/E851BD5302E77D82852575020014A85B/$FILE/2008_China_Semicon .pdf.

7. "China's impact on the semiconductor industry," *PriceWaterhouseCoopers*, op.cit., p. 7.

8. Geoffrey James, "Piracy on the high SystemCs," *Electronic Business*, August 2005.

9. A Reed Electronics Research estimate reported in "38% of global electronics output now produced in Asia Pacific," *emsnow.com*, July 14, 2006.

10. These figures were arrived at by McKinsey based on a survey of HR managers at multinational subsidiaries in these and other countries which asked the question: "Of 100 graduates with the correct degree, how many could you employ if you had demand for all?"

11. Data from National Science Foundation, *Science and Engineering Doctorate Awards: 2005*, accessed online at http://www.nsf.gov/statistics/nsf07305/content .cfm?pub_id=3757&id=2 Tables 3 and 11.

12. See AnnaLee Saxenian, "International mobility of engineers and the rise of entrepreneurship in the periphery," UNU-WIDER research paper 142, November 2006.

13. Data from National Science Foundation, *Science and Engineering Doctorate Awards: 2005*, accessed online at http://www.nsf.gov/statistics/nsf07305/content .cfm?pub_id=3757&id=2 Table 13.

14. Based on Global Semiconductor Alliance data.

15. Cited in "Taiwan ranks 4th in the world in US patents received," *Taipei Times*, October 17, 2006.

16. J. Robert Lineback, "UMC to merge joint ventures, speeding capacity expansion in foundry arena," *Semiconductor Business News*, June 14, 1999.

17. "TI-Acer: A Profitable Diversion," *Electronic Business*, June 1997.

18. Data from Fabless Semiconductor Association.

19. "Taiwan makers to produce 90% of all notebook PCs in 2008, says paper," *DigiTimes*, December 26, 2007.

20. 1999 figure from Taiwan's Industrial Technology Research Institute cited in Chang and Tsai (2002, tab. 5); 2006 figure from Taiwan Semiconductor Industry Association (2007).

21. "Trends in SOC design unthaw at SOC 2004," *EDN*, December 9, 2004.

22. Chikashi Horikiri, "Taiwan transforms into IC development center," *Nikkei Electronics Asia*, February 2006.

23. SoC Technology Center interview, March 2005.

24. Dylan McGrath, "Study: China consumed one-third of chips in '07," *EE Times*, November 18, 2008.

25. Mike Clendenin, "Analysis: background on TSMC, SMIC lawsuit," *EE Times*, January 5, 2004.

26. Jason Dean, "TSMC reaches a settlement in patent aase against SMIC," *Wall Street Journal*, January 31, 2005, p. B6

27. Mark LaPedus, "TSMC files suit against SMIC, says report," *EE Times*, August 27, 2006.

28. Dylan McGrath, "Datang to acquire 17% stake in SMIC," *EE Times*, November 10, 2008.

29. Mike Clendenin, "Deflated expectations in China's IC biz," *EE Times*, August 28, 2006.

30. "CCID consulting examines global, Chinese foundry developments," *Tech-On*, July 31. 2007.

31. Ibid.

32. Fieldwork interviews in Tianjin and Beijing, Summer 1997, and in Tokyo, Summer 2004.

33. "Motorola to sell China fab to SMIC," *EE Times*, October 23, 2003.

34. "Buying out local partner, NEC moves deeper into China," *SinoCast China IT Watch* (via Nexis), December 24, 2003.

35. Mike Clendenin, "Intel confirms $2.5 billion fab in China," *EE Times*, March 26, 2007.

36. Peter Clarke, "Gartner analyst revamps analysis of Intel in China," *EE Times Europe*, April 3, 2007.

37. "China's impact on the semiconductor industry, 2008 update," *PricewaterhouseCoopers*, op.cit.

38. Bill Roberts, "An offshore test of IP rights," *Electronic Business*, May 1, 2004, p. 19; and "SigmaTel sues Chinese chipmaker over IP," *Electronic News*, January 10, 2005.

39. Assessment of Byron Wu, iSuppli analyst, reported in Mark LaPedus, "China's IC design houses struggling for survival, says iSuppli," *Silicon Strategies*, May 20, 2004.

40. Based on information from Global Semiconductor Alliance.

41. Ikutarou Kojima, "Chinese fabless semiconductor manufacturers' sales to reach $2.8 bil. in 2007: iSuppli," *Tech-On*, August 20, 2007, and Mark LaPedus, "iSuppli lists China's top fabless IC rankings," *EE Times*, April 21, 2006.

42. "China's fabless revenue grows 55 percent in 2006," www.euroasiasemiconductor.com, March 2007.

43. Richard Goering, "Running start helps clear 90-nm hurdles," *EE Times*, April 3, 2006.

44. Her sample of 70 design firms included 85 percent of all known Shanghai IC-design firms in 2005.

45. Calculated from Obukhova (2007, fig. 1).

46. "Synopsys teams with China's Ministry of Science and Technology, SMIC," *Nikkei Electronics Asia*, March 21, 2003; "An uneven playing field," *Electronic News*, July 3, 2003; "China nurtures home-grown semiconductor industry," *EBN*, December 8, 2003; "China government to support Solomon Systech, Actions and Silan," *DigiTimes*, April 14, 2005.

47. "China to form R&D fund to replace VAT rebate, says report," *EE Times*, April 15, 2005.

48. "China's impact on the semiconductor industry, 2008 update," *PricewaterhouseCoopers*, op.cit.

49. "China backs off of WAPI proposal," *Electronic Engineering Times*, April 21, 2004.

50. "Story behind the story: Design in China is growing, but not exploding," audiocast by Bill Roberts, Electronic Business, September 1, 2006, http://www.edn.com/article/CA6368425.html?text=%22design+in+china%22#

51. "More overseas Chinese students returning home to find opportunities," November 16, 2003, http://www.china-embassy.org/eng/gyzg/t42338.htm.

52. "More overseas Chinese students return home," January 1, 2004, http://www.china-embassy.org/eng/gyzg/t57364.htm.

53. C. Chitti Pantulu, "Reliance looks abroad for semiconductor unit," www.dnaindia.com, November 10, 2008.

54. Data from Frost and Sullivan, in Chitra Giridhar, "India design firms as product innovators," *Electronic Business*, July 18, 2006.

55. K. C. Krishnadas, "Indian design business reached $6 billion in 2007," *EE Times*, April 22, 2008.

56. "Rick Merritt, India's people power is also its problem," *EE Times*, March 28, 2008.

57. Sufia Tippu, "MosChip proves India and semiconductors mix," *ITwire*, August 8, 2006.

58. "Study: Indian design firms prefer time and material model", *EE Times*, September 22, 2006.

59. Dossani (2007) provides a thoughtful overview of the role of religion, the educational system, and other institutions in India's development into a global high-tech powerhouse.

60. Personal communications in Bangalore, November 2005.

61. Personal communications in Bangalore, November 2005.

62. Don Clark, "Intel has big plans for small chips," *WSJ.com*, February 21, 2008.

63. Claire Sung and Emily Chuang, "TSMC and UMC to see handset chip orders from TI grow 40% in 2Q, says sources," *DigiTimes*, April 17, 2007.

64. SEMATECH is a US-based industry-funded research consortium (http://www.sematech.org/); SELETE is a Japan-based, industry-funded research consortium (http://www.selete.co.jp/?lang=EN); and ASET is a Japan-based, government-supported research consortium (http://www.aset.or.jp/english/e-index.html).

65. R. Colin Johnson, "Is the US falling behind in chip R&D?" *EE Times*, November 24, 2008 provides an overview of R&D at Intel and IBM and their partnerships with universities.

66. Peter Clarke, "Russia lays plans for 300-mm wafer fab," *EE Times*, June 18, 2007.

Conclusion

1. Quoted in John Walko, "Intel's Barrett berates US government policies," *EE Times Europe*, September 23, 2008.

References

Afuah, A. 1999. Strategies to turn adversity into profits. *Sloan Management Review* 40(2): 99–109.

Angel, D. P. 1990. New firm formation in the semiconductor industry: Elements of a flexible manufacturing system. *Regional Studies* 24(3): 211–21.

Baron, J., and D. Kreps. 1999. *Strategic Human Resources*. New York: Wiley.

Bassett, R. K. 2002. *To the Digital Age: Research Labs, Start-up Companies, and the Rise of MOS Technology*. Baltimore: Johns Hopkins University Press

Berglund, C. N. 2003. Trends in systematic nonparticle yield loss mechanisms and the implications for IC design. *Proceedings of SPIE* 5040: 457–65.

Borrus, M. 1988. *Competing for Control: America's Stake in Microelectronics*. Cambridge, MA: Ballinger Publishing.

Braun, E., and S. MacDonald. 1978. *Revolution in Miniature: The History and Impact of Semiconductor Electronics*. Cambridge: Cambridge University Press.

Brown, C. 2006. Managing creativity and control of knowledge workers. In D. H. Whittaker and R. E. Cole, eds., *Recovering from Success: Innovation and Technology Management in Japan*. Oxford: Oxford University Press, pp. 145–65.

Brown, C., and B. Campbell. 2001. Technical change, wages, and employment in semiconductor manufacturing. *Industrial and Labor Relations Review* 54(2A):450–465.

Brown, C., J. Haltiwanger, and J. Lane. 2006. *Economic Turbulence: Is A Volatile Economy Good For America?* Chicago: University of Chicago Press.

Brown, C., and G. Linden. 2006. Offshoring in the semiconductor industry: A historical perspective. In L. Brainard and S. M. Collins, eds., *Brookings Trade Forum 2005: Offshoring White-Collar Work—The Issues and the Implications*. Washington, DC: Brookings Institute, pp. 279–333.

Brown, C., and G. Linden. 2008. Semiconductor engineers in a global economy. In Committee on the Offshoring of Engineering, National Academy of Engineering, *The Offshoring of Engineering: Facts, Unknowns, and Potential Implications*. Washington, DC: National Academies Press, pp. 149–178.

Brown, C., G. Linden, and E. Yamaguchi. 2005. The role of Japanese start-ups in high-tech innovation. *Doshisha University ITEC Policy Brief.* http://www.itec .doshisha-u.jp/03_publication_03_policy_main.html.

Burgelman, R. A. 1994. Fading Memories: A process theory of strategic business exit in dynamic environments. *Administrative Science Quarterly* 39(1): 24–56.

Butz, W., T. Kelly, D. Adamson, G. Bloom, D. Fossum, and M. Gross. 2004. *Will the Scientific and Technical Workforce Meet the Requirements of the Federal Government?* Santa Monica: RAND Corporation.

Cappelli, P. 2008. *Talent on Demand.* Boston: Harvard Business School Press.

Chang, P.-L., and C.-T. Tsai. 2002. Finding the niche position—Competition strategy of Taiwan's IC design industry. *Technovation* 22(2): 101–11.

Chesbrough, H. W. 2003. *Open Innovation: The New Imperative for Creating and Profiting from Technology.* Boston: Harvard Business School Press.

Chesbrough, H. W., and R. S. Rosenbloom. 2002. The Role of the business model in capturing value from innovation: Evidence from Xerox Corporation's technology spin-off companies. *Industrial and Corporate Change* 11(3): 529–555.

Christensen, C. M. 1997. *The Innovator's Dilemma.* Cambridge: Harvard Business School Press.

Chuma, H., and N. Hashimoto. 2008. Moore's Law, increasing complexity, and the limits of organization: The modern significance of Japanese chipmakers' DRAM business. RIETI discussion paper series 08-E-001.

Cohen, W. M., R. R. Nelson, and J. P. Walsh. 2000. Protecting their intellectual assets: appropriability conditions and why US manufacturing firms patent (or not). Working paper 7552. National Bureau of Economic Research, Cambridge, MA.

Cole, R. E., and T. Matsumiya. 2007. Too much of a good thing? Quality as an obstacle to innovation. *California Management Review* 50(1): 77–93.

Curry, J., and M. Kenney. 1999. Beating the clock: Corporate responses to rapid change in the PC industry. *California Management Review* 42(1): 8–36.

Defense Science Board. 2005. Defense Science Board Task Force on High Performance Microchip Supply. Washington, DC: Office of the Under Secretary of Defense for Acquisition, Technology, and Logistics. Available at http://www.acq .osd.mil/dsb/reports/2005-02-HPMS_Report_Final.pdf.

Dossani, R. 2005. Origins and growth of the software industry in India. Working paper. Shorenstein APARC, Stanford University.

Dossani, R. 2007. *India Arriving: How This Economic Powerhouse Is Redefining Global Business.* New York: AMACOM.

Flamm, K. 1996. *Mismanaged Trade? Strategic Policy and the Semiconductor Industry.* Washington, DC: Brookings Institution Press.

Flamm, K. 2004. "Moore's Law and the economics of semiconductor price trends. In D. W. Jorgenson and C. W. Wessner, eds., *Productivity and Cyclicality in Semiconductors: Trends, Implications, and Questions*——*Report of a Symposium.* Washington, DC: National Academies Press, pp. 151–70.

Fransman, M. 1990. *The Market and Beyond: Cooperation and Competition in Information Technology Development in the Japanese System.* Cambridge: Cambridge University Press.

Fransman, M. 1995. *Japan's Computer and Communications Industry: The Evolution of Industrial Giants and Global Competitiveness.* Oxford: Oxford University Press.

Freeman, R. B. 2003. Trade wars: The exaggerated impact of trade in economic debate. Working paper 10000. National Bureau of Economic Research, Cambridge, MA.

Freeman, R. B. 2005. Does globalization of the scientific/engineering workforce threaten US economic leadership? Working paper 11457. National Bureau of Economic Research, Cambridge, MA.

GAO. 2003. H-1B foreign workers: Better tracking needed to help determine H-1B program's effects on US workforce. *GAO Report* 03-883. Washington, DC: US General Accounting Office

Gawer, A., and M. A. Cusumano. 2002. *Platform Leadership: How Intel, Microsoft, and Cisco Drive Industry Innovation.* Cambridge: Harvard Business School Press.

Gereffi, G., and V. Wadhwa. 2005. Framing the engineering outsourcing debate: Placing the United States on a level playing field with China and India. Engineering Management Program, Duke University. Available at http://www.soc.duke.edu/resources/public_sociology/duke_outsourcing.pdf.

Grindley, P., D. C. Mowery, and B. Silverman. 1994. SEMATECH and collaborative research: Lessons in the design of high-technology consortia. *Journal of Policy Analysis and Management* 13(4): 723–58.

Hall, B., and R. Ham Ziedonis. 2001. The patent paradox revisited: An empirical study of patenting in the US semiconductor industry, 1979–1995. *Rand Journal of Economics* 32(1): 101–28.

Ham, R. M., G. Linden, and M. M. Appleyard. 1998. The evolving role of semiconductor consortia in the US and Japan. *California Management Review* 41(1): 137–63.

Hemani, A. 2004. Charting the EDA roadmap. *IEEE Circuits and Devices* 20(6): 5–10.

Henderson, J. W. 1989. *The Globalisation of High Technology Production: Society, Space, and Semiconductors in the Restructuring of the Modern World.* New York: Routledge.

Henderson, R. 1995. Of life cycles real and imaginary: The unexpectedly long old age of optical lithography. *Research Policy* 24(4): 631–43.

Henisz, W. J., and J. T. Macher. 2004. Firm- and country-level trade-offs and contingencies in the evaluation of foreign investment, *Organization Science* 15(5): 537–54.

Hilbert, J. L. 1991. Introduction to ASIC technology. In N. G. Einspruch and J. L. Hilbert, eds., *Application Specific Integrated Circuit (ASIC) Technology.* San Diego: Academic Press, pp. 11–16.

Hong, S. G. 1992. Paths of glory: Semiconductor leapfrogging in Taiwan and South Korea. *Pacific Focus* 7: 59–88.

Howell, T. R., B. L. Bartlett, W. A. Noellert, and R. Howe. 2003. *China's Emerging Semiconductor Industry: The Impact of China's Preferential Value-Added Tax on Current Investment Trends.* San Jose: Semiconductor Industry Association.

Hurtarte, J. S., E. A. Wolsheimer, and L. M. Tafoya. 2007. *Understanding Fabless IC Technology.* Oxford: Newnes.

Hutcheson, G. D. 2005. *The R&D Crisis, Doc: 600201.* Santa Clara: VLSI Research. https://www.vlsiresearch.com/public/600201_r&d_crisis.pdf.

Iansiti, M., and J. West. 1999. From physics to function: An empirical study of research and development performance in the semiconductor industry. *Journal of Product Innovation Management* 16(4): 385–99.

International Business Strategies. 2002. Analysis of the relationship between EDA expenditures and competitive positioning of IC vendors: A custom study for EDA consortium. http://www.edac.org/downloads/resources/profitability/HandelJonesReport.pdf.

Jorgenson, D. W., and K. J. Stiroh. 2000. Raising the speed limit: US economic growth in the information age. *Brookings Papers on Economic Activity* 2000(1): 125–235.

Katz, R. 1997. *The Human Side of Managing Technological Innovation.* New York: Oxford University Press.

Kim, L. 1997. *Imitation to Innovation: The Dynamics of Korea's Technology Learning.* Boston: Harvard Business School Press.

Lazonick, W. 2008. The quest for shareholder value: Stock repurchases in the US economy. Working paper. Center for Industrial Competitiveness, University of Massachusetts, Lowell.

Leachman, R. C., and C. H. Leachman. 2004. Globalization of semiconductors: Do real men have fabs, or virtual fabs? In M. Kenney and R. Florida, eds., *Locating Global Advantage: Industry Dynamics in the International Economy.* Stanford: Stanford University Press, pp. 203–31.

Lewin, A. Y., and C. Peeters. 2006. Offshoring work: Business hype or the onset of fundamental transformation? *Long Range Planning* 39(3): 221–39.

Levin, R. C., A. K. Klevorick, R. R. Nelson, and S. G. Winter. 1987. Appropriating the returns from industrial research and development. *Brookings Papers on Economic Activity* 3: 783–820.

Linden, G., C. Brown, and M. Appleyard. 2004. The net world order's influence on global leadership in the semiconductor industry. In M. Kenney and R.

Florida, eds., *Locating Global Advantage.* Stanford: Stanford University Press, pp. 232–57.

Linden, G., D. C. Mowery, and R. Ziedonis. 2000. National technology policy in global markets: Developing next-generation lithography in the semiconductor industry. *Business and Politics* 2(2): 93–113.

Linden, G., and D. Somaya. 2003. System-on-a-chip integration in the semiconductor industry: Industry structure and firm strategies. *Industrial and Corporate Change* 12(3): 545–76.

Linden, G., K. L. Kraemer, and J. Dedrick. 2009. Who captures value in a global innovation system? The case of Apple's iPod. Communications of the ACM 52(3): 140–44.

Macher, J. T., D. C. Mowery, and A. Di Minin. 2007. The "non-globalization" of innovation in the semiconductor industry. *California Management Review* 50(1): 217–42.

Macher, J. T., D. C. Mowery, and D. A. Hodges. 1999. Semiconductors. In D. C. Mowery, ed., *U.S. Industry in 2000: Studies in Competitive Performance.* Washington, DC: National Academy Press, pp. 245–86.

MacMillen, D., M. Butts, R. Camposano, D. Hill, and T. W. Williams. 2000. An industrial view of electronic design automation. *IEEE Transactions on Computer Aided Design of Integrated Circuits and Systems* 19(12): 1428–48.

Malerba, F., R. Nelson, L. Orsenigo, and S. Winter. 2008. Public policies and changing boundaries of firms in a "history-friendly" model of the co-evolution of the computer and semiconductor industries. *Journal of Economic Behavior and Organization* 67(2): 355–80.

Mathews, J. A., and D.-S. Cho. 2000. *Tiger Technology: The Creation of a Semiconductor Industry in East Asia.* Cambridge: Cambridge University Press.

McKinsey Global Institute. 2005. *The Emerging Global Labor Market.* San Francisco: McKinsey.

Monteverde, K. 1995. Technical dialog as an incentive for vertical integration in the semiconductor industry. *Management Science* 41(10): 1624–38.

Moore, G. A. 2005. *Dealing with Darwin: How Great Companies Innovate at Every Phase of Their Evolution.* New York: Portfolio.

Moore, G. E. 1965. Cramming more components onto integrated circuits. *Electronics* 38(8): 114–17.

Nakata, Y.-F., and S. Miyazaki. 2007. Has lifetime employment become extinct in Japanese enterprise? An empirical analysis of employment adjustment practices in Japanese companies. *Asian Business and Management* 6(suppl. 1): S33–56.

Nakata, Y.-F. and S. Miyazaki. 2010. Increasing labor flexibility during the recession in Japan: The Role of female workers in manufacturing. In C. Brown, B. Eichengreen and M. Reich, eds., *Labor in the Era of Globalization.* Cambridge: Cambridge University Press, ch. 5.

National Research Council. 2000. *Forecasting Demand and Supply of Doctoral Scientists and Engineers*. Washington, DC: National Academy Press.

National Research Council. 2001. *Building a Workforce for the Information Economy*. Washington, DC: National Academy Press.

Okimoto, D. I., and Y. Onishi. 1994. R&D Organization in Japanese and American semiconductor firms. In M. Aoki and R. Dore, eds., *The Japanese Firm: The Sources of Competitive Strength*. Oxford: Oxford University Press, pp. 178–208.

Porter, M. E. 1985. *Competitive Advantage: Creating and Sustaining Superior Performance*. New York: The Free Press.

Prestowitz, C. V. Jr. 1988. *Trading Places: How We Allowed Japan to Take the Lead*. New York: Basic Books.

Rumelt, R. P. 1987. Theory, strategy, and entrepreneurship. In D. J. Teece, ed., *The Competitive Challenge: Strategies for Industrial Innovation and Renewal*. Cambridge, MA: Ballinger, pp. 137–58.

Sawicki, J. D. 2004. DFM: Magic bullet or marketing hype. In L. W. Liebmann, ed., *Design and Process Integration for Microelectronic Manufacturing II*. Proceedings of the SPIE 5379, San Diego: SPIE Press, pp. 1–9.

Saxenian, A. L. 2002. Transnational communities and the evolution of global production networks: The cases of Taiwan, China and India. *Industry and Innovation* 9(3): 183–202.

Saxenian, A. L. 2006. *The New Argonauts: Regional Advantage in a Global Economy*. Cambridge: Harvard University Press.

SIA (Semiconductor Industry Association). 2003. International technology roadmap for semiconductors: Design. http://www.itrs.net/Links/2003ITRS/Home2003.htm.

Taiwan Semiconductor Industry Association. 2007. *Overview on Taiwan Semiconductor Industry*. Hsinchu, Taiwan: TSIA. http://www.tsia.org.tw/Eng/.

Task Force on the Future of American Innovation. 2005. The knowledge economy: Is the United States losing its competitive edge?" http://www.futureofinnovation.org.

Teece, D. J. 1986. Profiting from technological innovation: Implications for integration, collaboration, licensing and public policy. *Research Policy* 15(6): 285–305.

Thursby, J., and M. Thursby. 2006. Where is the new science in corporate R&D? *Science* 314: 1547–48.

Tilton, J. E. 1971. *International Diffusion of Technology: The Case of Semiconductors*. Washington, DC: Brookings Institution.

Wadhwa, V., A. L. Saxenian, B. Rissing, and G. Gereffi. 2008. Skilled immigration and economic growth. *Applied Research in Economic Development* 5(1): 6–14.

Warshofsky, F. 1989. *The Chip War: The Battle for the World of Tomorrow.* New York: Scribner's.

Wesson, T. 1994. Toward a fuller understanding of foreign direct investment: The example of Hyundai's investment in the US personal-computer industry. *Business and the Contemporary World* 6(3): 123–36.

"Vanguard International Semiconductor" 2007 Annual Report http://www.vis.com.tw/annualreport/2007/english/pdf/en/vis2007_en.pdf.

Whittaker, D. H. 2009. *Comparative Entrepreneurship: The UK, Japan, and the Shadow of Silicon Valley.* Oxford: Oxford University Press.

Young, R. 1992. Structural and ideological mismatch: a study of US–Japan competition in the high technology food chain. Unpublished manuscript. UC San Diego.

Yunogami, T. 2006. Technology management and competitiveness in the Japanese semiconductor industry. In D. H. Whittaker and R. E. Cole, eds., *Recovering from Success, Innovation and Technology Management in Japan.* Oxford: Oxford University Press, pp. 70–86.

These are the URLs for the online press sources cited in our footnotes.

Online News Sources Used

The following list provides Internet addresses for the online publications cited in our endnotes. In some cases the original Internet site that we used to access the article has been folded into another. The current site is the one listed here. Some of the articles are also archived at third-party sites such as findarticles.com, so it is generally simplest to search for the article title as an exact phrase. Articles older than five years may no longer be available online.

Bloomberg News http://www.bloomberg.com/news/index.html
BusinessWeek.com http://www.businessweek.com/
Chip Scale Review http://www.chipscalereview.com
Control Engineering http://www.controleng.com
Design News http://www.designnews.com
DigiTimes http://digitimes.com
EBN http://www.eetimes.com (formerly separate publication, Electronic Buyers' News)
EDN http://www.edn.com
EE Times (also Electronic Engineering Times) http://www.eetimes.com
Electronic Business http://www.edn.com (formerly separate)
Electronic News http://www.edn.com (formerly separate)
Electronics Weekly http://www.electronicsweekly.com
Forbes.com http://www.forbes.com
Information Week http://www.informationweek.com
IT People http://www.itpeopleindia.com

ITwire   http://www.itwire.com
Nikkei Electronics Asia   http://techon.nikkeibp.co.jp
San Francisco Chronicle   http://www.sfgate.com/chronicle
Semiconductor Business News   http://www.eetimes.com (formerly separate)
Semiconductor International   http://www.reed-electronics.com/semiconductor
Silicon Strategies   http://www.eetimes.com (formerly separate)
Solid State Technology   http://www.solid-state.com
Taipei Times   http://www.taipeitimes.com
Tech-On   http://techon.nikkeibp.co.jp
The Register   http://www.theregister.co.uk
WSJ.com (formerly Wall Street Journal Interactive)   http://online.wsj.com

Index